Musica ex lumen

Know thyself and you will know the Universe and the Gods.

Temple of Apolo, god of Light and Music, in Delphi.

Treatise of

Hermetic Music

As sounds the Heavens,

Sounds the Earth.

By
Magister Artium &
Magister Scientiae

Jasper C. Hernández

Year   2024

Vol. I

✕✕✕✕✕✕✕✕✕✕✕✕✕✕✕✕✕✕✕✕✕✕✕✕✕✕✕✕✕✕✕

Translated from the

original

"Música Hermética"

✕✕✕✕✕✕✕✕✕✕✕✕✕✕✕✕✕✕✕✕✕✕✕✕✕✕✕✕✕✕✕

Sefarad
Moncayo-Axis Mundi

Title: Hermetic Music. As sounds the Heavens, sounds the Earth.
Author: Jasper C. Hernández.
Publisher: Jasper C. Hernández (Cronocratores collection).
ISBN: 9798324873844

Hermetic Music Series, as the Sky Sounds, So Does the Earth.
Cronocratores Collection

Index

FIRST VOLUME

Praeludium   **13**
*To the Reader/ What is Hermetic Music/ Origin of this Book/
A matter of great power/ The Musical Speculatory*

Brief Introduction and Basic Concepts   **27**
*Vibration in music/ The Spheres-Sirens/ Intervals/ Harmo-
nic Series/ Series of Chronocrators/ The tradition overlooked*

Corpus Musicum   **37**

Pentalfa of the musical body   **39**

i. Light and the Vibratory Phenomenon. Fundamental **42**
definitions.
*Vibration in Hermeticism / Neoplatonic Spheres / The light
wave of the year / Circle of diapentes*

ii. Tetractys and the Music of Numbers   **61**
*Numbers and waves in the Tetraktys/ Seven/ The twelve no-
tes/ Notes and planets/ Scale of the spheres*

iii. The Scale   **72**
*Creation of the Scale/ The Pythagorean Scale and the herme-
tic incursion into Robert Fludd's works/ The five-note scale/
The system of 22 shruti or tones of India. Carnatic Music/
Ontological nature of musical notes*

iv. Music and Memory   **91**

Memory of the planets around the Sun/ Of geniuses, initiates, and prophets/ Musical-mnemonic map exercise/ Non-hierarchical neuronal memory/ The circle of diapentes and the hand model/ About the shadows and lights of musical ideas

v. Mirror   **125**

King Solomon's mirror/ Solar order: the twelve diapentes in the zodiacal journey. Comparison with lunar scale/ Periods of the solar system/ The mirror, its function, and wave attunement/ In conclusion

Conferentiae de Musica Hermetica   **137**

Initial Commentary   **139**

C.I. TOTAL NUMBER OF POSSIBLE MELODIES. MUSURGIA   **141**
UNIVERSALIS [I]

The musical bird/ Hierarchy of Hermetic ascension/ The Hermetic wave/ Music Magnifica/ Combinatorics with music notes

C. II. INSPIRATION IN KIRCHER. MUSURGIA UNIVERSALIS   **157**
[II]

Orpheus/ Mother of the Muses/ Circumference that inscribes the soul

C. III. INSPIRATION AS THE CHOOSER OF OPTIONS. DIS-   **167**
CERNMENT

Discernment/ Tabula ii/ Combinatory table/ The sense of spirituality/ Man does not perform discernment

C. IV. GAFORI'S MUSES AND COMMENTARY 187

Apollo/ Charites/ Muses/ About the musical modes/ Apollo's Cycle

C. V. ROBERT FLUDD I 203

What is the macrocosm, and what is the microcosm/ The Macrocsmic pyramids/ The quantity of light and the direction of the pyramid/ The Philosophical Hero

C. VI. ROBERT FLUDD II 221

Tuning/ Derived: pi number and the wonder of musical coordinates/ On the Nature of the Musician

C. VII. THE NECESSARY PRESENCE AND NATURE OF ARCHETYPES 232

About the quest for each sphere: the musical sky/ On the predominance of lights and the nature of skies/ Map of benfical attributes/ On the timelessness of the musical experience. Thalia/ The Eight Spheres of the Eight Quests

C. VIII. MUSICAL ECSTASY 255

Light, heat, and moisture/ The Opus of Chaos/ Natural perfection

C. IX. JACOB'S LADDER AND MUSICAL INITIATION 262

The Pythagorean lambda/ Visual analysis/ Athena and her counterpart, Apollo/ The time of the Conservatoires comes to an end/ The initiatory musical education

c. x. ASTROLOGICAL SIGNIFICATORS OF MUSIC 279
Reasons for its Study/ Correspondences of the art of music and of Heaven

c. xi. QUADRIVIUM 283
Introduction/ From heaven to earth/ The ideas of music/ Study from a new paradigm

c. xii. NUMBERS 294
Nature of number/ Numbers and their hierarchy: causes and consequences between them/ Instrumental and comparative study of intervals/ The four elements on the Classical Guitar

c. xiii. TREE OF LIFE AND MUSIC 317
Introduction or transition to music/ Relating to music: second insights/ Structure of the Tree/ The Hermetic Musician's Kabbalism/ Mnemonic Diagrams

c. xiv. STRING THEORY AND 432 Hz TUNING 333
Musical String Theory/ How to reconcile this theory with music?/ 432 Hz Tuning/ The archetypal diagram of diapents: A as an universal note

c. xv. Κάλλος καλλατοσ. MUSES OR THE RAPTURE OF MUSICAL DIVINITY 346
The 'Gratias'/ Rapture/ How does one become a prey to divine love?/ Meaning of the number of the Muses/ Are the Muses real? Physical effect/ Muses's Undullatory

Appendix 371
Bibliography 377

HERMETIC MUSIC

The intellect of music begins anew, revealing what will replace the Conservatories.

What is Hermetic Music?

It is a musical system of thought that revives the hermetic tradition, originally encompassing music and harmonizing matters of the soul and spirit with those of the body to make the teaching and learning of music and its powers complete.

And the Hermetic musicians?

Those who dwell in the rapture of melodies that balance the inner and the outer with the harmony of the Universe.

Praeludium

In the Beginning there was the Verb,
in the beginning there was the Number,
in the beginning there was the Sound.

To the Reader

The mission incumbent upon each individual with this tome is a deeply personal affair. Foremost, I anticipate its integration into one's library, by which I mean its harmonious inclusion within the literary corpus, naturally resonating with the affections of discerning readers and avid scholars alike. Secondly, I hope it serves as a beacon of hope for both academic and non-academic aficionados of music, catering to both professional musicians and amateurs; appealing, in general, to those with a cultivated and inquisitive intellect. Thirdly, and perhaps ambitiously, I wish for it to be read slowly and deliberately, with an understanding that it is not merely for entertainment, but rather for the dissemination of profoundly serious subject matter, underscored by cultural and speculative heights that are undeniably paramount.

The path traced by this volume would rather be settled along the course of inspiration and memory, a river of vivid perception and ontological delineation in earthly materiality, whose waters precipitate all the sublimation of the harmonic particle. In terms of instruction, we address the transition from the conservatory to the musical realm of natural law.

I must say that the journey through the musical particle has its wide spaces and also its narrow (and inaccessible) areas; its lights and its shadows, as befits any human work. In this landscape, there are high mountains whose peaks better collect the light. There would even be corners whose vision seems remote, and if that were to happen, my plea to the reader is not to falter. At certain times, the caves, also present in the relief, may simulate a lack of light. Ensure that your pupils remain for the prudent period to begin to discern the forms...

What is Hermetic Music?

Hermetic music encompasses the tradition of the soul regarding the operation applied to it by music. Thus, we could initially state the present occupation to distinguish, on the one hand, the idea of operating on the soul and, on the other hand, the sonic praxis that executes it. We would synthesize in movements and resonance everything that brings the individual closer to what governs them (destiny), to then propose that these resonances produce alterations in the movement and destiny of the human being when properly employed. When we think of music, we barely consider the sonic and sensory manner in which the order of movements manifests. These movements belong to the macrocosm and the microcosm, and by moving, they belong to the realm of the soul (anima).

In this book, the aim is to provide a clear understanding of what this is and what it studies: not just a branch, but rather the trunk, roots, branches, and even, why not, leaves and fruits of the hermeticism of music. The choice of its format was the first consideration, ultimately settling on compilation rather than mere compilation. It consists, on one hand, of the precise notions that students must contemplate as the common trunk, common to other hermeticisms as well as speculative music, a musical body or *corpus musicum*. Then, various streams and lectures conducted on different digital platforms are transcribed, covering a multitude of authors and topics within the subject (*conferentiae*). Finally (in the second volume), material is employed that is both combined and perhaps conjured from Plato's renowned work, the Timaeus, and a central question of this treatise called the Hermetic Wave.

It is therefore fundamentally a book designed to recover as best as possible the hermetic, gnostic, and Pythagorean musical tradition, from the era in which we live, and aims to bring its *genius loci* closer to the growing number of individuals interested in the spirituality and symbolism of music. I have also taken the liberty to expand and construct several hermetic musical studies from scratch, which had not been aired until now and which essentially constitute the bulk of the book, agreeing that they not only contribute cohesion to the matrix but often constitute the creation of new colors and authentic artifacts for the mind of the musician (the hero-musician or hermetic musician), who will know how to employ them over time and with adherence to all this metaphysical-musical coherence. As will be seen, there are both basic and advanced concepts, but always with an advantage, in that instead of proceeding in increasing order of difficulty throughout the entire journey of the book, it does so rather within each topic, as if it were a compilation of stories, constituting a single myth.

To create this corpus, at its content source, 108 hours of lectures and an equal amount of course classes have been transcribed, edited for reading comprehension (which is not the same as listening comprehension), and expanded upon, totaling approximately 216 hours, of which every effort has been made to present them as structured parts. In some cases, the structuring has been quite a puzzle, as when speaking, ellipses are much more frequent than when writing, and an individual like me, influenced by Mercury, has had serious issues dealing with this. I want the labor to be appreciated, I do not say this ironically. It is also needless to omit expressing gratitude to all those who were present, and to all the students of the courses.

Origin of this book

The writing of this volume arose in the same year that 'La Lira de Hermes' was published, under the aegis or also the tide that the foundation itself of the Pythagorean and Hermetic School of Cittara, also the origin of the Musical Speculatorium, and made a year earlier. In reality, everything is part of the same, of the same corpus, and if I have to highlight important differences between the former and this volume, they are undoubtedly the approach of many of the issues to more earthly realms, allowing people from the broad musical sphere to combine the ideas of the existence of 'something more' with the answers - if any are given - from this book.

With this, the idea is twofold: on the one hand, to enunciate the precepts of a new type of musical education more in line with the emerging new time; to underline the perfectly studied foundation from ancient times of the qualities that music has and what effects it produces on musicians, listeners, and scholars of it; and to continue the line of the hermetists of the past who did so much to preserve the ancient tradition of Egypt in their studies.

One of them, Robert Fludd, is highly admired and extensively reflected in this work, as well as in all the means of disseminating Hermetic Music that I employ. But he is not the only one. So that the reader realizes the scope in which we are moving, both Fludd and others were members or sympathizers with initiatory schools of knowledge, such as the Rosicrucians. Rosicrucian readers and Masons of this volume will find valuable information for their growth, without my daring to say more or less than in 'La Lira de Hermes', what happens to be undoubtedly enough to say for this humble scribe speaking to them.

A matter of great power

With the permission of the Muses, I have focused this work on providing the musician with the tools to evolve from their conservatory education -and derivatives- to the correct approach for our time. To justify this assertion, I have taken into account the cycles that affect Human History, as extensively studied by figures such as Pierre D'Ailly or Demetrio Santos, unknown outside the realms of the Lodges, and applied them to the History of Music. Speculative and hermetic or Pythagorean music studies the power of music from the traditions of the West and the Near East. These matters are not foreign to the Vedic tradition (India), and together they move music to the place it deserves as a *language beyond language,* so to speak. Music is the manifestation of the idea in the auditory realm. Without it, ideas would not flourish inside the human mind, and progress and recapitulation would be impossible and unfeasible. This is why its selective prohibition, like that of literature, has been so characteristic of tyrannies throughout history.

The ability of music to awaken internal dynamics and, thanks to this, lead us to the heroic path ("know thyself"), is astonishing. I spoke about this in 'La Lira de Hermes', a previously published book on the initiatory journey of the hero-musician. Triggering the journey towards the center of being becomes the very origin of the disposition of what surrounds us, empowering us by the absence of fear, death's quintaessentia. Fear aside, and with a *hand full of music*, it won't come to pass the worst of possibilities. We have to be creative, because this brings us closer to musical comprehension.

The following discourse preceding the content may seem unjust to those who attend or belong to conservatories. It should be stated upfront that the writer does so from the knowledge of matters beyond the pride that may arise from having completed all conservatory education with the highest grades. That's water under the bridge now, and everything has changed, so whether the brightest minds or not the best-oiled machines thrive does not depend on me, but is a fact that will unfold in the world of musical education by laws far beyond my desires. As it often happens. Let it be clear, no offense intended, as much ego has been built on something that is soon to disappear. This is the real Classical Music.

The Dawn of the Musical Mystery Schools and the Decline of the Conservatoires: the Musical Speculatory

It makes no sense for the music taugh in conservatoires to be called classical music, as it would be a neoclassical achievement and only as a brief period under a similar name, not comprising Baroque, Renaissance, &c. Considering the idolatry prevailing in conservatories, I would rather say that it is called Idolatrous Music, and that conservatories manage to preserve this rather than the classical, that is from Greek and Rome, which they lost if they ever had it. They are Idolatrous.

I have previously mentioned the convenience of real studies for the musician, based on the fact that we are entering a new temporal cycle, an era, as we call it, or a subcycle of an aeon, as it was said in ancient times. As I delve into the numerical analysis of this later on, and measure it with the historical example of another Empire that also seemed eternal, I must now outline the flavor of this change. Conservatories emerge and develop under the dual premise that those with the most technical ability learn music; and those with the most resources also learn music. Both serve the same end, which is the earthly, the Earth as a classical element.

Physical structures such as conservatories correspond well with an education based on physical qualities (dexterity, resources). And, as a counterpoint, intellectual and innovative qualities, related to ideas and intellect, are summarily set aside: education is developed by and for technique on the instrument. It may be difficult for us to observe at first glance that music encompasses more than physical excellence on the instrument. Matters of the spirit are not addressed in conservatories, nor even the origin, selection, and function of Inspiration. At an intellectual level, conservatory musicians do not necessarily have to be intelligent. In fact, the notions of physics and mathematics that are necessary for understanding acoustics, a subject taught with little emphasis, are entirely baffling for the minds that are molded in these schools. The mind is exercised subordinated to the best use of the body, which is optimized to excellence. Whether it's a guitar or the voice, all physical instruments are perfected.

Therefore, it will be understood that both the institution and the students' access to it have had a raison d'être: matter, the earthly element, which is absent from the light of Reason (from Logos). In a previous tradition, we've had the Quadrivium, in which the four classical elements are treated in relation to music. It is nothing more than the way in which the wave divides into four (or reaches its fourth wave or third harmonic), producing the fundamental intervals (foundation of matter :: foundation of music).

If the era of the conservatories belongs to the earth element, then the one that has begun belongs to air. The institution is digital (the sign of Aquarius) for the next 20 years out of a total of 240 years; then transitioning to forms not yet seen. Over the next two centuries, which constitute the entire cycle, a teaching based on Intellect will be consolidated, where the access of the students will be determined by their mental capabilities, because of their ideas, and perhaps because of their belonging to one thought, ideology, or another. Imagine homogeneous groups of students, each one belonging to a school of musical thought well defined from the others. In fact, this will inevitably lead to competition in the realm of ideas, as it did in the Middle Ages with theological questions. For this reason, because History always repeats itself and the laws are there, it is that I stablished this school, the first Musical Speculatorium. And now, I will say that I write this book - though it's always the Muse who truly does.

As a corollary, we will find that the new institutions will be primarily online, in constant communication with each other like a nodal network on a global scale. The exchange of ideas, as well as their safekeeping, will be the hallmark of these schools. If virtuosity was once a measure (and still is, despite the distressing state of classical music concerts) of quality, now it will be intelligence; thus, the most intelligent will indicate the rules and paths (initiatory schools) for those entering their institutions.

I don't place much faith in schools governed by a solitary figure, but rather in collectives, although there will undoubtedly be individuals possessing the requisite acumen to cultivate multifaceted thinking within the uniformity of a collective ethos. Furthermore, I anticipate a climate of information censorship, with music education aligning itself with political doctrines, perhaps focusing on issues such as climate change or the advocacy for marginalized groups. Such myopic perspectives may serve to segregate individuals initially, yet ultimately, unifies them. However, it is conceivable that, at various echelons of visibility, ideologies more redolent of clandestine societies than educational establishments will emerge. While this outlook extends over a span of 240 years, it behoves the reader, whether a musician from the 'old guard' or a newcomer to this paradigm, to discern the prevailing winds.

The hermetic tradition has not left music aside, despite my first impressions 10 years ago on this matter. The institutions in charge of teaching music are the ones that have ignored the classical & metaphysical character of music, sound, and unfortunately overlooked learning their ways. We have the Greek myths, whose current analyses may indeed have overlooked the musical aspect, but when Pico della Mirandola dramatizes them in the Renaissance, music takes centre stage. It's no wonder that nowadays, major films, those whose significance lies -or lied, before *woke* culture arised- in their cohesion with the hero myth, feature soundtracks that constitute the majority of the dramatic object. Music enhances the vision, that is, the depth of sight. When observing the sequences, the characters acquire their complete archetypal garb, not only through their dialogues or appearance, but also through the music associated with them by the composer. The definition of heroic archetypes and the multiplicity of mythic faces are delineated or limited by the musical theme. It is thus an organiser of symbolic hierarchy, a veneer that transforms the physicality of light into the metaphysicality of the light's veneer. This veneer is responsible for imagination, and hermeticism works on it with the symbols we'll explore here.

Apart from Joscelyn Godwin's thorough analyses, it is indeed certain that music would have been susceptible to having its boundaries blurred, perhaps due to its own nature, perhaps due to its esoteric character. In a sense, the hermetic tradition utilized music to imbue its practitioners with a veneer and to inspire them. We are not discussing matters aired to the public, to the common folk, but rather knowledge that would often remain concealed due to its transmission in secretive form or passage, breaking more times than counted, thus breaking **orphic golden chain.**

Lastly, and before beginning the dissertation, I must emphasize that the basis of music theory as such has nothing to do with the true meaning of learning music, returning the slap of the unnatural to those who tried to enter into it and were scalded. It has therefore been necessary to underpin some basic principles. Principles that music students must be acquainted with, encompassing both its aesthetic and spiritual depths. These fundamental concepts are exemplified throughout this work, articulated and illustrated by numerous diagrams and figures that uphold the continuity of the longstanding hermetic tradition.

Once the principles are understood, the text is enriched with the ministers in the praxis of hermetic music in a myriad of subjects of which the knowledgeable audience of the Cittara™ corpus can now see all that knowledge expanded. Thus, I build a bridge between digital content and the classic book, for the good of all those interested in the matter. As I said, in these contents a clear vision of musical secrecy and its application is achieved.

My motivation for this writing is to continue serving the purpose of shining a light on the transmission of knowledge. Nevertheless, now, the hermetic question of music begins in earnest. I hope it clarifies many doubts for you and, above all, raises many new ones.

Book started on December 21, 2020, and finished its written corpus on April 12, 2022, towards the river banks of the Eridano. Finally tanslated in 2024 to English language.

Salutationes Orphicae

I dedicate this book to the woman that is the Door of Haven; the Strength; G.od's very Face. To Gabriela.

Baruch HaShem

.

Brief Introduction and Basic Concepts

*

* *

There exists the possibility, however uncertain it may seem, that the reader perusing this text may not yet be acquainted with the initial keys required to delve into these realms. We will discuss this, forming a pentalfa of tools, but first, let us understand that when we speak of hermeticism, it is one thing; whereas "material" music is another.

Music is grounded in notions of harmony, waveforms, and names and numbers to designate one or the other. Thus, for harmony, we have intervals, which define what sounds pleasant to the ear and what does not. Those interested in this book will want the introduction to be as comprehensive as possible, without being burdensome to read, so several key concepts that are of paramount importance and assist in discernment for what concerns us will be synthesized. I caution, and he who cautions is not a traitor, that this text will delve into the symbolism of hermeticism and, imbued in music, will sift through much thought; for they contain clues about musical ideas that, over the years, are bound to solidify

First and foremost, it is to bring all of this forth into nature, like any living being. Otherwise, the intellect lacks substance to nourish it and merely constructs artificially every journey in pursuit of the music of the spheres, or the musical ecstasy. This results in multiple styles, none of which are valid, as the being needs to earn a place in nature to avoid the sin of rushing to destroy it with the distortion of its fantasy. Therefore, we must place each piece in its proper place, building a structure that is difficult to dismantle, for at least a quarter of a millennium.

Vibration in Music

We begin by discussing vibration. The initial wave emerges from a complete absence of vibration, giving rise to a dynamic preceded by the tension of opposites. When two opposing forces collide, they create an oscillation that amplifies their opposition. Put differently, motion arises from a crisis and resolves it within the same movement.

The first hertz (oscillation per second) represents the first note, albeit inaudible. It is a C. This designation may be purely coincidental historically, or perhaps because ancient artifacts or resonators existed that indicated oscillations per second, allowing for calculations extending into the inaudible range. Indeed, anything below approximately 20 Hz is imperceptible to the human ear.

I OSCILLATION IN T SECONDS

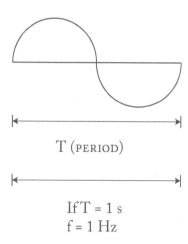

T (PERIOD)

If T = 1 s
f = 1 Hz

Figure: definition of Hertz.

Frequency, therefore, represents oscillation and is measured in Hertz (Hz = oscillations per second = second^{-1}). A visual example can be found in a guitar string, which vibrates like a skipping rope. From tens of cycles per second for low pitches to hundreds for high pitches, the higher the vibration, the sharper the note, and consequently, the higher its place in the hierarchy we will later discuss: that of the spheres.

The Spheres-Sirens

In the myth of Er, by Plato[1], Sirens are creatures that sing from each of the planetary Spheres (Moon, Mercury, Venus, ...), following each other in a hierarchical order, and that appear in the transit of the soul of this warrior. Every sound that is heard obeys to an oscillation, a time period, correspondent to each siren, also harmonically united into a whole chord according to the spindle of Necessity. The Music of the Spheres is the general harmony of all the moving bodies of the Universe, and it has both an exoteric and an esoteric study variants. The first of these is studied here The second is hinted at, not written, in any book as such.

Intervals

A note has more than just one frequency; it has a series of frequencies placed in very specific locations naturally configuring what is called the harmonic series. Each component of the harmonic series is a wave that has a numerical relations-

---

1   Plato. Republic. Book X, 614a-621b.

hip with the previous and the next. These relationships or ratios are called intervals. An interval, therefore, is the ratio between two pure sounds, initially, although it extends to any sounds. For example, among the first harmonics of a note, we find the ratio 3 to 2, meaning 1.5 times the original oscillaton. Well, this interval is a perfect fifth, a musical fifth. While this is not a book about basic music theory, it is significant to formulate intervallic understanding. I gather and discuss, therefore, with a series of clues, the nature of musical intervals.

[Hint 1] If a subject is represented in its predominant quality by one note, and another subject is represented by another, the interval or ratio between them would measure the degree of affinity for both qualities of both subjects.

[Hint 2] These basic intervals are:

Octave	Fifth	Fourth	Tone
Diapason	Diapente	Diatessaron	Tone

[Hint 3] There are perfect consonances, and the further the interval is in the harmonic series, the more imperfect (dissonant) is the ratio of the sounds.

[Hint 4] There are three ways to name an interval: by **number**, by **name**, or by **ratio**:

By number: the notes that mediate between two are counted: for example, between a do (C) and a fa (F) there is a fourth (do1 re2 mi3 fa4). By name (greek): diapason, diapente, diatessaron, ditone, semiditone, tone and semitone correspond to fractions between whole numbers that perfectly determine the wave na-

Diapason	2 a 1 (2:1)	octave
Diapente	3:2	fifth
Diatessaron	4:3	fourth
Diatria or Ditone	5:4 or 81:64	major third
Semiditone	6:5 or 32:27	minor third
Tone (epogda)	9:8	tone
Limma	256/243	semitone

Figure: intervals, the reasons of music.

ture of the interval. By proportion (latin): dupla, sesquiáltera, sesquitertia, ... although they have little use. Most importantly, the Greek name for the numerical ratio. Hence the table.

[Hint 5] Intervals, moreover, are formulated as fractions of two whole numbers. An interval can be indicated as 4/3, 5/3, etc. Starting from the origin of the harmonic series, what does this mean? Simply put, if a note vibrates at a certain frequency (Hz), when multiplied by such and such an interval fraction, another note is obtained, not an anonymous intermediate sound. The second note is at a certain interval from the first.

For example, if I play an A vibrating at 216 Hz, multiplying its frequency by 3/2, I get 324 Hz, which is an E. From A to E is a perfect fifth. As a result of this, the sound changes its name for the first time. In the harmonic series of the note C, for example, we have C C' G' C" E" G" B" C"', D"', E"', etc. The perfect fifth is the first note that varies from the fundamental (G in the example). The connotation of this is deeply mystical and gives rise to the so-called circle of fifths as a variation of the qualities of music that gives rise to the names (notes) of the sounds. Without this first interval different from the octave (which always yields the same note in name), music does not unfold.

But since this is an introduction to hermetic music, it is enough now to convey the idea that nature creates the harmonic series, and from there we extract, with reason and by reason itself, the intervals.

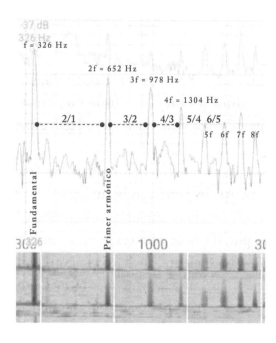

Figure: complete sound, with fundamental and harmonic series (where it says 'primer armónico', read 'first harmonic').

Harmonic Series

Sound, as it contains its name in the first instance and the unfolding of its attributes (harmonics) in the second, formulates order within itself. In the figure, you can see the example for a slightly high E note at 326 Hz. The spectrum[2] analyzer shows peaks where there is energy, that is, at double, triple, quadruple, etc., of the base frequency. This phenomenon is the harmonic series of a fundamental wave, and it is the most impressive and wondrous quality of nature.

Series of Chronocrators

For subsequent notes, it will be useful to include the dynamics of time in the numerical equation of hermetic music. There are cycles of approximate virtue that ring bells every certain number of years, which are 238 or, to simplify, 240 in the case of what are called *grand conjunctions*, 960 in the *maximum conjunction*. The starting cell of all of them is the conjunction between Jupiter and Saturn[3] ("cronocrators") that occurs every 20 years, which is the minor conjunction.

There are other conjunctions, such as the 30-year conjunction between Saturn and Mars, or the intermediate 60-year con-

---

2   Spectral or frequency analysis serves to observe the vibrations 'individually' of any sound. This can be done for a specific moment, as shown in the figure, or for the analysis of the sound over a certain period of time. It follows the principle that frequency is the inverse of the period ($f=1/T$), meaning that the number of waves per second is precisely what is represented by each peak (energy).

3   Pierre D'Ailly. Imago Mundi. Ed. Antonio Ramírez de Verger, Tabula Americae.

junction between Saturn and Jupiter . What will matter here is as a measure of time, since *chronocrator* denotes fatefully its meaning as a measurer of time. The foundation, so that you can understand where this comes from, that after 240 years with conjunctions in an element (fire, air, water or earth), then the chronocrators move on to the next element in the list of triplicities. That is, first 240 years combined in Fire sings, then another 240 in Earth signs, 240 in Air signs and 240 in Water signs, making a total of 960. There are overlaps and it is not that simple, but the rule is firm and in accordance with the *lex naturalis*.

Finally, to conclude the understanding of this, let's see where the cell comes from, which, after multiplying (harmonics), will lead to the great conjunctions and their periods. This cell, of approximately 20 years, is calculated as the synod of Jupiter and Saturn, that is, the time that elapses between every two encounters of the great gaseous giants of our solar system. For this, known the period of Jupiter around the Sun, which is approximately 12 years, and that of Saturn, which is approximately 30 years, its synod is calculated - approximately, as we are just beginning - as follows:

$$T_{conj} = \frac{30 \cdot 12}{30 - 12} = 20 \; years$$

Phormulae of the synod of Saturn and Jupiter (simplified).

When considering its twelfth harmonic, we come across the cycle of triplicity of each element of 240 years, $12 \cdot T_{conj}$; and the millennium cycle, $48 \cdot T_{conj}$.

The Tradition Overlooked

We must include in this brief introduction one of the reasons for the corpus you hold in your hands. In the year 1600, Giordano Bruno was burned at the stake in Campo di' Fiore by the Holy Office, which would set a precedent for the Hermetic tradition to carry out its hidden practical work from the ecclesiastical powers. Thus, in the following two centuries, Freemasonry (first grand lodge in 1717) and the Rosicrucians (Fama Fraternitatis, 1614) emerged as secret orders in communication with the Brunian reform. In the centuries from 1800 to today, the character of these orders shifted from an interest in the intercession of light with the physical world to an interest in dominating societies through their politics, with ideas of Hermetic and hierarchical emanation.

If we focus on music in its theurgical or symbolic-practical component, it was not integrated into secret societies, although it may have existed until the end of the Renaissance. Thus, the non-practical or speculative symbolism of music survived until today in the so-called speculative music. Authors after 1800 address this issue by stripping music of Hermetic practicality; the previous ones, such as those we will study here, still convey the light of the divine and archetypal ideas through music (1600-1800). Now, as a scholastic continuation - not narrative - of 'La Lira de Hermes' (The Lyre of Hermes), this volume makes the effort to revitalize the musical Hermeticism that was, on one hand, overlooked and, on the other hand, stripped of its power over the sonic and musical object. Music is, and will be, the greatest power that humanity can know, and it can lead to excellence if it is just, or to destruction if it is impious. The reader will realize that the book revolves around the solar idea, the just ordering of light in the human being, and the profound understanding (essayist) that Hermetic music requires from the student. Read, reread, and you will find.

```
          *
       *     *
    *     *     *
 *     *     *     *
```

CORPUS MUSICUM

Pentalph of the Musical Embodiment

For centuries, the West has embraced a musical doctrine detached from the soul through conservatories, despite having one of the most invigorating spiritual traditions of the human spirit. Thus, the emphasis on the material has allowed the validation of what would otherwise be unthinkable. Still, stemming from a tradition rooted in a time prior to the governance of cycles ruling now, the music inherited from the devic period (India) and religious era (Egypt) perpetuates the sense that once permeated the West (Greece), the inseparable purpose of music: to convey an intention imprinted from the divine or archetypal realm. If we aim to take the natural step towards the re-spiritualization of music, the structure must be built upon the ancient rules in which it was upheld, sometimes latent, sometimes living, for millennia.

In shaping a musical corpus that embraces the natural laws to be unfolded, the structure venerates the parts that constitute it with the number of Man. Thus, the number of matter -four- and quintessence produce the major themes of study and form the basis of hermetic music. Five pillars, reminiscent of ancient lodge principles, for in this aspect, the focus is on reintroducing the ancient to *equip* the modern musician - and non-musician alike - with the appropriate tool for such purpose.

Far, perhaps very far from my intention is to proclaim the sufficiency of the corpus that is presented, since only the number is enough. The parts that compose it are:

[1] Light and the vibratory phenomenon. Fundamental definitions.

[2] Tetraktys and the music of numbers.

[3] The Scale.

[4] Music and Memory.

[5] Mirror.

Understanding the natural system of music is fundamental for it to serve as the garment of Nature and to do so in the most harmonious manner possible. Thus, we speak of the relationship between what we observe in our daily lives and music; of the cycles of time and the vitality of ideas in harmony with music; of where and how music is processed in our bodies, and, in sum, music in its structural aspect within the processes of our minds and Nature itself.

Throughout the treatise, efforts will be made to link with classical knowledge what is necessary for music to regain its place in the Hermetic tradition. This tradition was severed in the 17th century and survived with specific figures that we will study on one hand, while on the other hand, the knowledge of the Hermetists, Kabbalists, and other such classifiable heterodoxes from this century onward, passed into the fickle clandestine realm, as has been mentioned. The figures represented in the pentacle are the classical virtues[4] and the Sun, symbol of Truth. The latter should refer to the first body, and the virtues to the others by their quality. These types of diagrams contain an explicit exoteric part, as it refers to each of the five parts or bodies that will form the musical body as such, and another esoteric part, which is not explained but which I trust can be sufficiently

---

4   In order: Justice, Temperance, Fortitude, and Prudence.

understood towards the end of the volume. So that a correspondence can be established:

1. Light = Truth (the whole)
2. Tetraktys = Justice (reason over the whole)
3. Scale = Temperance (serve yourself from the whole)
4. Memory = Strength (preserve the whole)
5. Mirror = Prudence (contemplate the whole)

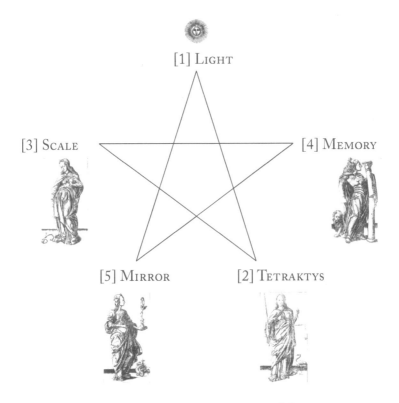

Figure: musical embodiment pentalpha.

I. Light and the Vibrating Phenomenon. Fundamental definitions.

The principle of all hermeticism is the movement particle that we call 'oscillation'. Without this idea, logical deficiencies crowd at the door of the student who tries to unravel a set too complex to glimpse an easy solution. Everything oscillates at different levels and with different qualities of vibration. The whole is hamonic to a certain degree and also allows the contemplation of its internal harmony at the same time. The phenomenon of vibrtion passes from the subtle to the physical and then to the subtle, so many times. The adventure of knowing, of delving into the depths of the unknown, training in the two-way gaze and unraveling the qualities of being through friction with life itself is a privilege of the living. Light needs the experience within matter to make the powerful drama of the world prosper; light needs life. It is therefore the right of every living being to enhance its brilliance in the incessant change within the unfathomable darkness of the universe.

1.1. Vibration in hermeticism

Vibration is every oscillation, and oscillation is the movement originated in the force of opposites. Two emerging particles arising from the desire of the previous monad or unity to exist in the physical realm. Tradition speaks of masculine and feminine principles stemming from an androgynous entity, and in 'La Lira de Hermes' this matter is well documented. From the two distinct particles, movement blossoms, for their opposition generates the dynamics of things, giving rise to the wave. To begin with, one must understand the sequence:

[1] There is the One, the indivisible force, the whole, which emanates from the Nothingness through the *desire* of light to manifest itself in the World.

[2] From the Necessity of the One arise in turn the two opposing antagonistic principles that shape the World.

[3] These two principles define, through their opposition, the tension that generates the first Movement.

[4] This movement, in turn, initiates the movement of all things that exist as consequences in the mind of the One, thus:

[5] All movements are originated. This occurs successively and without time or space.

[6] All these things vibrate in different ways and speeds.

[7] Part of all that vibration is audible to beings.

[8] Part of all that vibration is visible to beings.

[9] Part is perceptible to beings in other ways.

Now we need to understand the terms that completely shift the focus of what will be concretized later. There are three ancient precepts that converge into one solution. Firstly, hermetism designates all vibration as light, so that light spectra beyond the eye are also light, and most importantly, sound vibration, sound, is also light. Secondly, it follows from the Pythagorean perspective: everything that vibrates is sound, meaning all oscillation is viewed in terms of sound. The third consideration is Gnostic, which sees all vibration as a time aeon -total or in its partials-, as temporal cycles ranging from the everyday to the galactic, consonant with Hindu doctrines. Light, sound, and aeons are the true considerations of vibration. As can be deduced, they all embed each other particularly and as a whole, thus fulfilling the identity of all others. We can illustrate this with an algebraic theorem: if a set A is contained (its elements) in B, and B is contained in A, with A and B being two sets or spaces of the same dimensions, then A = B.

The implications with the three elements seen, mutually related as stated by this theorem, are manifold. The most important of these is, then, *what is music?* Since the stage on which music moves is the multiplicity in harmony, it is only possible to contemplate it from this plane, which is that of Creation. Everything that moves and therefore vibrates is interconnected by music both within the same being and with other beings. A physically simple being contains less complexity in its vibrations, therefore less musical complexity, than one with more complex biology. Hence, ideas are often associated with musical purity, because it is through atomization that man reaches his ultimate cognitive frontier, where he dissolves into the unknown whole (myth of Butes). As an example in human biology, there is a harmony between the senses of hearing and sight, with configurations in each based on octaves of vibration (1 octave for sight, 10 for hearing)[5].

Each one of us, thanks to the internal multiplicity of sounds, lives *a* harmony or lives *in* harmony. The correspondence with similar harmonies makes us resonate and therefore produce a movement in the world generated by that resonance. Music is the use of internal harmony, its dynamization endowed with intentionality. It is clear that music (from the Hebrew root *mosh*, water; or Latin *moys*, water as well) is the fluctuation of harmony composed of internal sounds in collusion with the vital journey that combines them with external ones. I will simplify it: harmony is an absolute that generates internal movements and resonances corresponding to vital experience; music is the result of these movements and resonances.

Seeing music as a natural result of the configuration of the human being at all levels, subtle -spiritual, electrical- and physical -biological-, is undoubtedly something interesting to imagine. Music becomes like the sea, where everything is interconnected with everything through waves ('oceans of time'). We could talk about similes unconsciously created by poets, like the one for the Moon, but there is already much written in later regions of this book for such a formal explanation.

Sufficient is then to say that when we talk about music, we point at a result of the movement of light; at a result of its own creation of temporal aeons; and then a result of life itself that reproduces it and continues reproducing it, through the cycles of cycles (*in saecula saeculorum*). Because everything

---

5   Factor of approximately 2^{10} for the sound spectrum (20-20000 Hz) and 2 for the visible light spectrum (760-380 nanometers).

plays its own music. Because every being, given birth by a mother (water, moys, music) and therefore a holder of an imprint of that light in its biology, experiences that same imprint through the movement of tension-distension (waves), where the soul expresses itself.

It is, perhaps with all certainty, the intellectual capacity of the human being that can consciously immerse him/herself in the divine language hidden within music. Hence the teaching of the **matematikoi**[6] in contrast to the **akousmatikoi**[7]. The latter would be experimenters of external sound, while the former are knowledgeable about it at an internal level.

Tracing a reverse path with the previous points, music would not exist except in the multiple, and as we ascend into levels-of the-subtle scale, only the interval, or interval-idea, would exist. We will discuss much about this, and it is interesting from the outset to think of the monad, indivisible unity, as the unison interval, and duality as the octave, both with vibration relationships of 1 to 1 and 2 to 1, respectively, understanding in the same language (number) music and idea.

1.2. Neoplatonic Spheres: analogies with the previous statements

Neoplatonists, followers of the doctrines of Plato and especially the Timaeus, deduce different degrees of ontological reality that we call Spheres, which are analogous to what we

---

6   The knowing ones; operators of the idea-number with a mystical character. Close associates of Master Pythagoras.

7   The listeners; the esoteric teachings were forbidden to them, but not the practices around number nor the way of life of the Pythagorean community.

have just recounted. What first exists as knowable is the first cause, a level that is not a consequence of any other and is the cause of all others. This is -behold- the Pythagorean Monad. It is followed by the first mover, the sphere of the fixed stars (firmament, *rakía*), and the seven spheres of the visible planets, including the Sun and the Moon. The correspondences with the previously mentioned points are direct, and it deduces that the fixed stars, which are ultimately the first visible, hide duality and de facto exhibit the multiplicity of matter. The connection of these two parts is something called *form*, which refers to the spiritual immanent in the world: the Holy Spirit. The Trinity of Catholicism exemplifies it, for is triune and geometrically triangular. It is also the Masonic triangle, that is, a representation of divinity as an archetypal image. Also the third level of the Tetraktys, a figure that we will see later.

1.3. The light wave of the year

One of the phenomena of vibration is the harmonic. Each note seen as a primarly or fundamental vibration (oscillation) possess a series (array) of harmonics that follow it. I am sure that many of you will know what the harmonic series is, but I am going to explain it here in such a way that it is understood at a knowable level, close to the syncretism that we were talking about between light, sound and time. For this we are going to take the model of the year, whose light measured in daylight hours is increasing and decreasing in function of the solstitial axes. When the Sun is at the winter solstice (Northern hemisphere), the light is minimal[8], both in height and in radiation time. This affects all eco and bio-systems under it, then the world is governed by the light of the year.

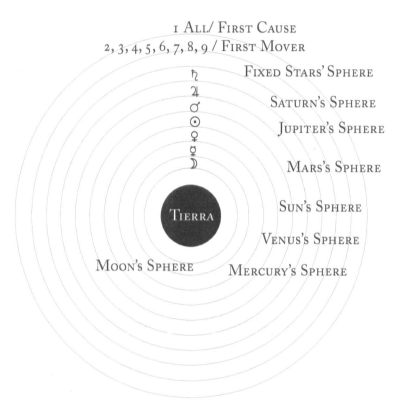

Figure: neoplatonic spheres.

The light's zenith is at the summer solstice; its nadir at the winter's, and both dates mark the beginning of the zodiac signs Cancer and Capricorn, respectively. This allows us to trace a half-wave of light[9] along the entire zodiacal set.

---

8   Referencio a latitudes específicas del hemisferio norte, todo es a la inversa para el hemisferio sur.

9   The half-wave or semiperiod is taken as the fundamental frequency, O1.

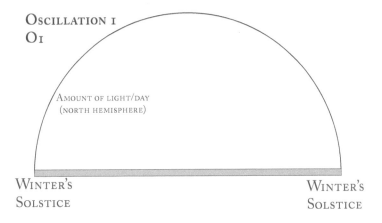

OSCILLATION I
O1

AMOUNT OF LIGHT/DAY
(NORTH HEMISPHERE)

WINTER'S
SOLSTICE

WINTER'S
SOLSTICE

Figure: first wave O1, in relation to the light of the year.

Now we turn our attention to the first derivative of the matter[10]. Light ascends in hours and altitude throughout the year from the winter solstice to the summer peak; from there it descends to the winter solstice again. In other words, each day in the first half of the period is brighter than the previous one, and in the second half, it's less bright. This variation in light is called the 'light gradient', indicating that there will be two zones in the year of opposite nature based on that variable. Since we represent the first wave, we now do so alongside the second, observing the same wave phenomenon but unfolded initially. This second wave, O2, is a harmonic of the first, and its frequency is, as can be seen, twice as much. The octave or diapason has been born, dividing the year between increasing light and decreasing light.

---

10   The derivative refers to the variation of the function. In this case, it 'derives' more at the beginning and end of the year, and not at all towards the middle. This is better represented by twice the period (rather than a cosine function) as it combines both the harmonic series and the light phenomenon, marking not only the variation but also its nature.

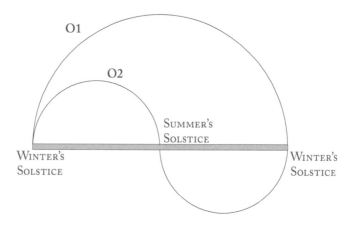

Figure: waves O1 and O2.

Following this same rule, if at double the origin vibration of the light we have another wave with a natural direction in the year (light gradient), applied a factor of 3 we will have triple the vibration of the origin wave, which will leave three semicircles displayed throughout the year. This third wave divides the year between (1) humidity, (2) dryness and again (3) humidity; or if preferred, reception of waters, harvests, and sowings.

After O3 comes O4, which is derived from O2 and quadruple vibration of the original. The intervals of fifth and fourth, diapente and diatessaron, or harmonics at three times the original frequency and double octave of the original frequency, unfold over the year. Both will have natural significance. Thus, O4 marks the four seasons with each zero crossing[11], and this is the most visible. Oscillation O3 has another connotation not so trivial, as it comes from the form (number 3) and is not treated here in all its depth. Suffice it to say that light follows the natural order when

---

11   The zero crossing is the passage through the null value of the function, when the wave is neither positive nor negative.

unfolding in factors of 2, 3, and 4. Light also shows time structures delimited by the four qualities of matter when unfolding in O4, as it becomes evident that winter (cold and dry), spring (humid/moist and warm), summer (warm and dry), and autumn (cold and wet) perfectly divide the year. A student of hermeticism sees in that thing which is light the cause of this. That is to say, the harmonic of the light constituted by the O4 produces, in fact, the qualities of matter: warm, cold, moist and dry. It is not lost on anyone that things divided into four parts, like the directions (cardinal points), the houses (walls), etc., obey this harmonic of light, and therefore exist as an idea (*ratio*, reason) in our intellect.

Seeing the seasons depicted in undulating waves intertwines seamlessly not only with the temporal eons but also with the mystic realms of musical theory. This doctrine is steeped in Pythagorean wisdom, where the synthesis of vibration -light, time and sound- finds its essence in number. For the ancients, number is - or embodies - the Logos, giving birth to the very fabric that imbues meaning into the vast cosmos. While we comprehend binary time divisions with ease, the ternary remains a mysterious triad, akin to dawn, day, dusk, night. Yet, this triadic division, although I've reserved a separate volume of a religious-musical nature for its elucidation, may allude to the spirit's cravings, the soul's motions. These are the yearnings for material acquisition driven by an impulse or vital force, echoing in the cyclic rhythms of harvests and growth.

The day can be divided into three parts: day, night and twilight. Objectively speaking, sunrise and sunset are a period of the day with common characteristics in terms of the height (angle) of the light. Not in terms of the sign of its gradient, but its intensity[12].

---

12 The light variation at sunrise and sunset is similar, albeit the former entails

It is sufficient to point out the common to classify as one (common feature: horizontal incidence). Now, what distinguishes the moment of twilight from the ordinary moments of day and night, on a mental level? That the energy and dynamics at those points vary significantly with respect to the others. It is an internal effect that produces the third wave, a difference in the quality of being, *the qualitas*. This internal mutability, this very musical dynamic is going to take place in the odd waves and, before that, it will be the very basis of music. Regarding the even waves, they will refer to the physical, to the material product of the waves of light, either O2, O4 or if we extend the model, O8, O16, &c.

Seeing it as a frequency, the year would vibrate according to its O1, which would be its fundamental oscillation. A wave has positive and negative half cycles, which expresses duality in its first form. If the year is expressed with a single hemicycle, it is because it represents unity, where there are still no principles divided into opposites[13]. With this natural example I have deduced for your better understanding that each fundamental vibration has replicas at double, triple, quadruple, and beyond, its frequency; giving rise to the environment as we see it. Then, if a C vibrates at 64 Hz (fundamental frequency f), this favors the development of a component of the note at 128 Hz (2 times f), another at 192 Hz (3·f), at 256 Hz

---

it positively (increase) and the latter negatively (decrease).

13   One of the main differences between two of the most important doctrines of the cycle, Pythagoreanism and Gnosticism, is that the former sees the whole (Universe) as unitary, and from there successive ontologies derive into matter, which is embedded in a single process. Conversely, Gnosticism, the latter, indicates the soul-body division and this duality as its foundation. Hence, its ontological exegesis of the wave (positive semicircle and negative semicircle), and with it the other doctrines of number that supposedly influence (Kabbalah).

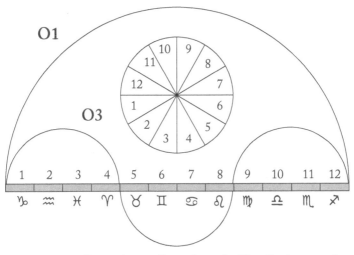

Figure: year according to its quality, where the 12 split signs can be seen.

(4·f), 320 Hz (5·f),... -up to a finite and unlimited frequency term with less and less amplitude. Therefore, the harmonic phenomenon gets explained by the multiplicity of orders (Cosmos) of life. It suggests exactly that, that music points to how the strata of life are constituted, and since everything moves, everything has a soul, and is therefore part of a movement, which is music. For the Pythagoreans, the Universe was included in a great Animal (it is Plato who explains it, although the substratum was Pythagorean), analogy with soul, soul, movement. And that this animal, like a great whale -corresponds to the Hebrew Leviathan- harbors the drama of the stars and life.

Understanding well what has just been explained regarding the light of the year implies delving precisely into the consciousness of the natural, as examples emerge like the day, which we can contemplate with its harmonics analogous to those of the year, unfolding to complete, in stages, the set:

O1 (fundamental oscillation) = natural day.
O2 (first harmonic) = day and night according to light; Sun and

Moon according to governance.

O3 = formal division in light, wetness, and heat, of the day.

O4 = angular division of the day = dawn, zenith, sunset, nadir.

Natural, luminous, and angular divisions define the waves of the day as a microcosm of the year, so it is not difficult to understand that the harmonics, nature of sound, unfold in what is marked or subject, measured by time.

For the hermetics, the focal point of the universe is humanity. Within humanity (hence the Renaissance Humanism's avid embrace of hermetic translations), influences converge. Broadly, these extend to communities, nations, and on a global scale, to beings and the Earth itself. Now, the life of a human being, while marked by the threshold between stillness (death) and motion (life), unfolds in continuous movement. Thus, their first wave (O1) is intertwined with every movement, encompassing pulse, breath, and more.

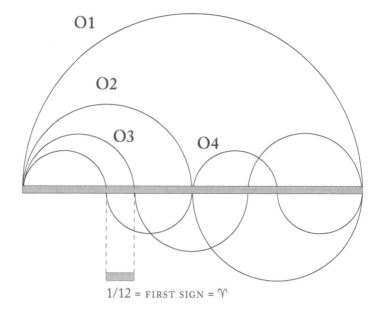

1/12 = FIRST SIGN = ♈

Figure: year according to its quality, where the 12 divided signs are appreciated.

The two material waves, O2 and O4, denote distinct phases in a person's life. The former signifies the midpoint, while the latter represents a quaternary division. These are physically discernible stages: a private and familial sphere contrasts with a public one, and a phase influenced by external factors (family, nation, ...) differs from one where the individual is the agent of change or relocation. For instance, it is at a certain age that one transitions from being a member of a family to establishing one's own. The fourth wave encompasses the four pivotal moments of individual crisis:

O4 (human):
O4.1. Birth and infant life.
O4.2. Adolescence and sexuality.
O4.3. Adult life, marriage and children.
O4.4. Contribution to society, legacy and eventually death.

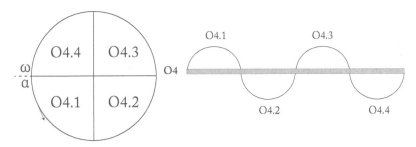

Figure: vital eons of the human being.

The cross that delineates these four phases of the wave points to those four moments of crisis, initiating them. The model originates from Demetrio Santos' C60 and, in broad strokes, indicates the ages of transition or crises at approximately 0, 14.5, 29, and 44.5 years of age for the individual, marking the 'death' within the cycle, around[14] age 60 (hence the name). As the individual is embedded in society, this knowledge, which was understood, underpinned what are known as rites of passage.

Ancient societies produced rites between these stages, some of which still offer us reminiscences today (baptism, circumcisions, military service, marriage, ...). It would be worthy of study which of these crises are not overcome in the society's unconscious due to lack of rites of passage, but as long as it serves as an idea, I am content. It's natural that these examples sound 'traditional', as it is precisely the sense of tradition to offer rites at critical life points. What rites of passage achieve is to prevent the somatization (illness, death) of crises, so their utility is fundamental not only at an individual level but also at a social level, as society also somatizes and does so in psychological forms: collective psychosis, fear, docility, in the negative; momentum, expansion, and birthrate (continuity of the community), in the positive.

A society like the Western one, now characterized by its low birthrate, thus exhibits a symptom of psychological mourning that stems from not resolving crisis points. It's unnecessary to see how in Eastern European countries, where teenagers face military service (initiation into adulthood) and have a strong institution of marriage (initiation into the public sphere), the birth rate is high. I am aware that the portrayal sounds discordant, but precisely there lies History to give us the guidelines to follow. Unless, of course, we think that human beings have evolved somewhat in our atavisms or our biology as much.

---

14 58 years according to the initial idea from Demetrio Santos, only that 60 better explains the onset of old age.

Ignoring the third oscillation O3 in the human life cycle would be a mistake, as it provides the most insight into the subject matter of this book, which, apart from branches like the previous one, is none other than the true functionality and meaning of music. The third wave impacts the internal plane, affecting emotions, thoughts, ideas, and, in general terms, the human spirit. The number three balances the life narrative, doing so unconsciously and perpetuating itself in spheres that fertilize thought: narrative works have three parts, as do films and their direct derivatives, artistic or entertainment events (streams, concerts, shows, videos), and songs, to name direct examples. Similarly, a conversation follows this 'pattern,' with greetings at the beginning and end; and conversation in between. Can anyone imagine doing it differently? It's natural, what the internal number makes us manifest. If we find this structure in art (and music in particular), it's because we need it to move through life. Without anything other than material cycles (O2 and O4), life lacks substance, preventing the individual from being fulfilled. It is in the third wave where the *qualitas vitae* resides, thus the essence and movement of the thing.

1. 4. Circle of Diapentes

From the third oscillation O3, which governs the movement of the soul or internal variation of being (vital processes)[15], we bring into musical consciousness the diapente. Remember, it is called so because there are five notes between

---

15   Consider, for example: childhood, adulthood, old age; seed, plant, reproduction. &c.

the origin and destination notes of the interval. It was called diapente by the Greeks, which means "through five," and later the perfect fifth, and determines entry into the sonic quality. The first distinct note arises with the perfect fifth. It differs in quality, hence its name (C, G, D, A, ...). Arithmetically, it arises from multiplying the vibration by 3, or 3/2 if we adhere to the definition of diapente inscribed within the octave (diapason), the usual one. The number 3 pertains to form, and it is the first masculine number of the Pythagoreans (1 is androgynous, 2 is feminine, 3 is masculine), which effectively configures the diapente as the architect of the generation of the sonic event. Hence arise the 12 notes, going from perfect fifth to perfect fifth until completing the 12 quantum sounds.

If we then multiply the vibration of C by 3, we have that of G^{16}; if to this by 3, the one of D; successively until reaching again a C, only 19 octaves higher than the first C although not quite the same[17]. The total interval is covered by 12 diapentes but it is not, however, a result of 19 perfect octaves, for the Pythagorean comma ('CP') stands out, as it is called, resulting as the distance with respect to the perfect 19th completion of the diapason:

$$CP = \frac{3^{12}}{2^{19}} = 1.013643265$$

---

16   C-do (1st note) re (2nd) mi (3rd) fa (4th) sol (5th).

17   With these multiplications by 3, we increase by one diapason and one diapente each time (disdiapente), so that finally we will have increased approximately 19 octaves by the Pythagorean comma. That is, if we ignore the Pythagorean comma, 19 disdiapentes are equivalent to 12 diapasons.

However, at a nominative level, and although this comma bears profound significance, our interest lies in the 12 diapentes. We are concerned with the fact that these 12 notes complete what is called the Circle of Diapentes or Circle of Fifths. The first is the appropriate way to name it as it alludes to its original name and quality; the second is the *schematic* way of doing it. The musician knows it by heart, but little is known about the relationship with the number 3, and hence the connotation derived from O3 or the third wave of light. It can be understood that if 12 sounds are necessary for the musical structure, the diapente produces the distinguished sound quality (a different note) and completes the series in O12, which produces the zodiacal system. Both, the system of 12 diapentes or simply the notes, and the zodiac, are intimately related through the same root idea.

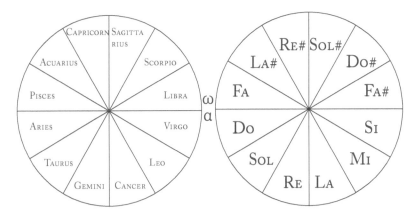

Figure: Circle of Diapentes and Circle of Zodiac Signs.

In these figures, we take the corresponding division into 12 parts (O12) of the harmonic-zodiacal set, to indicate within it the division of time and space carried out by music, which acts as the formal language of number for discerning the cosmos. The equinoctial beginning serves as a model, and from the starting point of the winter solstice (beginning of light), another could be indicated, although with the natural order of sounds (successive diapentes or circle of diapentes), the same natural succession of the zodiac signs, or the 12 portions of the skies, is understood. They correspond to each other through movement, not so much through the names of the notes, and through the number of elements. Movement because it reflects the natural order: neither going backwards in cyclical time is natural, nor is the reverse listening of the circle of diapentes; and number, because 12 is the continuous order upon which the cosmos is sustained, by matter (4) and by astral force (3).

II. Tetraktys and the Music of Numbers

Figure: pythagorean tetraktys.

The divine Tetraktys is an ontological diagram, in image of the Creation of the World. It does not hold the representation of the world only visible but the invisible. This figure is also named Mnemosyne, *Memory*, and at each point houses a deity. We will not linger on this, but the notion that number is an idea and is divine is with this figure explicitly stated. As for the emblematic sum of the perfect number, the decade (10), starts from the first four natural numbers, endowing them with a clear symbolic magic for the Pythagoreans: 1+2+3+4=10, the completeness, the scalable whole. Thus, it is inscribed in the four levels, the created universe. There is a method of verifying in this the coexistence of the physical and the metaphysical: the geometric. Neither an isolated point (higher level), nor a straight line (second level), nor a plane (third level) are physically reachable; On the other hand, a volume (four points) is, since four points are necessary and sufficient conditions to form a volume, physical object and allegory of the tangible. All levels exist but the last one is both matter and a consequence of the other three (form/ causes). This simple reasoning that uses the idea of the minimum number of points that define a volume, a plane, a line and a dot, serves perfectly the purpose of exemplify the interconnection of everything created, whether we can physically verify it (scientific method) or not.

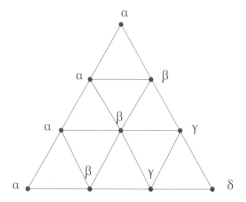

Figure: tetraktys as geometry emblema[18].

In the tetraktys, the relationship between the fourth level and the first is one of disdiapason, double diapason, double octave, 4 parts opposed to 1. It is between the third level, in the form o triad, and the fourth (tetrad), which appears the interval diatessaron 3 to 4 (or 4 to 3). And from the level of the dual to the trine 2 to 3 (or 3 to 2), diapente. The sequence is therefore diapason-diapente-diatessaron.

---

18 Unfolding the 10 points in hierarchy, the process involves recognizing the geometric nature of each one: first the point (α); then two points (α, β) are needed to form the line; then (α, β, γ) the plane; finally (α, β, γ, δ) the tangible volume.

Considering harmonic series up to its twelfth term (oscillation) O12, the zodiacal divisions and the harmonic wave will coexist. It is in this "moment" that music defines from the roots its fundamental matrix as syncretic with time. The 12 eons participate in the twelve divisions of the ecliptic of musical discourse. But why twelve? Up to now, this number has been introduced as the quintessential triumvirate of identities light::sound::eons, but ideas intertwine in the mind in ways that are not easily explained. What we do observe is its consequence in music.

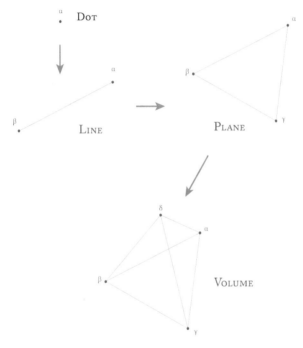

Figure: Unfolding of the geometry of points (point-line-plane-volume).

The panoply of possible sounds for scales and modes is twelve (excl. Hindi music). From the 12 sounds as formants of all the quantum possibilities of sound vibration, the order imposes the use of 7, which are those of the scale, mode or swara. In one of the most successful videos on the Cittara Musica Hermetica YouTube channel, he argued the relationship between note systems and the quintessential Pythagorean figure: the tetraktys. I transcribe here with certain adaptive modifications to the style and purpose of this book what was its text, adding part that was not issued and that was kept private in the original, seeing the light in this case.

2. 1. Numbers and Waves in the Tetraktys

Enigmatic figure whispered among Pythagoreans, offering as its primary power the attainment of musical intervals, and its foremost act the use of the monochord. Let us delve into this mysterious realm. The octave (levels 1 to 2), the fifth (2 to 3), and the fourth (3 to 4) function akin to the earlier discussed waves (oscillations) O1, O2, O3, and O4. It is fitting to classify it thus, for the number is nothing but the idea resting in memory after comprehending the phenomenon of cycles and harmonics. Expanding upon this notion, numbers would not exist as such but as images produced within our intellect, where Memory resides, and as a veneer in the mental image created upon understanding cycles. The cycles do exist, **physically as waves, and metaphysically as numbers**. And, behold, the Tetraktys was known as Mnemosyne (memory).

On another note, let us begin with the obvious. There are two key numbers to define music: 7 and 12. Seven are the notes of the scale; twelve, the total possible notes. Among these, we take the first to create scales and tonalities, underlying a vector from chaos to order, from the total sound of

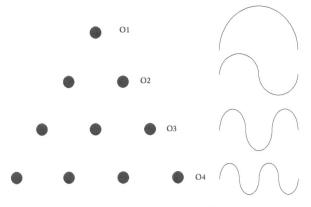

Figure: tetraktys and its oscillations.

12, requiring order to produce effects on the individual, on the ensemble (subset) of 7 sounds guaranteeing such order. Always, a subset of 7 of those 12 notes is employed (in Western music). However, in Carnatic Music of India, there exist 22 possible notes called shruti, of which 12 would be a subset. This is because the intervals of the Pythagorean scale are a subset of the intervals that make up the 22 shruti. We'll delve into this later. We embark on a journey through the numerical realities of our music, and it is to teach us both simplicity and significance simultaneously.

2. 2. Seven

The addition of the points at the 4th and 3rd levels of the tetraktys mirrors the contemplation of the superimposed waves O3 and O4 (representing diapente and diatessaron, movement, and the physical), establishing a correspondence with the harmonic seven that sustains nature. Seven notes are formed within the scale by the interaction of the diapente and the diatessaron, creating the tone, which serves as its foundational element, resulting from the diapente between the diatessaron. Additionally, considering that each level of the tetraktys holds symbolic significance, the summation of two levels also carries meaningful implications.

Focusing on these levels requires their definition. The fourth level is that of matter, since 4 are the constituent elements of this (fire, earth, air and water); the third is associable to the tripartite substance Body-Soul-Spirit, a kind of seat level of the paradigm for harmony whose virtue lies in its quality, which is formal, of light, and therefore balances the previous, the biological. This leads to movement both external (movement, audible sound) and internal (anima, inaudible sound). Certain texts intertwine both meanings in the following way: earth + water = body; water + air = soul; air + fire = spirit. This serves as a foundation to move from one level to another. However, the interdependence of the different levels of the tetraktys does go further.

The sum of the two levels, that of matter and the first level dedicated to spirit (form), aligns with the total number of notes on the scale. Consider that the scale serves as the indispensable and comprehensive unit for musical composition. With seven notes, melodies and harmonies are crafted, establishing the essential framework, as observed in tonality, to create a closed and coherent system—a work reflecting creation within its defined boundaries, marking both the beginning and end of the model.

Therefore the music that is born from this union has a material and a spiritual component. The material aspect we contemplate has, thanks to physical phenomena: acoustic listening, the instruments with which it is performed, the human body, and sound waves as a physical phenomenon. The spiritual part would reside in the emotions that its execution transmits, the evocations that it produces when being played, those that the musician receives when being inspired, as well as the impulses of transcendence of the limitations that it inspires in the musician, performer or listener, listening to music and everything that connects with the "rapture" of inspiration.

The culmination of these two tiers, as previously mentioned, delineates the musical composition, or what it is meant to be. A system with a commencement and conclusion, an alpha and omega, yet one that solely possesses them to recommence afresh with another set of seven, is consequently enclosed within 7 notes. And this cycle never ceases, octave after octave. The same phenomenon applies to the sequence of seven days known as the septimana (week), which perpetually recurs as a local unit of time measurement.

At a more subtle level of understanding lies the melodic foothold of the significance of seven. Three and four are aligned to make seven, and thus the dimension remains. Therefore, every melody is **horizontal**, meaning it follows a pattern that allows projection onto the horizon, like the outline of a mountain range.

2. 3. The twelve notes

The 4th and 3rd levels, O3 and O4, again -but now multiplied- give the 12 possible notes: the sound matrix. From this we draw the initial conclusion that music is therefore circumscribed to these two levels of the Tetraktys. This time, being a product, the implications are different. The lowest metaphysical level and the physical level interact, not aligning each other in the same dimension, but placing one orthogonal to the other, thus generating a larger dimension than in the previous case. This dimension is harmony. Music, in this context, progresses vertically, with notes layered atop one another, subsequently generating melodies. Both harmony (of 12) and melody (of 7), understood as concepts, embody their entire speculative significance, defining the essence of music. The problem is circumscribed to the deep understanding of the tetraktys, something that was exhaustively worked on in 'La Lira de Hermes', the initiatory journey of the hero-musician.

Harmony in classical music, its physical concept, is built as several melodies one on top of the other, complying with certain rules. That is to say, that the melody proves that it is a subset of the harmony, or the 7 notes are a subset of the 12, as also happens at its purely rational- Pythagorean level.

Music runs like this, it runs vertically: notes on top of other notes, which in turn generate melodies. Harmony is thus vertical. Both, the harmony, of 12, and the melody, of 7, understood as ideas, shed their full speculative meaning of what music is, and the problem remains circumscribed to the deep understanding of the tetraktys and what each level and each particle means in extension, something that exceeds the purpose of this writing.

2. 4. Notes and Planets

The notion that melody involves the number 7, in ancient science, is associated with the 7 visible celestial bodies, and therefore with the 7 days of the week (or septimana): the Sun, the Moon, Mars, Mercury, Jupiter, Venus, and Saturn. Harmony, on the other hand, would serve as the context for these 7 spheres, the places where they "resonate," much like how it provides support to melody in worldly music. And where do they resonate? Perhaps this is the most beautiful aspect of all: there are twelve divisions of the sky along the so-called Ecliptic - as we have seen - which is the region where millennia ago, the constellations of the zodiac were identified. Seven celestial bodies within twelve zodiac signs-cons-tellations that have served since ancient times to measure what? The cycles, the events, the periods, ... or the synthesis of all this: time, aeons, light.

Thus, music and perhaps as I say this is the greatest possible conclusion, is circumscribed to the temporal universe, and is in-capable of de facto transcending it. But that is its limit and it also relies on it to create the sensations of 'fleeting passage of time', 'heavyness', 'joy', 'melancholy', all of them implying subjectively a distortion of the perception of time. So, not being able to change it de facto, at least music acts in -and strikes to- the human psyché making that man has a totally speculative idea of the relativity of time, being able to *peek* the superior dimension where it no lon-ger exists. A dimension claimed by the mystics and that without a doubt would have been transcended by notoriously very few people throughout history. This is where music connects with mysticism.

2. 5. Scale of the Spheres (and introduction to the next point)

When we combine the four notes with the three, we gain a faithful understanding of how the mind structures or articulates the material with the spiritual. Initially, it places the dense, the four, and then closes the group with the formal. The scale from the fundamental vibration to a higher diatessaron encompasses progressive heights from the former to the fourth note; this would correspond to four of the spheres. The last three notes would correspond with the other three. The 7 notes are:

[a] The **Four** astronomical planets of rapid cycle: spheres of the Moon, Mercury, Venus, Sun (Neoplatonists' view).

[b] **Three** of slow cycle: Mars, Jupiter, and Saturn.

I've taken the liberty to introduce a variable, which is the speed of the cycle, so that a problem can gradually permeate it, which we will address when we explore the Music of the Spheres. As a consequence, what we have referred to by the names of the notes would allude to the stars. The Gnostics already deal with this, and it's no wonder, as it allows us to address the 'mirror' existing between the seven sounds (deduced in this number by the Pythagorean scale as we will see shortly) and the seven moving celestial bodies.

Figure: clestial bodies and scale.

This view of the notes can serve to contemplate the germ of the music of the spheres. It is obvious that the first four are syncretised with the material (four elements), and of the remaining ones the spiritual, and I state this with two corresponding figures: square and triangle. You can imagine the notes you need, but under the aegis of the major scale or Pythagorean scale, as it serves as a model. There is no suggestion of a unique allocation for each planet-note, since the divergence between what reflects the material (first diatessaron) and what the formal (last ditone) is of greater appreciation, and how they underpin the union of the 7 elements of astral quality. What will be of interest to the reader, already aware of celestial mechanics, is that as the orbit size increases[19], the vibration decreases as the period becomes longer, and therefore the note becomes lower, not higher in pitch. But it must be remembered that the number of variables here is immense, and if it were resolved by a simple logic problem, no symbol would have been constituted thereby. It will become clearer as we proceed. Let's now move to the next principle.

---

19 The "orbit" of the Sun would be that of the Earth, we are dealing with Neoplatonic cosmogony.

III. THE SCALE

Seven sounds embedded in a hierarchical structure based on their vibration produce a scale. Hierarchy and ladder are resonant, sympathetic, analogous terms, pointing towards a process of ascent and descent through the souls of the spheres and through the material and formal worlds that the same scale traverses. Sets of notes intertwine their possibilities through music, which is the expression of their movement; water, which is an ocean capable of linking the different ports found in the idea of each note. If the archetypes, the gods, the music of ideas, have long soaked up the expressible, physical and metaphysical language, or the projection of the Logos, the scale **illuminates** their foundational words, vectors towards the Logos itself with the greatest purity among all things of the sensible world.

The allegory is very ancient, and we must focus on the numbers that compose it to decipher its formal part. Before clearing its placement on the wall of memory, the one that allows the next floor to connect with our feet, let's clarify its few figures:

[1] There are two *diatonic* fractions: **9/8** and **256/243**.

[2] The number **9**, seen as an absolute frequency, corresponds to the note D; 8 vibrates as C-do, just like 256 (do). The number 243 corresponds to the note B-si[20].

[3] This implies that the tone arises from the numerical relationship between D-re and C-do, and the semitone between C and B, with this trio of notes serving as the foundation of the model.

---

20 Measured in Hz, cycles per second, 8 Hz, 9 Hz, 256 Hz, and 243 Hz correspond, respectively, to C, D, C, and B.

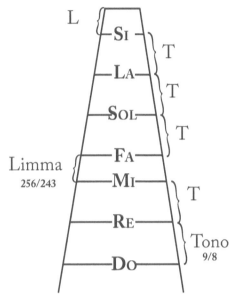

Figure: scale I.

3. 1. Creation of the scale

Let's pay attention to the two steps that create the scale from the basic intervals that we find in the tetraktys. The limit will always be the diapason, indicating that the universe of experience, the spectrum of visible light, and the musical octave, constitute the same universal idea, the limit within which the vibration occurs.

[1] With the diapente and the diatessaron, 5a and 4a, we obtain the tone.

[2] With the diatessaron and two tones (ditone), we obtain the semitone or pythagorean *limma*.

73

Arithmetically or arithmologically, to the fifth or diapente 3/2, if we operate it by reducing it by a diatessaron or fourth 4/3, it results in the ratio 9 to 8 or tone. By concatenating two tones we will have 9/8 times 9/8, equal to 81/64. The **ditone**, extracted from the diatessaron, produces the semitone ratio 256/243, limma:

$$limma = \frac{\frac{4}{3}}{\frac{81}{64}} = \frac{256}{243}$$

Phormulae: pythagorean limma.

In these two steps one travels from the harmonic series (nature of sound, of vibration therefore), unlimited, to the musical organization within a limit: the diapason. This step is given in the image and likeness of the Logos, whose minister in man is the intellect. Trying to suggest that nature creates physical scales is to ignore that music acts from an intelligible level, and for this reason it derives from movement the placement of the harmonic series in seven sound archetypes within each octave.

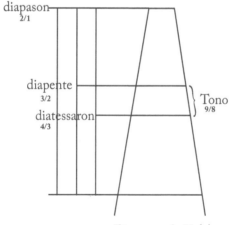

Figure: scale II (a).

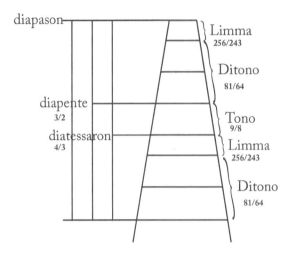

Figure: scale II (b).

Let's revisit the whole set to link together tones and limmas in a scale-array: {9/8, 9/8, 256/243, 9/8, 9/8, 9/8, 256/243}.

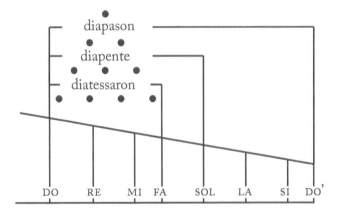

Figure: scale III.

We call this scale **diatonic** in terms of the structure of tones and semitones (two types of interval, dia-), and Pythagorean in terms of its nature, for this very reason (emphasis on the numerical structure of each interval). The starting note naturally coincides with the C, so when the notes were named they were done in a manner consistent with the arithmetic ratio of the scale.

And what about the rest of the twelve sounds? All the positions of the scale are covered by the Pythagoreans, summoned by its ratio. To have the first semitone, let's say if the reference is C, the C#, it will be sufficient to apply 256/243 to the vibration of that one. For the D#, limma and tone make a fraction of 32/27; for F#, typically 45/32; for G# 128/81, or 8/5 if we are in just tuning; A# last is the ratio 16/9. Since we have not yet placed the fractions of the natural notes, we put their sequence into fractions without missing the opportunity to emphasize their numerical-archetypal significance.

3.2. The Pythagorean Scale and the Hermetic Incursion into Robert Fludd's works

- [tone] 9/8
- [ditone] 81/64
- [diatessaron] 4/3
- [diapent] 3/2
- [sixth] 27/16
- [seventh] 243/128

Or in the form of array: {9/8, 81/64, 4/3, 3/2, 27/16, 243/128}, these ratios starting from the fundamental vibration of C produce D, E, F, G, A and B, respectively. There seems to be no other philosophy around the scale than a progression of these numerical ratios. In fact, let's think of it in these terms: one learns the ratio and understands how much the value of a vibration increases. For instance, if 243/128 applied to C gives B; then applied to the vibratory image whose object we can delimit, produces a transformation of the quality of said object. In other words, through the process of the intellect, and because it is from this that the scale derives, we can transform an idea and increase (or reduce) its vibration. This hermetic art comes to fulfill the process of making matter subtle and/or densifying the spirit. The first diatessaron (C, D, E, F) contains notes linked to matter and the following interval diatessaron (G, A, B, C') linked to form (spirit). By applying the ratios we overcome the statics of the model, we travel (Hermes) between one and the other, Heaven and Earth, speculatively speaking, and our mind then understands a memory process that operates in the Pythagorean conception of matematikoi, that is to say, it accesses the sacred patina of the scale, the note and the number/interval.

Every process of the intellect unequivocally concerns memory; even more regarding Hermeticism, which we will further expand upon. I need to mention in passing what will later become one or more substantial topics regarding the Englishman Robert Fludd. There is a peculiarity in this character that, with the permission of the reader, I overlook, and that is that its scale -hence I come up with it- he states as original begins with the note G. Numerous compliments arise, among them the esoteric ones that I will analyze later. However, here I place the arithmological aspect, which is a necessary and sufficient justification for its scale, akin to Kepler's, to originate from the note G.

Given that the tone arises between the diatessaron and the diapente, that is, between the fourth and fifth sounds, the figures 9 and 8 correspond respectively to the limit of this note diapente (9) and the note diatessaron (8). Thus, straight forward, this fourth note is a C, since 8 Hz is its natural vibration, and the fifth is a RE-D at 9 Hz. Since the semitone is obtained as mentioned above, and the third note fits perfectly being close to the fourth, it remains to be noted that its number, 243, vibrates as a SI (B). However, going down to the origin of the fingerboard we find the note SOL (G), as we wanted to show.

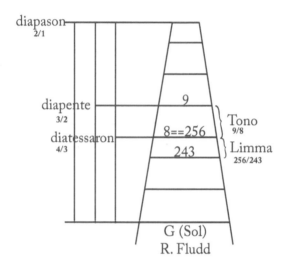

Figure: scale IV.

3. 3. The 5 note scale, or Pentatonic

Bone flutes of vultures from the Paleolithic period have been found tuned to the pentatonic scale. The same raga used for invocations to Lord Ganesha, a foundation in Hindu ritualistic practice, is pentatonic. African chants that gave rise to the *blues*, intended to alleviate earthly sorrow (slave labor), were pentatonic. Perhaps this is the oldest sophisticated tuning system, and perhaps also the most common worldwide, used in cultures mistakenly labeled as uncivilized such as African tribes, or as the musical basis in sophisticated China. It begs the question if the melodic origin of humanity, I speak of genesis, wouldn't precisely be the five notes, just as the symbol of man, both the number five and the pentagon are.

As it has to resist the obvious musical relationship of numbers 7 and 12, as sum and product of matter and form levels of the tetraktys, the number 5 will have to be understood in the figure in the same way. We've observed the Pythagorean system's internal coherence, which is symbolic, and for this reason it must serve us to define these cases as well.

The temptation to include levels 2 and 3 of the decade diminishes upon considering that doing so would detach music from its material dimension (the fourth level, that of the elements). Consequently, music would not be physically 'transmitted' (belonging to the world of forms and geometrically existing as the intangible line and plane). That is not possible. We need the physical environment to access the experience that is beyond it and for this reason, the fourth level must be included in the sound idiosyncrasies of the pentatonic scale.

Five is the number associated with Man through his four extremities plus his head, and with Venus since the ancient cultures of the Goddess. It refers to what we move with and come into physical contact with the World, the legs: land and water. To our work, our work on it, made with our hands: air and fire. And to the element that coordinates everything, the head, fifth element. Hands and feet are in the world of matter, interacting with it at all times. This world is composed of the four elements, four points of the lower tetraktys. But what about the head? That which originates the human being with his higher consciousness resides in his mind. And even though the mind is something that encompasses more physical places in the body, the head is one of those that has symbolically transcended as symbol of the mind. Another is undoubtedly the heart, to which we could also assign this fifth element because of how head and heart are connected.

Fifth element, or quintessence, is the synthesis of the four elements, the germ of their transcendence to another plane and therefore the divine power that resides in matter and that allows acting on it, transforming it. It is the transforming agent of the material world, and thus the five sounds would reflect the exoteric way in which primitive man realized himself in his interaction with the world... and his effect on it, too! The man, with the extremities and the head, forms the pentacle. Thus, we have to find the fifth point in the center or heart of the Tetraktys, as a primal incursion towards that third level, which, added to the four of matter, would complete the system in one sense. Or, as I say, exoteric, not esoteric. The pentatonic scale is, therefore, a scale whose objective was to connect what happened in the world, with the sacred, and to do it through the rite, by using this scale in the rite and thus print the genius loci in men. That is the numen, or also the celestial object or moment, in the hearts of primitive, ancient and modern people, which in turn allows serving as sourdough to create the myths of the collective unconscious. Playing the 5-note melodies in a certain place would be done to bring in the "mind" from the place, that is, the genius loci, and to be able to obtain his favors or powers from it.

In an esoteric level, the tone of the quintessence is inaudible, and yet it reverberates in the clean waters that flow from the earth, whispering the names of the nine muses so that their healing power is matured and understood.

Playing an instrument with certain intention requires at first knowing the quintessence of sound, which is only perceptible through the Venusian archetype of Harmony. If the dodecahedron is the figure that Plato ascribes to quintessence, it is only because the pentagon itself refers to Venus, thus to all the healing and feminine places in Nature (fountains) that have been valued so much since ancient times. Twelve times the pentagon is the invitation to consecrate each month, to heal it, each sign belonging as 1/12 of our calendar. Twelve signs are represented in the dodecahedron, whose faces are those that inscribe man into each zodiacal aeon. Perhaps from this creative way of living in accordance with natural law, the Chinese lü were born. These tubular bells were played each month in a China very different from the one it is today. Twelve tubular bells with the twelve tones, played one at the beginning of each celestial month. Everything in the human being refers to consecrating his passage through time and space, then music, subject to and within the limit of these, should only be the main crown of this: the instrumentalist will know the essence of his physical will, and through it he will be able to endow what he touches with intention.

This would mark one of the significant divergences between the teachings of the conservatory and those of Speculatory of music. It is appreciated that the intent of this writing is constructive, hence I have refrained from the impulse that the reader can imagine and that on the other hand is non-existent in the one who writes to articulate a large section dedicated to the defects and errors of music theory or teaching current regulated as such. Nothing further, because it would make this writing worthless. The meaning is to shed light to what is in the darkness, not to merely point out the darkness itself. This, like the shadow with the Sun at its zenith, disappears from the body. Having said this, what can really train the musician without knowing himself, without knowing about the essence that forms him? For this and many other issues 'I' (it was really the Muse) wrote 'La Lira de Hermes', since the musician has to be made in an internal process to the heroic mode, that is, solar. The object will be double: to know the value of doing it, in order to project its intention through the musical; and to discern between the authentic and the useless, the latter being a teaching that ignores vital issues.

Perhaps the reader could understand that if there is one musical tradition that has been able to keep this vital concept of transmitting the intention and have incorporated it into the essentials of its teaching, this is that of Carnatic music in India. In reality, the Western cultural sphere appears to have undergone a period of uncertainty over the past two centuries, precisely because of the lack of *"spiritual north"*. Evidence of this is found within the musical influences form the East, localisms and nationalisms, of the last two centuries. Examples of what I say -to continue with the observation- we hace granted with generosity. When equal temperament was adopted, it was done to homogenize the tunings and thus allow ever larger instrumental ensembles: the grand (symphonic) orchestras of the 19th and 20th centuries.

On the path, the colors to which just intonation (precedent) subjected the scales are lost, with a scale of E major not sounding the same as one of C major even if the instruments tune E and C to the same frequency. At that moment, nuances relative to the ear, the organ of physical and metaphysical listening, were lost, and its relationship with the spiritual (tuning, attunement) is remarkable. If we diminish colour, if we 'grey out' the auditory experience, the spiritual also suffers. Thus, it has happened that there are musicians without hearing who perform at major events. Without hearing, the musician who is trained is more like an automaton than an enlightened man in music. But we saw it coming, if the sign of musical education is earthly (resources and technical ability), an organ of the nature of water (internal ear) and air (external ear) was not going to be a vital differentiating element among musicians. Earth, earth, and more earth. So, the West has colonized as well as created the great symphonies, sublimating the essence of its aeon in nations whose essence was precisely that. Now everything changes, and the cycle of air also modulates the center of the globe.

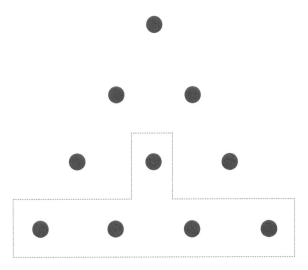

Figure: pentatonic tetraktys.

3. 4. The system of 22 shruti or tones of India. Carnatic Music

In India, tradition allows a glimpse into the metaphysics of sound. The 22 notes used in Carnatic music of India are its 22 possible sounds. From these 22 sounds, normally 5, 6, and more commonly 7 are chosen to compose a *swara*, equivalent to a scale. With the *swaram*, each *raga* is formed, a kind not of scale but of mode, linked to ceremonies, rituals, and the induction or enhancement of sensory faculties of various kinds, as numerous as the ritual moments for which they were conceived (Melakarta, 72 ragas). I delve into the numerical-Pythagorean essence of the matter again, and we will see what it leads to.

If the Tetraktys is a diagram of the Universe, and if Pythagoras clearly elaborated the scale with numerical proportions, a subset of those that make up the sequence of the 22 shruti, then there must be an ultimate meaning for this musical system integrating the Tetraktys. Now let's remember that the 3 main notes of every scale in the West: the 1st, tonic, the 4th, subdominant, and the 5th, dominant, corresponding as a whole to level 3 of the Tetraktys. There are no musical works with only those notes, because they lack of "matter", because they lack a "context" where they can enhance their spiritual strength. Remember the beginning of the music piece "Also Sprachst Zarathustra" (R. Strauss) in the film '2001: A Space Oddyssey' and how the opening motif, formed by the intervals of the Tetraktys, acquires its full effect when cadencing the last two notes. Go listen to it and come back here later. The three primal notes cannot generate a whole without the materiality offered by the other four positions of the scale. They need the material part. Well, in the Indian system, the total of 22 possible sounds undergoes a much more impressive analysis than in the Western system.

The reasoning is as follows: melody (7) and harmony (12) are present, to which we add the idiosyncrasies of the three pivotal notes of all raga: Shadja (Sa), Madhama (Ma) and Panchama (Pa).

[a] $4 \cdot 3 = 12$;

[b] $4+3 = 7$;

[c] $12+7 = 19$;

[d] $19 + 3 = 22$.

Adding everything up, we obtain 22. It is clear that it is a sum of everything that is possible, of the entire encompassable musical universe. That's the crux of the matter. And it shows the full range.

As we said, pieces with 22 different sounds are not played; one chooses from these 22 sounds to, through swaras, make the *kirtans*. But another option arises later, and this one involves all the elements of the tetraktys, that is, 10, the perfect, the oneness. If we add 10 to the number of harmony, 12, which refers to the (musical) context where totality lays, we obtain the 22 sounds. The meaning of this is that harmony, or the union of heaven and earth (O3-O4), will always be present in the music produced by humans. However, due to its inherent connection to ritual and religiosity, it seems to extend further, as its melody encompasses both the audible and the inaudible, reaching higher realms. This is how the system of Carnatic music is perceived: it naturally expresses itself within the human and temporal limits of the 12 notes while also drawing from the divine light encompassing *all* creation.

In the number three resides the astral force, materializing in the structure of music with three notes. Whether depicted as tonic-subdominant-dominant, diapason-diapente-diatessaron, or shadja-madhama-panchama, the trimurti, already in context and syncretism of the West, is the triumvirate of life, that is, the three necessary forces according to Neoplatonists—light, heat, and humidity—for life's existence. As far as its force is given in harmony, begets life in the world, ergo giving birth to music. Carnatic music embodies this allegory within its three notes as the divine trimurti: creation, conservation, and destruction (light-moist-heat), Brahma-Vishnu-Shiva. In this way, he endows his music with an ontological difference that becomes evident in the physical sound through musical intention. The whole ensemble, its union granted by its symbolism, can articulate what the music of the West lost with equal temperament tuning. Lastly, not wanting to entertain the reader any longer than needed in this part, to briefly touch on the tetraktys, the three cusp points may be allegorical representations of the Trimurti.

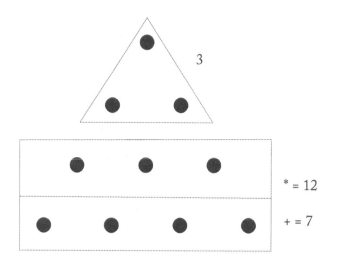

Figure: carnatic tetraktys.

3. 5. Ontological nature of musical notes

One wonders about the passage from number to name. How from the harmonic set of 7 sounds ordered by Light, their names are given. First is the discernment of the parts in which the whole is constituted. In this case, the colors of light, or the notes of sound. But these quantum states of sound, conditioned to the harmony that they have to make resonate internally (microcosm, psyche), come to be named after becoming patent; definitely become visible.

Quantized sound → name

We name something by the evocation that the symbol of the named object exercises in the imagination. That is to say, in some way, regardless of the historical moment, the names of the notes do accurately and quasi-univocally name their representations. We note the affinities revealed by both Western and Hindu systems (commonly used syllabic abbreviations for their application to each sound): DO RE MI FA SOL LA SI / SA RI GA MA PA DHA NI.

1. The second note begins with the sound "R."
2. The fourth note opens with the sound "A."
3. The sixth notes are phonetically similar: "L" is alveolar, "Dh" is similar to "T ", both dental, with the difference being a slight relocation of the tongue.
4. Both end in "A" sound.
5. The seventh name coincides in its term and is the only one ending in "-I" in the Hindu system.

Besides the fact that both systems refer abbreviated to longer non-syllabic names, the similarities can be found interesting, to say the least. The geographical and cultural traits will make a difference in the texture (phoneme) that in the end will reflect the written letter.

There is no doubt that at the cognitive level at which the symbol operates, sound, color, planetary period, and everything we observe with a division of seven qualities, coexist. It almost consists of tracing backwards from observing the world to pick up these associations. However, the layers that influence the observed and the observer are so particular to each one that we will only see the number as absolute, and not even that, since absolute is only a number or its absence: 1 or 0.

For this reason, if we intend to associate notes with planets, we will have to frame the context in which said frame moves very well. Attending to a first level or cognitive layer that includes mythology as an input to a natural look at the notes, we can propose:

a. C. DO = **Jupiter**. Zeus is the most important god. Origin of other gods and father of heroes, who are nothing but *conquisitor*, seekers of the truth. It is therefore appropriate to the cause of deployment of the scale.

b. D. RE = **Mars**. Re, red, sound with the same 'r' vibration as Mars or Ares. All this is enough for the mind to classify it, delimit it, sharpen it.

c. E. MI = **Mercury**, Hermes. That same '-i' sound signals its acute (intelligent) nature.

d. F. FA = **Venus, Aphrodite**, where the former gives the clue that the latter word covers up. The sound "f" is linked to the sexual and sensual, not in vain not only does it sound like a soft and homogeneous expulsion of the internal breath, but it is used to hang out and its current synonyms, both in Spanish as in English.

e. G. SOL. Together with do, it is a syllable ending in "-o", which can indicate masculinity. The "s" is doubly seen as Sol, Sun and

Surya (Sanskrit for sun). It does not follow the mythological sense, since in this, Apollo, Helios, ... they are faces of the Sun
god, much older (observations and calendar), just like the
Moon.

f. A. LA. Together with fa, it is feminine, the "-a" denotes
the gender, like the "-o". Selene, **Luna**, la, reverberate in the
same stratum of the quality of the observable world.

g. B. SI. It is unnecessary to combine the name with **Saturn**, although I think that name is problematic and a better
choice should have been 'Se', instead of 'Si'. In this way, it is
reciprocal with Mars (Re) by its natural malignancy and by
its ontology it links the name to Seth, which is Saturn 'co-
rrespondante'. In addition, Mercury (Mi) has its own idiosyncrasy, likely for the case not having to share a vowel, since
it is an interplanetary traveler (mythology : Heaven-Earth
traveler).

In short, I propose or suggest: *DO RE MI FA SOL LA SE*. In
any case, this nomenclature is not used in this writing. The
ends of the scale would be given by the two chronocrators,
something that seems to be a correct interpretation of the
symbol of the note since Saturn and Jupiter encompass all
the interior spheres, in the same way that between do and
si takes place the full set of note names. The note at the
center would symbolize the greatest harmony within the
scale due to its balanced position. It represents a central
point where equilibrium exists among the notes. As a name,
the FA, although I considered in 'La Lira de Hermes' the
FA# because of its exact centrality. Time will have to place
constitutive causes of this fact. At the center lies the note

of Venus, in addition to the fact that for Venus we have the same aesthetic and semantic question of the harmonic. Even the synodic kisses of the planetary meaning follow the defining pattern of beauty, the golden canon, approximated by the 8:5 ratio. The classical modes that we will study contemplate the same notes to the planets with the exception of Sun and Mercury, which are interchanged as MI and SOL, respectively.

IV. MUSIC AND MEMORY

Scales, music comprehension systems, none of it is really useful if it doesn't serve memory. The *raison d'être* of the spiritual part of music, power of the intellect, is to serve it, since this is what the human being uses to enhance its meaning in the world, its meaning as incarnated light, as a multiple leveled vibration with which we interact through our internal light; and from that interaction we receive the external one.

Crises are remembered for the deep levels at which its profound impact takes place, transcending conscious biology or, let's say, conventional medicine. The biological levels that medicine does not know go very deep towards the molecular atomic, towards the electrical that governs it, the magnetic that transforms it, and the gravitational that coheses it. If we could see the magnitude of the body in all its sub-levels we would not be able to comprehend it and would suffer mystical madness and perplexity. The reality of all those levels -and I mean the distance of understanding- lies in the images of the world that make them up. Life lives itself, just as love saves itself as the first action to arise again in a person. That is magnetism, it is the structure of the oscillation, its cause.

Movement agitates and vivifies memory, since everything that still moves is remembered, be it ideas or biological traces that are passed from generation to generation. The absence of movement preambles -and even causes- movement, since it contains the desire to manifest itself. But to do so, you need a memory, a foundation, an archetype. This is the engine of the world, and memory is the vehicle where it works. Without memory, the archetype of the madman (of the Tarot) appears, and the undefined idea runs wild. Memory directs the various dimensions of being towards whatever it is that needs to be lived by the light itself.

Due to changes, to the eternally changing disposition that governs us, music appears -it always was- and sounds from its frictions. Without change there is no music because the movement needs to be lived and the experience resolved in memory. Music celebrates its greatest finesse in the greatest crises, since the terrible movement determines its assimilation to the highest level, to the level of the highest spirit, singing or playing with the intellect placed in the high spheres where to tune in and safeguard the biological physical cohesiveness. Crises that affect and even destroy the individual, also can redeem him with music, are expressed through music, are necessary as music.

We remember, yet it's not so much a matter of places within the brain, as commonly presumed, as a result of the spirit-matter dissociation that exerts so much vilification on the structure of the human being. It is, on the contrary, within us; it vibrates, and therefore sounds, illuminates, illustrates, and is in tune with the cycles and rhythms of the macrocosm. Tuning the input to the registers is the key sentence to contextualize the memory. We experience tuning in with people, with situations, but little is the notion, perception and acknowledgment of syncing with the cycles of Heaven.

If we structure our weeks and months based on cycles of 7 and 12, reoccurring each year, why not accepting that we are living, for this latter case, according to the Sun? If this is so, as indeed it is, commencing the year on January 1st is nonsense. The Sun begins its year at dawn on December 25. A proper alignment, a right tuning, implies starting with something as simple as this. Beyond the solar aspects of living, don't we visibly deal with lunar, Venusian, &c. archetypes? In a thousand ways; and most of the time we do it without bringing it to consciousness. Not surprisingly, many classifications come out, all moved by necessity, and running into the classics is that they find a resting point. Why not revisit them? The archetypes will still be there, will persist. We must constantly remember that the number is the residue of the cycle in our memory.

We must also comprehend that the memory of the stars is another part of the tuning that we have to carry out to *anchor* the mind with the spheres. Planetary apparent periods imprint their light's significance upon us, for each planet has apparent periods that produce other "years" in us. Thus, they act as mnemonic clocks whose memory traces the meanings of their light. The great scholar Demetrio Santos proposed for the chronologies of the Biblical patriarchs that they be lunar years instead of solar. Methuselah, said have lived 969 years old, would have lived 78 solar years in those 969 synodic[21] lunar cycles 24 based on the fact that in ancient times the lunar calendar was followed (antediluvian era, also according to Demetrio). If instead of the Moon, which in fact serves as an account of time in the Paleolithic, we used Venus, whose period is 0.615 years, a person like Jesus Christ, 33 years old at the moment of his death, would have 54 Venus' years. If tradition revered a fertile goddess instead of a masculine deity, perhaps it would depict Jesus's passing at 54 years.

4.1. Memory of the planets around the Sun

Memory of C ; Mercury: 0.241 years
Memory of D Venus: 0.615 years

---

21 $969 \cdot 29,53/365,25 = 78,34$ years. Synod: 29,53 days.

Memory of E Mars: 1.88 years
Memory of F Jupiter: 11.86 years
Memory of G Saturn: 29.45 years
(Memory of O Earth: 1 year, 365.25 days)

These are the exact periods of the planets around the Sun. We celebrate the year by virtue of the Sun. However, alongside this significant year, there exist secondary cycles—attunements—between the cycles of Venus, Mars, and others. They all suppose a memory loci linked to their number, their note. We arrive at the matter therefore ritual, because nothing other than ritual is also New Year's Eve or the solstitial passage. Mars, for example, makes us a 'birthday' every 1.88 revolutions around the Sun. Celebrating by staging it properly every 1.88 years will mean tuning in with its energy, memory, *place* and quality. In the projected memory, the *imago*, imagination, the adequate martial archetype, the warrior, and as much as I wield accompany him, must be perfectly drawn. In modern society we find athletes or martial artists, in addition to soldiers, as agents of Mars. The Olympic Games, celebrated every 4 years, would align more closely with this concept if held every 1.88 years, or perhaps every 2 years approximately, which coincides with the Mars-Jupiter cycle.

What would this iteration produce? Ritual entails a sacrifice that attracts celestial favor, as believed by ancient civilizations seeking glory and triumph. In Rome, this idea was transferred to the military (Mars, *triumphus*[22]). While avoiding wars might

---

22 In these celebrations of military success, a connection with Jupiter was established through both accessories (laurels, purple or dark red toga) and the location of the ritual sacrifice, the temple of Jupiter. Since the nature was military, the parade itself belonged to Mars.

not seem like a significant reason, the premise holds importance. War stems from Mars, dragging its conflicts toward all beings. The sacrifice of athletes in the Games, both mental and physical, is a form of harmonious sacrifice. The Greeks found a certain balance between war and sports, training for both as if they were intertwined. Glory, analogous in both war and games, is linked to divine favor associated with Jupiter. Earlier, we mentioned the nature of the third wave linked to shape, humidity, inspiration, etc. Considering Jupiter's cycle analogously to a year, its O3 signifies the Olympics cycle:

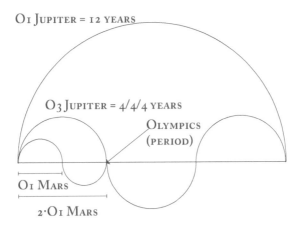

Figure: memory I (periods of Mars and Jupiter).

Modern societies are barbaric compared to that of Greece, since their rulers are not educated in reason and philosophy. So much so, they are perfectly manipulated by people who do know certain issues and who do not stumble at all with incorruptible minds. It is therefore a direct relationship with wars without any benefit for the individual who fights them, as it indeed happened in other periods of History. The Olympics should currently be held every two years for this purpose. A staging every 12 years produces harmony with the planet Jupiter. Note that at all times we are talking about a subject of musical resonance, where the musical is inaudible but exists; and the resonance, which spaces and surrounds the place of memory, is our tuning in with this musical essence. Thus says Demetrio Santos:

> *"The vital period of a living being resonates within those periods of influence closest to its own since its vital period is a consequence of their influence. Consequently, if an animal lives for 12 years, the resonant planet or period for it is Jupiter. This will be fundamental for the animal in its transits and aspects, as it does not repeat itself during its lifetime."*

And continues stating:

> *"For a fly, the annual cycle of the Sun is important, fundamental, and it will also be the lunar one, because they are the closest to its vital period : the fly, in effect, is incapable of overcoming the annual cycle.[23] We can also apply this law to other living beings, which respond with special intensity to certain periods due to resonance effect."[24]*

The human being is a complex entity, whose life span covers about 60, 90 or 120 years[25] (as a future trend) depending on many factors. Thus the cycles of heaven take place as vital influences. And isn't it reflected in how our being is operated

---

23 It is suggested: thus, it passes its memory to the next generation, unable to confine itself to an outdated cycle of the Sun, but encompassed within it.

24 "Investigaciones sobre Astrología", by Demetrio Santos Santos. Vol. I p. 260 Ed Ciclos del Cosmos.

25 All these cycles are the complete turn, turn and a half, and two turns, respectively, of the C-60 cycle determined at the radix of the person at birth. They are cycles of Saturn, hence the god of time for the classics and of death in old age for the Neoplatonists.

by these sounds? Consider this: as we mature, these celestial cycles dictate our thoughts, morals, impulses, physical conditions, and even crises that manifest at each nodal point. These cycles, which we can associate with governing archetypes, mark pivotal moments in our lives.

All this system of eons, contemplative of harmonics and composed of these and their bases, finally form the multilevel memory that affects the body. The 12-year cycle of Jupiter is in charge of the studies: secondary school plus higher education cover that number, likewise an individual spends from the age of 18 to 30 studying if he or she carries out studies at the highest level (doctorate), thus completing the 12-year cycle of an academic signifier such as Jupiter in traditional astrology.

The truth is, only the intellect—the human reasoning found in some individuals—exists in a way that surpasses the unpredictable changes of biological life. Its cause is not in the body but in the spirit. That is why these individuals seem to possess a unique gift that keeps them observant of the physical while aligned with the intellective, the archetypes, conquering themselves and the physical universe that surrounds them. This, if done unconsciously, is called genius; if the man becomes conscious according to a doctrine, is called an initiate; and if he is made conscious from oneself, a prophet. It is in these cases that the eon or archetype is transcended rather than one being governed by it. This is the spark of the human being, signified by Uranus, who is *from heaven*, the creative ray, and whose corporeal period covers a human life (84 years). Urania, also from heaven, will represent the same memory (Muse) that transgresses the biological limit of Saturn, minor orbit.

4.2. Of geniuses, initiates, and prophets

We're entering lands of great erudition when we delve into topics such as memory. Giordano Bruno managed to draw maps that exceeded the minds of his time -and ours-, reaching our days with treatises of enormous complexity and intellectual versatility, such as The Shadows of Ideas or the Epistle (*The Expulsion of the Triumphant Beast*). The truth is that in the images that he exudes there are powerful ideas that determine the dynamics of being and make matter imbue the spirit in the way that the spirit lives in matter. As a consequence, harmony blurs the limit between one and the other. That is why it is inharmonious to think of a spirituality alien to materiality, or vice versa, to seek material profit without offering food for the soul. Of great virtue is therefore the scale when conjugating one with the other, the notes-beam of matter with the notes-beam of the spirit. All like beams of light varying in density. Recognizing this common thread in vibration is crucial.

So the notes originate from memory, as a conversion of the internal cycles and their harmony into the scale of the living (material and spiritual) beings. These notes are structured, as we've discussed, and is in that order they allow Bruno's dream of spiritualizing matter and materializing spirit. The vividness of the colors penetrates the psyché, human soul, setting the number for these in seven, just like the spheres -with their attributes, the cycles-, and it does so while recalling the cathedral's order that imbibes spirit and matter together through numerical significance. Does it not seem that light speaks the language of music and vice versa?

Through hues, the image is indelibly imprinted upon the mind, akin to the memorisation of a moving artefact. Motion and colour are akin entities of luminescence, for colour arises from the variance in movements (vibrations), and the motion of every entity infers its purpose by the object of that motion. The avian creature that ensnares its prey, the ram that fiercely charges, the lion that resoundingly roars... there invariably lies a purpose from the subject that hastens recollection, impregnating it towards the image. To utter 'lion' differs from pronouncing 'yellow lion'; to articulate 'book' diverges from voicing 'crimson book'. Introducing motion envelops it and secures it more robustly in memory (the process of categorisation).

Subsequently, it undeniably holds true that we grapple with a profound quandary concerning order, with Justice, when dictating actions (motion). It is this hierarchy that posits a moral order, and said moral order is conspicuously absent if the hierarchy is non-existent. The hierarchy begets hierarchy; thus, individuals with acute audition, and particularly those endowed with absolute pitch, possess a distinctly lucid internal hierarchy of their functions and are less susceptible to vacillation. Hesitation equates several possibilities against an outcome, rendering them equally significant, equidistant, and commensurate in resonance.

Memory is a storehouse of these aforementioned options, therefore without a hierarchy associated with it -which on the other hand is its own-, the doubt is great in the individual. If the doubt is small, certainty allows solidity of purpose and path, and if the doubt is great, the individual is subject to the rest. It is as if a musician plays without knowing which note comes next, thinking of two options with the same probability of occurring. The Universe doesn't doubt, normally. The vicissitudes become crystalline in the presence of the inspiration phenomenon.

Thus, doubt does not exist in the balanced state of mind, so if doubt is an anomaly -necessary by contrast- and the lack of hierarchy supports it, then prioritizing memory will minimize it, leading the individual to make the right decisions. It is obvious that this has nothing to do with music for someone who does not know what we're talking about here, but it does. Music prints the most powerful hierarchy: sound. From there the interval and the scale are their children and from them shines an order consecrated to the natural that will lead, through discernment, to making the right decision. Let's give an example, and in it, consider the positions of the scale from fundamental to fingerboard:

- (Fundamental) Lion
- (Tone) To hunt
- (Ditone) Yellow
- (Diatessaron) Roar (intermediate between the physical and the metaphysical)
- (Diapente) Fear
- (Canon) **Courage**
- (Seventh) Fear
- (Fingerboard) Sun

The keynote designates the animal, the lion; the following, the tone, to an activity: the lion moves, making its activity its function, the hunt. After the most obvious, its colour, which also imbues the animal with vibration (light). From light we move to sound, its roar, imprinting a scale of vibration on the lion. The ear, receiver of sound, and the acoustic phenomenon itself, possess the virtue of straddling two worlds, the physical and the metaphysical (music of the spheres). It is precisely because of the hierarchy that this is so, relying on the fact that each note symbolises a part of the mnemonic object. As a result, the lion 'lives' in the intellect, so much so that it becomes a totem, transformed into a place. The notes must be conceived as a process that imbues this meta-process in turn.

From the spiritual (the last three notes) arises the fear that this animal instils in beings, which allegorically represents valor (let us remember the Wizard of Oz). It instils fear as its counter-function, its dark function. And this fear spreads like the rays of the Sun. Placing the Sun in the octave obeys that a new scale begins and what is in an octave is the sublimation of the previous one.

A learning model based on memorization must be grounded in music as a premise, as it not only better comprehends (numbers 3, 5, 7, 12, ...) but also tunes, equals, and connects ideas from different substrates. Discriminating between two options requires placing each of their objects on a point of the scale, in an interval. If object A has a lower vibration than object B, and the question pertains to matter, A will be the logical choice; if it concerns the spirit, it will be B. It is understood that they are the question, the possible answers, and the final answer; the three phases of the mnemonic movement. Inspiration reduces them to one, hence its wonderful influence.

Memory is what the Pythagoreans called the tetractys; Mnemosyne, the mother of the Muses, and that with Zeus. The divine breath (air::Zeus-Jupiter::ruaj) imbues the rules of memory (intervals) into 9 parts, called with receptive, feminine, watery names. Life flows anew in each of them, and they are associated with trades and musical modes in harmony with their abilities. In 'La Lira de Hermes,' I extensively discuss the 9 Muses.

So, what is proposed? That everything observed be transposed onto a scale and equated in hierarchy with other elements. By having the classical four virtues hover in the models, they acquire a spiritual sense that helps balance vital behavior. For example, with the former, we can change it. From the four virtues, Fortitude, Justice, Temperance, Prudence, we take Fortitude.

- (Fund.) Lion
- (Tone) To hunt
- (Ditone) Yellow
- (Diatessaron) Roar (intermediate between the physical and the metaphysical)
- (Diapente) Fear
- (Royalty) Courage
- (Seventh) **Fortitude**
- (Fingerboard) Sun

Fortitude stands just before the Sun much like as its rays, as its light. Therefore it is its most direct influence, favoring the named virtue through the reason process. Remember that for the ancients, the Sun is an unappealable, sovereign archetype, defining what is real, royalty and good. From good, strength, hence valor. Obviously, if we continue the previous sequence, we'll contemplate again the correct descending order from the Sun: Sun (→Light) → Strength → Courage → Roar → Yellow → Reign → Hunt → Lion. This significantly omits the element that was left over, Fear, although perhaps Terror would have equally fit in the first sequence.

Be that as it may, the scale becomes more refined as the thought itself does, delving deeper and deeper into the original idea. It is a gauge of the fineness that thought is acquiring in the interval game (mediation between ideas). Outlining each model can actually lead to a dynamic process in memory, progressing from an initial E1 scale to a final E10 scale, an actual reflection -manifestation- of the psychic movement of this deepening. In summary, a macro-process $E_1:E_2:E_3:E_4:E_5:E_6:E_7:E_8:E_9:E_{10}$, where each Ei signifies a scale with 7 word-ideas that are evolving, tempering, specifying their places. The most interesting thing is that this process is in itself an internal way of knowing oneself, a way of knowing the internal movements of the light of the intellect: internal music.

4.3. Musical-mnemonic map exercise

From time to time, in social networks, I enjoy to put exercises that help to understand complex things. Making the complex concept simplify through the image of memory increases intelligence, and with it discernment, a quality that we discuss in one of the transcribed stream conferences below. For now let's do this exercise. These are what we can call Brunian associations.

1. Dog → Moon → Gray → Barking → Protection → Home → Diatessaron

2. Lion → Sun → Yellow → Roar → Alert → Diapente

3. Serpent → Galaxy → Wave → Green → Cicle → Stage → Diapason

It's noteworthy that, although it is indeed a complex matter, the logic behind transitioning from one word to another is relatively easy to visualize, employing the language of movement. Logical thought is for this reason that it slips and does not allow the dynamism of memory or the internal movements of the psyche; and for this reason it is also confusing to think that mind associations are using logic in a standard way. Once the exercise is done, we can agree that the sound of a diapente contains that of the diatessaron in the same way that the lion stands out over the dog. The quality that makes him stand out is strength -underlined in the former more than in the latter- a virtue represented by a lion. The serpent is by all means more powerful than the lion because in fact it can put an end to his life. He does not do it with force, but with poison, which is blood associated, and fire associated too (its burn effect). Hence, the snake triumphs over the lion by means of a more subtle fire (poison) than the one displayed by the lion (strength). This establishes a diatessaron::diapente::diapason system that is displayed in memory.

4.4. Non-hierarchical neural memory

With twelve notes, it is indeed feasible to engender a mnemonic system. Furthermore, the circle of fifths, which shall serve as the foundation, bestows equal hierarchy upon each constituent element; thus, the twelve ideas that shall comprise it shall undeniably be on par in significance. Within this concept lie: the twelve tribes of Israel, the twelve signs, the twelve Apostles, &c. In all such instances, the same idiosyncrasy arises, taking diversity in quality rather than level. We revisit, in almost harmonic terms (twelve), and melodic terms (seven), as in the numerical analysis of the tetraktys.

Mnemonic rules employ celestial resources such as stars or constellations to establish ideas. Supposedly, an idea emerges from the whole, leading in turn to a broader consideration of the archetypes that strongly compresses the ideas as the overall figure progresses. It's like the spheres; if once all the constellations of the night sky are learned, it triggers a greater understanding, something we previously couldn't have seen, this would be an idea that would allow for the passage to the next cognitive level. Like so many other things, until they are employed, their power remains unknown, their worldly arrangements are overlooked.

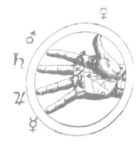

Figure: "The hand of chiromancy" engraving by Heinrich Cornelius Agrippa von Nettesheim (1486-1535) 'De Occulta Philosophia libri tres,' published in 1533.

4.5. The Circle of Diapentes (fifths) and the Hand Model

Consider, by way of illustration, the diagram with the 12 fifths or diapentes converging at a central point akin to a wheel. The equidistance to the centre suggests centrality; the centrality implies the origin of coordinates, the place where the totality of sounds radiates outward. The perfect analogy is that of the Sun, a note that would be unpronounceable, whose rays in the visible realm we identify as the 12 physical and producible notes. Our hand cuts through some rays and casts shadows, thus selecting seven. To select seven notes, it discards five, which are cast as shadows. All music henceforth emanates from the light of that centre, yet the shadows that the hand, with its five fingers, projects. Five shadows are matched by the five fingers, and henceforth they shall reveal which sonic absences, which silences, refer to which stars, for the fingers are the stars. A scale can not therefore being a consequence of matter, but of the way of light to trespass it.

In ancient wisdom, the pinkie is attributed to Mercury, the ring finger to Jupiter - hence the weddings -, the middle finger to Saturn, the index finger to Mars, and the thumb to Venus. The light of twelve rays is the Sun, and the scale with which music is created (the remaining seven rays) is the Moon. We move our hand as if playing an instrument, and each mudra produces a scale, a mode that exists only in the Moon, the archetype of our emotions and the nurturing binding force of light. We can envision it as if that Sun were an internal Sun and the Moon were an external sphere receiving the rays that an intermediary hand does not obstruct.

The 'musical hand', as it covers specific rays of the Sun, it also hides notes from the visible world. The Sun and its light are the constant, therefore constitute an ontology, an absolute center, a god; but the hand obstructs the lumen of the twelve rays, not being able to do it with all but only five, leaving the seven notes unobstructed. A natural mode, such as major C, lacking sharps or flats, implies that notes F#, C#, G#, D# and A# are obstructed, and that this is the physical realm that covers their rays. This works as a natural phenomenon, since the hand is like the Earth (matter) between the Sun (light of the

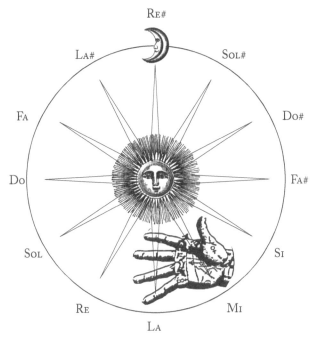

Figure: the Musical Hand (the author).

spirit) and the Moon (illuminated soul). Not by any means randomly, the pentagon emerges as Earth, being the symbol of Man; and the 7 rays Star symbolizes the Spirit on the Soul -the Hebrew Shejiná or classical pneuma.

Moon = Soul = what the Hand (Body) lets pass of the light from the Sun (Spirit)

The light that follows, permitted by the hand, is that which penetrates behind the Moon into the different stratified corners of our substance. The part of fire, that of air and water (humid), and that of earth; they take over from one to the next, like different levels of vibration. The light of the intellect, of reason (ratio), gradually penetrates and produces different effects in one supersubstance and another. The latter

107

Figura: emblema XLV: "El Sol y su sombra completan la Obra". de Atalanta Fugiens (M. Maier).

are the repositories of memory, which is resolved by attracting the filtered light itself, so that the matter is organized to establish a certain destination (Hand of G.od = Hand of Fate) and thus urge the movement of the Moon-soul in one way or another.

Filtered note-images thus change the texture of being, the fabric of existence. This is fascinating, because the hand and the elements consubstantial to being are constituted simultaneously: they agree, and since one is the visible face of destiny and the other the invisible, both end up introducing the intellect, as lumen, into the notion of reality: light is embodied in the musical verb (scale).

We may fall into the temptation of outlining fingers in astral correspondence and we have to proceed in order: Mercury, Venus, Mars, Jupiter, Saturn. Musically, in the case of the Pythagorean scale, which is the natural one, the fingers will cover the following rays:

(Finger of) Mercury = FA#-F#

Venus = DO#-C#

Mars = SOL#-G#

Jupiter = RE#-D#

Saturn = LA#-A#

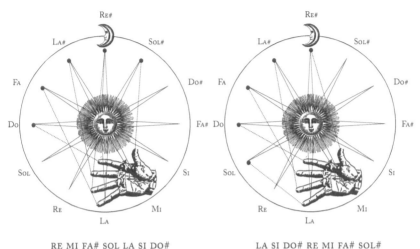

RE MI FA# SOL LA SI DO#   LA SI DO# RE MI FA# SOL#

Figure: scales projected by the Musical Hand (by the author).

Like so, C, D, E, F, G, A B (DO, RE, MI, FA, SOL, LA, SI) end up illuminating the Moon. Therefore, Sun and Moon sympathize more for their wide sound spectrum than each of the stars, regardless of the mode or scale that is chosen. They also match with the uttermost joy, for this is the natural or pythagorean scale, and also the Lydian mode, related to Jupiter by the original correspondences -not the newest wrong ones- by the Spanish Ramis de Pareja.

The hand can cover a single ray, eventually, but this would make the music more complex; It can still work by covering only four, and there is only one inharmonious element. There are five planets and the absences are felt as lack of balance of the whole. By covering certain rays, it induces one harmony or another, one way or another. As said, the previous examples are for the so-called Lydian mode in the 'octoechos', the standard nowadays major scale. In both examples, said harmony of the mode is followed, although since we are dealing with note-symbols we are leaving out the possible different temperament of the tones. They are two Lydian modes, but both, according to the correct tuning, would be of different colors. In reality they are proposed as ideas, since the mere notes subject to a temperament dwarf with respect to the notes-symbol. As we saw in 'La Lira de Hermes', the notes symbolize gods, and powers of number before those gods. So it is useless to treat the notes with respect to each other or use concepts like color here. The way of using the word 'color' within the dogma of the conservatory is merely aesthetic, programmatic, without any understanding of any source of light or relationship with it.

The hand represents the planets, and with that, the set of forces that modulate and carry the action of light itself and that constitute Fate. It is no coincidence that the Pythagorean pentalpha -number five- was the image to be internally understood by the Pythagoreans. If the hand is an obstacle to light with its body, it is also permissive of the former due to its absence. In the model, this translates into the matter-form duality, or more sensibly, 'physical reality' or 'negative' of that reality, exactly as explained about the arcana of the Hanged Man from the Tarot, in the previously quoted book:

> "The archetype of emptiness that has been detailed here turns out to be necessarily imbricated in a non-time and non-space stage. In the inverse vision of the World that surrounds us and for this reason it pays attention to the spiritual, not to the material; to empty himself, not to fill himself. This non-time is not easy to explain. Every moment of materialization, of entry into the visible world, occurs in circumstances in which the mind seems to be abstracted from everything that surrounds you, including time."

According to what was said and the present statement, the archetype of the Hanged Man is, in its image, equivalent to the inverse pentalpha, which although it is represented inverted as a symbol of the passage to the Underworld, represents an all-encompassing 'mold' of invisible daimonic reality. They are different things. In fact, it is possible to understand in modern representations that the inverted pentalpha was associated with the devil in a way that the right pentalpha also (hand::intercession / intermediary of light::Lucifer) does, leading to misconceptions, clouding certain ideas in people's minds and end up being stigmatized.

The Sun acts upon all things, but it passes through the void (negative of the Hand = the Hanged Man), impacting bodies (fate = hand) so that ultimately its light empowers the nurturing power of life (Moon). Archetypally, the entire environment between the Sun (which, if one observes closely, is internal) and the sphere of the Moon (external) represents the **cosmic egg**, and within it, the hand in its interaction with the rays is the *hero's journey* and, through the application of 'La Lira de Hermes', the same path as the Tarot or the 22 numerical[26] stages. Each of them is therefore represented in an aspect of the interior of that egg.

With this diagram belonging to the mentioned book, it is possible to understand what has been said, although it would have to be conceived unfolded in a specular way, with the soul housing the spirit in the center. What is of direct corres-

---

26 This would liken to the idea of the transition from shadow to light, from lunar to solar, and even from the deception of the sublunar to the clarity of the prophetic. Indeed, everything connects with the solar rite and the hero's journey, which in turn inherits the book of Thoth. In 'La Lira de Hermes' (The Lyre of Hermes), this process is specified in an intervallic manner.

Figure: domal diagram and of the hero-musician (La Lira de Hermes, Spanish ed.).

pondence are the notes as a symbol of different lights (hence colors) penetrating the biological body and produced by the notes.

In the space between the Sun and the Moon lies the filtration of light that sustains life, and this filtration is governed by fate. What hermetic music creates in the student is the dissected image of this, and thus music becomes both a science and divination at the same time, although I would prefer to say, and I believe it is more accurate, that it becomes a faithful tool in service of the motto 'know thyself and thou shalt know the universe and the gods' of the temple of Apollo, at Delphi.

4.6. About Sun and Moon on the Instrumentalist

For some years now I like to dramatize the Sun and Moon principles to my students in the following way: a guitarist plays the strings with his right hand, although it is with his left that modulates its vibration. The left hand's passive action makes the vibration change, for the note becomes sharper or flatter within the limits that the string imposes. The fingers of the left hand allow the speed of these light modulations, in addition to the color (height of the vibration), so we already have two variables. The right hand imposes the rays of light crackling from the mechanical traction, and without its action there is nothing but darkness, the silence of the string and the instrument. Then we already have the framework (finite universe) in which these two variables occur. The first of the two changes the note, and therefore the texture of the very matrix nature of the string, in the way in which the Moon exposes to the viewer a part or portion of the Sun, as well as an influence or another of the stars. The second of the two variables measures the intensity of that nature, its agitation: the placid or intense Moon are celestial scenes of this light gradient.

As I say, the guitarist then finds that his hands are (1) like the Sun (and therefore the stars, for both are light emitters) and (2) like the Moon and its effect on our soul -right and left hands, respectively-. We can apply this concept to various plucked and bowed string instruments, although none so fortunate. The right hand, active principle, masculine principle, corresponds to light (divine fire); the left hand, passive principle, feminine principle, to darkness (waters). The chord produces a celestial harmony in the mind and the difference between bowed and plucked instruments is indeed within the nature of the light.

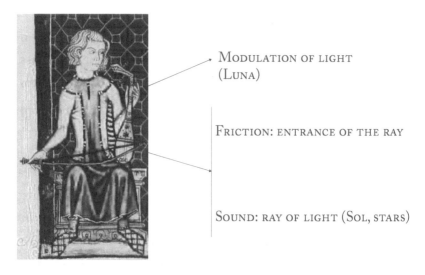

Modulation of light
(Luna)

Friction: entrance of the ray

Sound: ray of light (Sol, stars)

Figure: Sun and Moon within the music player.

[Dissimilarity between bowed and plucked string instruments according to this new light] By rubbing the string, two vibrations are produced: friction on the string, and sound; when pluck-pressing there is a slight percussion, but a sole vibration: sound. In the first case we have a principle analogous to that of wind instruments, whose blowing needs to generate a resonance to produce the standing wave that sounds. The "cerceo" produced by the bow of the viola or any other of the original family of the 'rabel' is symbolically analogous to the blow, which like a spark ignites the flame of sound. The analogy helps to understand that it is related to the divine spark that originates life. For the lyre, zither, guitar, &c., the pulsation is equivalent to the action of specifying light in matter, the **tzim-tzum** of the Hebrews or contraction of the Gnostics. The moment the kitharer plays, the image -which contains memory- becomes flesh.

In the instrumental set we'll find the same principles or common denominators, as who can deny the similarity between friction, pluck and breath? All of them are common to the moment prior to the inception of light, which is treated as vibration and transmitted through this communicating vessel, sound. But light is the appropriate term, since it starts from what we can consider the primordial sound (Genesis, 1.3):

Vayomer Elokim yehi Or vayehi Or.

ויאמר אלהים יהי אור ויהי אור

That voice of the verb, which is the Logos, equates to the friction:: blowing::plucking of the instruments, whose sound is the Or, the light. With musical instruments, the human being only emulates through the ceremony of performing this fundamental and foundational principle of life, but the awareness of it has long since disappeared, and it has never belonged nor will it ever belong to the conservatories. Sound and light are consequently vibration, as has already been said, and therefore allude to the vibrating ray that penetrates bodies and produces their animation, similar to the model of the egg or that of the hand.

By the effects whose cause is both hands' action when playing the instrument we can acknowledge the inside of the egg. While 'set of possibilities' might be an easier phrase to articulate concerning sound (such as modes, &c.) it lacks accuracy since is neither true nor precise. The action of the hands is a demiurgical mirror, and therefore playing is a form of theurgy in hermetic music.

In the diagram, both principles are symbolized by fire and water, which correspond to *sulfur* and *mercury* principles in alchemical jargon. Each arrow starts from a generative point and a modulative point of sound, such as the mouth of the guitar, which is solar, where the hand produces the contraction of the string that produces the sound.

A detail that surpasses the scope of a diagram is that of the air, which permeates all instruments in such a manner that the spark or contraction invariably ignites it. The soundboards and the tube constitute an indispensable microcosm. The sound-box adopts a shape that mimics a specific vessel or canopy, which accommodates or enables the accommodation of sound creation in a manner analogous to the macrocosmic universe housing the creation of light.

From all of this I hope that you, the reader, understands the good use that must be given to the instrument, since the treatment that we give to it dispenses in our favor the inspiration to do it with skill. With the use of instruments we're allowing our vital essence (internal sun) to reconnect with the universe (ordo caelis, celestial order).

4.7. About the shadows and lights of musical ideas

When the Sun moves along the Ecliptic, it focuses its brightness on each of the **rays** as its center, seemingly suggesting that it is this movement, that of the Sun, which determines the origin of the count of the rays; and that a fixed hand would always give a coherent tonality or music mode in which to move the music. However, it is not so, for the hand is mobile since its fingers are the planets. The Sun's rays, which constitute the lumen, do actually rotate counterclockwise like a crown of light. First, at the top, there is the ray of C, similar to Aries; then it rotates and is followed by G, representing Taurus; D, for Gemini; &c. The five fingers, as a variable, the 12 rays in coronary movement, as another, offer $(12-5) \cdot 12 = 84$ musical modes, and $5 \cdot 12 = 60$ shadows or physical bodies (that produce them). The sum of these two figures gives 144, which is $(3 \cdot 4)^2$. With this model, music is seen as a movement of the final notes, which are projected on the Moon. Music is the Moon in its movement, in its variations (phases). "Creating it" proved interesting to contemplate how the human hand reproduces the model of divinity seen in Robert Fludd and his monochord. The moving rays of light produce the modes in which music will precisely define that, a configuration of the hand. The hand is the physical body in the Brunian model of the Shadows of Ideas, and the Aristotelian matter. The conception that music is a consequence of the harmony of light in matter, of the spirit when it incarnates, is true, for it is mu-

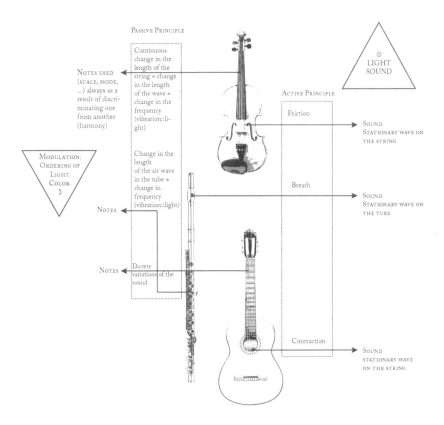

Figure: Idiosyncrasy of light and sound in musical instruments, and their demiurgic archetypes (with more detail in the book's annex).

sic that arises from the way the hand (body) produces when it obscures the intelligible rays of light. We must therefore know that music is the light we do not obscure, an outline of ourselves that delimits the constitutive frequencies of human memory (12 celestial signs = from the sky = memory).

Explaining this more broadly, we see the shadow as defining the contour of the body. The light that surrounds it is the musical model, and as the Spirit incarnates, it reveals the imperfections of matter, music ends up being the natural consequence of a kind of redemption of this fact, to allow vital drama and the continuation of the encompassing symphony. It is suggested that music appears to balance the internal shadow, which is the part of the intelligible light that we do not allow to pass from the Sun (Good). Music must move the hand so that this light reaches where there was previously shadow.

It is suggested that the music appears to balance the inner shadow, which is the part of the intelligible light that we do not let through from the Sun (Truth/Good). The music has to move the hand so that this light reaches places where before there was **shadow**.

But, what is the shadow? It is the fate which the planets impose on the human being. The five stars, subject to direct and retrograde movements, cast the resultant shadow of the being, that shadow C. G. Jung says it's necessary to recognize and to integrate. The Moon reflects it and the Sun redeems it, eliminates it from the sensible world. We must therefore nourish ourselves with the Sun, because that way the shadow vanishes and the heart loses its weight excess. Do we remember the myth of Ma'at/Osiris and the scales? Well, that's what it's about. There is no attainable peace if Good (internal Sun) does not triumph. The hand is therefore Fate (see how hand reading addresses fate understood; or the expression "Hand of G.d", to refer fate manifested), since it weaves with the rays of the Sun (notes) like threads, ropes, &c. And from this spinning action the shadow is defined in the tapestry of our reality. It can be said in another way, and that is that we inhabit the lunar, hence the ancients spoke of the "sublunary"; The solar archetype is the center of ourselves, our reason for being, our axis. The path of the hero is that of the intellect that surpasses the hand of destiny, and music is the system of comprehension of this quintessence (five fingers) to reach the glory that surpasses the astral bodies influence (heaven::superior cycles).

We return now to the numbers, which have thrown to be 60 for the *shadows*; 84 for the *lights*. The first will be the number of the physical world and the second of the form. The reader can take the 60 as anti-modes, and liken it to matter; 84 are the modes, and they are linked to light, which is therefore antimatter. The balance around the number 144 suggests that understanding all these modes and antimodes is equivalent to transcending the memory that we associate with the system. Understanding that is linked to the light-matter duality and whose transcendence implies the monad. The two opposites are conjugated around 144, note D (RE), and this would mean the previously said ontological monad represented as a physical note. The two cycles of Saturn, out of the shadows, express the generation of the limit, of matter (twice Saturn's cycle) in 60 years (cycles of the Sun); the light cycle of Uranus (Heaven), of 84 years, refers directly and inexorably to the stars (form::light::spirit). Nature's system is divine.

Saturn::darkness // Uranus::light // ratio of 7:5 (tritone).

Figure: saxtile.

Turning towards geometry, the number 60 correlates with the 60-degree aspect known as the sextile. The peculiarity of the sextile is that it corresponds to the way in which the water turns into snow, subsequently revealing the blueprint of the spirit's form, even leading to Kabbalah's teachings. Interestingly, 60 adds 6 and 84 adds double, 12, the number of sign-notes. Sixty refers to the aforementioned angular to 'flower of life'. In Hermeticism there are 60 concentric cycles around the Earth, equivalent to the 28 of Gnosticism or 10 of the Kabbalah. Regarding the sextile, Demetrio asserts:

> *"Due to the simplicity of its layout, and hence its very beauty that penetrates directly into the aesthetic and spiritual planes, it substitutes or replaces the sextile wheel in most cases, hence its geographical extension and its abundance.[27]"*

27 "Astrología y Gnosticismo" (Astrology and Gnosticism), Demetrio Santos. Ed. Barach.

The allusion to aesthetic beauty produces, when reading it - knowing the previous model - an evocation of how light is ordered.

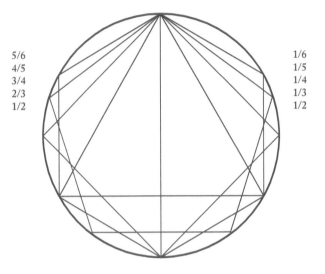

5/6   1/6
4/5   1/5
3/4   1/4
2/3   1/3
1/2   1/2

Figure: fractions of the circumference and intervals.

Indeed, a position of harmony seems to reign in the set given by the sextile. The primal force that denotes unites light and matter. Rationally, if the diapason responds to the 180° phase (opposition aspect), 120° to the diapente and 90° to the diatessaron, then the interval that corresponds to 60° is the semiditone[28]. The circumference-interval ratios would be {180°::1/2::diapason}, {120°::1/3::diapente}, {90°::1/4::diatessaron}, {72°::1/5::ditone}, {60°::1/6::semiditone}. The minor third, therefore, is the interval that represents each division of the sextile.

And to this purpose we have the following fact: it is not possible to divide the octave into fifths; it is not possible to do it in fourths; but it is possible in major and minor thirds: three major

---

28   1/6 of the circumference leaves 5/6 complementary, the ditone.

thirds add up to an octave and four minor thirds also. The ideas manifested with this can take us far. The first is that four, being the number of matter, and four being the times the semitone occurs to form the octave, make the figure of the Seal of Solomon, sextile, or **Magen David** in the circumference a symptom of beauty, indeed, and of order emanating from that beauty of the number. Again, 60 represents matter, with the addition of doing so in its blessed mnemonic place by light (ordered).

The human form (human spirit, pentalfa) remains in the aspect of 1/5 of circumference that corresponds to divisions of 72 degrees. Matter (four semitones = four elements) structured in separations of 60 degrees, and Man in divisions of 72 degrees, conjure two figures, **sextile** and **pantacle**, of great significance in the musical-symbolic realm. They exemplify how music supposes a vehicle of syncretism between the reality of the thing and the idea of the thing, because it will draw from the arithmological reasons of the intervals. Initially, one could have thought of the square figure for the four elements, and if so, the set would have value for four diatessarons, which are ten tones and a ratio of $(4/3)^4 = 3.16 = \pi$ which serves as an approximation of π pi, thus transitioning from the musical to the architectural. We have focused on the division with reference to the octave, in the diapason, in such a way that it is understood as a dwelling place and in it, as many numbers of its enclosures can fit as possible. The figures are sonorous, based on ditones (major thirds) and semitones (minor), as a cause image in turn for us to organize the chords according to them: music is the arrangement (geometric) of the inner light.

$$diatessaron^4 = \pi$$

We have focused on the division with reference to the octave, to the diapason, in such a way that it is understood as a room for as many as possible intervals to fit. The figures are sound, based on ditones (major thirds) and semitones (minor thirds), as an image that in turn causes us to organize chords according to them: music is the (geometric) arrangement of internal light.

Two sequences of angles, A = 30° - 42° - 18° - 54° - 6° - 60° - 6° - 54° - 18° - 42° - 30° or B = 60° - 12° - 48° - 24° - 30° - 30° - 24° - 48° - 12° - 60°, transcend based on the harmonics of the intellectual synthesis of matter and man. These sequences depict how divine essence inhabits humans, manifesting the organization of light through the production of music's fundamental chord types, major and minor, or ditone and disditone.

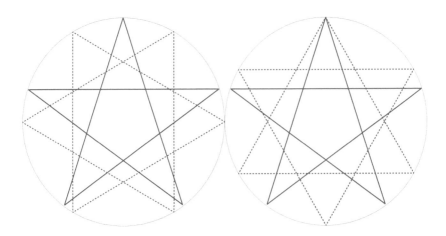

Figure: hexagram and pentagram, major and minor thirds, superimposed. From left to right, cases A and B.

In scenario B, where the vertices of both cusps overlap, a more distinct amalgamation of archetypes of natural force becomes apparent: the pentalpha and sextile in B serve only to evoke, in varying degrees, the significant ages of man and the cycles of the heavens. The latter, associated with Saturn (30 and 60) and Jupiter (12, 24, and 48), act as timekeepers, as previously elucidated - both in celestial spheres and on earthly realms. Meanwhile, the former delineates the stages of adolescence, fertility, marriage, societal zenith, and old age, marking the milestones of 12, 24, 30, 48, and 60 years respectively. Along the path of Saturn and its initial harmonic, and up to the fourth wave of Jupiter, these natural phases of individual existence are intertwined, uniting one's humanity (pentalpha) with the universal harmonious essence (sextile).

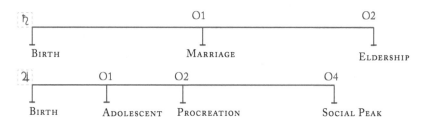

Figure: ages and waves of the chronocrators.

v. Mirror

5.1. King Solomon's mirror

It's believed that the governance of the stars was conducted through their images reflected in a mirror, simply bringing them to mind. This mirror, perhaps fashioned like a pool of water upon a mosaic of images, would reflect the celestial dome, with the advantage of containing Urania's geometric compass for accurate measurements of celestial movements. Its possessor, the renowned Solomon, would employ it to speculate on the heavens' secrets (measurements) or for the theurgic magic attributed to him by tradition. However, what's evident is that the mirror was what brought light (spirit) into the understandable, the concrete, the earthly (clay: earth and water). Thus, influenced by the stars, we are their mirror. By containing different planes of their movements (periods, harmonics of the periods, etc.), we have hierarchical systems to produce a coherent result for speculation. The Sun is always the center of the system, inspiring the heroic order (Hercules and the twelve labours) in reference to its annual journey. If we have twelve signs, it's because the docenary archetype resonates with the expansion of knowledge (Jupiter), something characteristic of the ancient priest, who knew the cycles of the sky.

Let's imagine we can gaze upon our life cycle in a mirror, where from all that movement springs a pattern that is harmonious, thus drawing a music. The light would be an expression of the potency of that music, and the mirror would be the instrument that brings forth the sounds that compose it. This is the concept of speculative music, an idea that, linked to the heroic, is what underpins The Lyre of Hermes ('La Lira de Hermes':): the initiatory journey of the hero-musician.

5.2. Solar order: the twelve diapents in the zodiac journey. Comparison with lunar scale

We are delving into speculative music, the speculum, the mirror, where in music, the definition of quality is given by the diapente (fifth), it is possible to construct the musical mirror with possible diapentes. The set of these is precisely twelve, and with twelve, the cycle of notes is complete (12 sounds).

Analogously to the journey of the Sun, music acts as the primary solar object, as the offspring of the Sun, being founded by each of the twelve parts it traverses in the sky. One note, one region of the sky, and its order given by diapentes (fifths). That is the speculative premise of Hermetic music that we present here.

We find the origin of the solar path in the note we call do, corresponding to 1 Hz of vibration, and from there the entire cycle of the Sun is built. The question arises as to what beginning we give to the year, since, though it may seem trivial, the year has begun in Capricorn (Solstice), Capricorn shifted (currently), Aries (Spring Equinox), Virgo (Egypt), Virgo-Libra (Rosh HaShaná of the civil year of the Hebrew people), at some point in Aquarius (Chinese New Year) &c. with different justifications in the meantime. The first distinction is made by solar or soli-lunar calendars, as well as other religious characterizations. Logically, it is the divisions that matter (number, interval) rather than a direct correspondence between these and musical notes. Each social macro-structure (civilization, race, religion, ...) possessing a natural mental framework of its own, adapts a different nominal structure to the group of twelve elements, hence the origin point of the circle depends on this. With lunar calendars, we do not complete the circle with twelve notes, as up to thirteen months may arise. This does not exclude the goodness of the system, as the Pythagorean limma fits exactly 13 times into the octave, and therefore a lunar calendar would be equivalent to the Pythagorean chromatic scale. Despite the exotic nature of the subject, I analyze it in the first place:

Moon 1: C, let's put it at 128 Hz 32[29].

L2: C#, at 135 Hz.

L3: D a bit low, at 142 Hz (vs. 144 Hz).

L4: D# at 150 Hz.

L5: E at 158 Hz, a bit low (vs. 162 Hz).

L6: low F, at 166 Hz instead of 172 Hz.

L7: high F, at 175 Hz.

L8: slightly high F#, at 184 Hz, vs. 182 Hz.

L9: G at 194 Hz (vs. 192 Hz.)

L10: G# at 204 Hz (almost identical to nominal 205 Hz).

L11: A at 215.5 Hz, rounding up to 216 to match nominal.

L12: A# at 227 Hz.

L13: B, at 239 Hz, 4 Hz less than B at 243 Hz.

---

29 We work with notes according to their natural tuning, coinciding in C and A with the much-famed 432 Hz tuning. C would be 128 Hz and A 216 Hz in this octave.

	DO	DO#	RE	RE#	MI	MIF	FA	FA#	SOL	SOL#	LA	LA#	SI	DO'
☽	DO	DO#	RE	RE#	MI	MIF	FA	FA#	SOL	SOL#	LA	LA#	SI	DO'

	DO	DO#	RE	RE#	MI	FA	FA#	SOL	SOL#	LA	LA#	SI	DO'
☉	DO	DO#	RE	RE#	MI	FA	FA#	SOL	SOL#	LA	LA#	SI	DO'

Figure: soli-lunar scale.

The note F is doubled, for there are a high-F and a low-F, center of the system above (seventh Moon). By having the reference, the deviation of the lunar scale with respect to the genesis of our solar scale, or Pythagorean scale, conjectures a correlation as in the figure, where a solar (12 notes) and lunar (13 notes) scales are represented. To complete the analysis, in the simplest case, corresponding to the tropical year that begins in the sign of Aries, the notes-symbols correspondence of the signs would be as follows:

C = Aries
G = Taurus
D = Gemini
A = Cancer
E = Sun
B = Virgo
F# = Libra
C# = Scorpio
G# = Sagittarius
D# = Capricorn
A# = Aquarius
F = Pisces

The additions to the model, alluding to Rigor, Mercy, Justice and Internal Music, encompass an esoteric aspect that

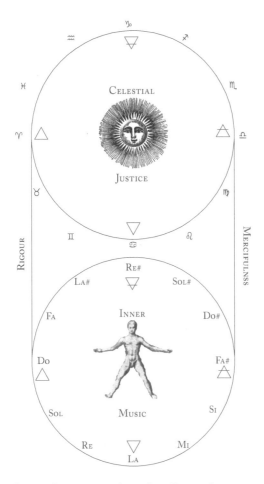

Figure: heaven-earth with zodiac and notes.

I leave out of this volume for simplicity, aware at the same time of the area where these issues are best studied. Man must internally reproduce the solar order that places the scale of twelve sounds in his internal dynamics (music), and this macrocosm-microcosm relationship must be harmonious, just, fulfilling in order and harmony the hermetic art (hermetic music). However, it's pragmatic to establish the level at which we're addressing these concepts.

5.3. Periods of the Solar System

If we take number as a mirror of movement and movement as the subject of the soul, that leads to the periods of the stars. For this reason, the hermetic musician must know them perfectly. Presented here are all the tools provided with some additional annotations.

Moon: it takes 27.32 days (sidereal period) to go around the Earth. Its phase looks the same again from the earth according to the synodic period of 29 days, this being the origin of the month.

Mercury: 0.2408 years (87.97 days) to go around the Sun.

Venus: 0.615 years.

Earth: 365.25 days (1 year).

Mars: 1.89 years. It can be approximated to 2 for certain symbolic issues, but it is preferable to stick to the exact figure.

Jupiter: orbits the Sun in 11.86 years, typically approximated as 12. Here the error is less than in the case of Mars, so the approximation is valid.

Saturn: 29.45 years, the 30s referred to as the Saturn cycle or 'Saturn return'.

Uranus: 84 years.

Neptune: 164 years.

Pluto: 248 years.

All of them govern the number of their period years. But not only that, but also in memory is impressed the harmonic series of these. From Saturn: 30, 60, 90, 120, ...; as well as its subharmonics: 15, 7.5, ... From Jupiter: 12, 24, 72, 48, 60; and its subharmonics: 6, 4, 3, 12/5, 2 .... As seen above, there are and will be coincidences, common places in the number symbol between harmonic components of one and the other planet. It also occurs with Mars and Jupiter, as the subharmonics 2 and 4 of Jupiter are the fundamental and first harmonic of Mars. The Universe is a network of interrelations, and this is an example in which this shines through.

5.4. The Mirror, its function and wave attunement

Every light possesses a harmonic series, harmonic components, which are perfectly visible in the Light-Wave of the Year. These are inherent to the image itself; therefore, it also has harmonics. If we pay attention to the levels of the harmonics, they go up to a finite and unlimited number, but numbers precisely arise from these waves. In other words, humans conceive numbers from waves; they do not exist as such but are the waves themselves, their vibration. The third of these waves, O3 (oscillation 3), is precisely the wave that we tune into when we observe something in a mirror. What we see in a mirror does not exist on a material level, so we must discard the idea that we tune into even waves, associated with matter (O2, O4, O8, ...). It is far too complex to tune into other waves (O5, O7, ...) where highly sensitive individuals may indeed tune in. And obviously, we would also be tuning into the first of the waves, O1, which carries the whole set.

The prime odd harmonic, and the one that should thus draw our focus, is O3, signifying form, signifying the soul. Hence, in the myth of Perseus, Medusa's own gaze reflects upon itself, turning her into stone. The stone is the matter, the Gorgon represents the cycles. Perseus contemplates only through the reverse of this mirror, that is, the inversion of the earth cycles (O2, O4, ...): the cycles of form (O3, O5, ...). Essentially, the mirror would relate to the soul. The soul is mirrored - redundant though it may sound - in that third wave, due to the dynamics it entails. In fact, in music, this third wave is what gives rise to the perfect fifth, that is, what gives rise to a different note. Music would provide here a specular image of the thing due to its formal quality, hence movement, thus soul. The mirror, the image of the mirror, the speculative image, would be an animic image. We would grasp it by tuning in with our soul. A mirror is never faithful to the material. When we observe ourselves in a mirror, the natural perception tendency is a subjectification of the physical subject, not aligned with other perceptions (photography, drawing, observer). Moreover, subject to the time of day, you see one quality or another. It is in constant motion when the material is fixed, and so should its reflection be. Devoid of materiality, it still possesses form. We cannot touch what the mirror reflects, but we can perceive its movement. This is equivalent to saying: (the mirror) does not tune in with O2, O4 waves and even harmonics in general, but it does with odd ones.

As a corollary, if we only have the odd ones, we have a system full of content but without structure, valid therefore for increasing the internal intensity of a person, but not without the danger of mismatching with their physical body.

Perhaps behind vanity lies hidden the distortion of one's own reality that induces the imbalance and falsity produced by the mirror. On the other hand, if you want to know the musical significance of this, you will have to find it in the reflection in the internal dynamics of being, and its music will be perceptible through the look in the mirror.

This conclusion affords the same with the musical mirror of the Heavens, as it reflects their souls. When forming the specular image of the stars in our mind, we endow it with movement to render it intelligible, to memorise their abodes, which is to memorise the souls of the stars, the souls of the spheres. Speculative music thus forms an image akin to a

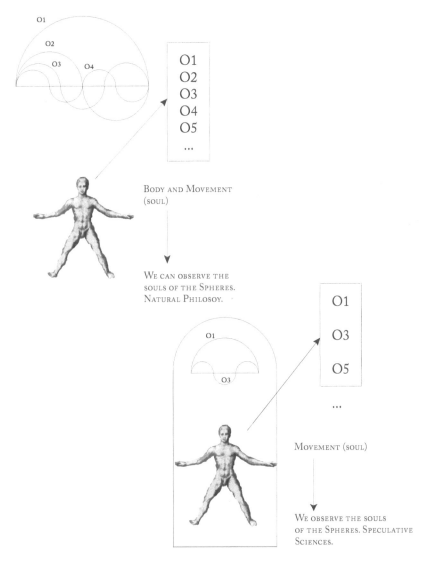

Figure: Odd waves and emotional involvement of the Mirror.

mirror, capturing or attuning to the formal part, the soul, of the movement of the stars, and leaving the physical part, for the process of imagining it in the mind lacks the tangible. By playing an instrument with knowledge of the philosophical doctrines that practically employ speculative music (hermetic music), then the imitation of the wave is complete.

5.5. In Conclusion

The five envisaged parts introduce and delve into the issues that are to underpin all current teaching of music. If one understands thereafter that the part which exercises the others, which directs and moves them as a whole with inspired artistry, is located not in the abdomen but between heart and head, one can access the line that hermetic tradition has bequeathed to us about the matters of vibration, sound, and aeon. Whether through the symbolic understanding of the act of playing, or through the study and virtue of memory and its hierarchical complexion, the student begins knowingly that they are breathing an electric fluid, capable of resonating in all facets of apparent and subtle reality. It is very likely that all these foundations will take time to be understood, but upon understanding, whether through reading and study or through study in the Speculatorium, they will serve as a point of access to the intellectual force of sound. To the musical secrets.

> *"Arimnesto, the beloved son of Pythagoras, made me an offering, for I discovered many secrets within the words"[30].*

---

30   Duris of Samos, speaking about Pythagoras. Lives of Pythagoras, Porphyry. Gredos Edition.

The speech, logos, the sword, discernment, inspiration, memory, spiritual hierarchy, ... all emanate from sound. A sound that is driven through the light of the intellect that we represent with the Sun and by the Musical Pentalpha. The student will find on the **tetraktys** the fundaments of discernment; in the **memory**, the permanence and solidity of the symbol; in the **scale**, the amphoras of his soul's journey; and in the **reflection** of the cosmos, the guide through all processes of hermetic music. This marks the completion of the rigourous part, where some may have stumbled; and where others may have successfully gotten themselves immersed into the subject.

CONFERENTIAE
HERMETICISMI MUSICAE

INITIAL COMMENTARY

I shall now endeavour to set forth what commenced through a series of digital encounters of diverse nature and platform. The conferences (videoconferences, streams, and seminars) unfolded from the months of October to December in the year 2021 until July 2022, and their content was predominantly of hermetic music. Initially, they were live with an audience, during which I transmitted my research in real-time. However, since the decision to transcribe and compile a book on the subject, the transformations, expansions, and documentations have turned the streams more into a homage to their origin than a reflection of the forthcoming reality. They are, unequivocally, comparative studies that have transitioned from the glow of the screen to that of the guardian candle, delving into either authors of the hermetic-musical tradition or my own contributions to the legacy corpus.

Concerning the renown authors, such as Athanasius Kircher or Robert Fludd, it is recommended to have some insight on their biographies. They are the ones that constituted the golden chain of the hermetic music though. In fact they are not only here but in the book as a whole in more than one section, since the student of Hermetic Music has to know them to ascribe his thought to the proposed system of this work.

Each and every one of them possesses a peculiarity: not only are they commented upon, but they also serve as a starting point for advancing in the hermetic-musical study process. These comparative studies ultimately form a unique work within this treatise, where the presence of wave theory and ontology, symbology, and Egyptian hermetic currents are constant themes. Thus, on one hand, it serves as a means to showcase works and figures that have delved into the musical Sophia, while on the other, it provides the gem that the Muse wished to impart on this occasion, for each of the commentaries and studies that enrich this treatise.

The interest lies, therefore, in the opening to another world and in the path to be traversed with the guidelines provided, in each instance. To whet the appetite, I shall begin by stating that the series of small chapters laid before the reader serves as both a reinforcement of the aforementioned Musical Body and an expansion. By expansion, I mean even innovation, within what may indeed be new and thus termed as such (circumstantial novelty). The reality is that the authors analysed, as well as the subsequent studies inspired by them, all have their foundation in the divine Muse, who truly inspires the consecration of the memoria mundi in the soul of the scribe of this work.

What unfolds before us traverses the minds of Kircher, Fludd, and Gaffurio before them, grasping almost to the blood of knowledge by links of the golden chain to forge a connection with the readers, so that adventure ensnares them, compelling them to delve deeper with each reading of each episode. To deduce from all of the above that what lies before us is new, as I say, would be an error, for there is truly nothing original as such; let us not confuse it - if at all - with unpublished. Nevertheless, I am pleased to bring certain reminiscences of the hermetic number and its music to the reader, and may they find favour in the reflection it induces. The whole section works as a single cohesive body of work, a second part in this book, and in a way that energizes not only the previously learned concepts, but also the psychic faculties that testify to the will to search and find the good lover of Sophia. he themes, as I say, inherit the previously stated ones. Without further ado, here and solely by the grace of the Muse and hermetic guide, are inscribed the treatises on hermetic music studies.

C:.I:. The total number of possible melodies. Kircher and his Musurgia Universalis, I

Or how the combinatorial approach that Athanasius Kircher brings us helps to understand the phenomenon of Inspiration

Figura i-1: Back cover diagram of the Musurgia Universalis, volume II, by A. Kircher.

We embark on a brief analysis of a text by one of the greatest compilers of knowledge during the Baroque period. Let us recall that this period spans from the beginning of the 17th century to the first third of the 18th century. This will be the stage for grand thinkers in the realms of hermeticism and music. Robert Fludd, Kircher, Kepler, all blessed by the sacrifice of the lamentable lack of will of poor Giordano Bruno, whose song was that of the swan and whose work became the greatest treasure during the tumultuous times that followed. We speak of a period in which two worlds coexist but do not peacefully cohabit. Kircher belongs to the scientific and theological domain, wherein the vigour of the new aeon of fire is evident, sublimating all possible knowledge into compilations.

Born in Germany and belonging to the religious sphere, he spoke Hebrew and Chinese, as well as German, English, Spanish... and of course Greek and Latin. We are talking about the most important languages, some not devoid of a spiritual and religious connotation, which resonate with the grand mind of this pioneering scientist. Regarding music, he authored a treatise called Musurgia Universalis, which is akin to a musical framework. The title reads *Athanasii Kircheri fuldensis societatis Jesu presbiteri Musurgia Universalis sive Ars Magna consoni et dissoni, translated as Universal Musurgia* or the art of consonance and dissonance, by the Jesuit priest Athanasius Kircher.

We will proceed step by step during the analysis of this section of his work. To do this, we will focus on a certain iconography of interest of what consists the proem of the book, which is combinatory. The conception of the Arts of Number is still going strong since if the hermeticist or student of these arts knows the number, he also transmits his intellect through the allegories that they carry.

1. The musical bird

The bird depicted below what appears to be a musical score following the title is striking. Kircher was passionate about Egypt and, in addition to his multilingual abilities, he was, to say the least, an instigator in deciphering its hieroglyphics. That's why this cartouche on the cover catches the eye. A cartouche is where the names of the kings and queens of Egypt were inscribed, primarily. It had a protective sense, as the circle is what surrounds the created, the realm. Our corvine friend, which is opening the scroll, possesses the will associated with that of the gods, announcing its desire to transfer the notes from the regions of the night, where they reside and transform the world of the dead, onto the paper where Kircher will circumscribe his text for the living.

Figure i-2: Musical Raven/Dove (Musurgia Universalis).

A stave yet to be written from which a single note appears. The parchment remains encapsulated, perhaps sacralized. It is possible that the bird is a raven, due to its color, or, on the contrary, a dove, perhaps judging it not by color but by the bulge of the skull (geolocalizer of the 'columba'). If it were to be the second case, it allegorizes the soul, the ba for the Egyptians, which is transferred to Christianity as the Holy Spirit. In the cartouche we could then read that the divinity on Earth, a sort of divine grace, deploys music based on its elements (we can guess notes on the stave). At the same time, we would read the transit, coming and going, of the deceased as a parallel to listening to the spheres (myth of Er). If it is a raven, perhaps it has a premonitory character, call or proclamation of the beginning of the work of which it is on the cover, and its symbolic use obeys a German cultural trait, where the raven is important in the pagan tradition, as well as an incursion into the emblematic alchemy.

There are some intriguing implications that allow for imaginative exploration. Kircher was a compiler of knowledge, and within that framework, he delved into these matters. However, the richness lies above all in the quantity and quality of what he bequeathed through the disciplines he touched upon. He was a man who immersed himself in everything he could, and he could accomplish much and had access to much through his religious order. Even in his critiques of other knowledge systems, he ultimately documents them, thereby bequeathing to us invaluable knowledge of other doctrines such as the Gnostic ones, present in his *Arithmology*[31].

2. Hierarchy of the Hermetic ascension

Here we have the circle where the music is going to be given —the germ of a tool dealt with throughout the entire text, which we can call Hermetica Circulorum. But let's proceed step by step. We can see that the motto below the dia-

---

31 Aritmología: "historia real y esotérica de los números" (Spanish Edition. translated title: Arithmology: "the real and esoteric history of numbers"). Ed. i.e. Maxtor.

gram says *'Musica nihil aliud est, quam omnium ordinem scire'*, which basically means 'Music is nothing but understanding the order of everything'. Within this circle there are three upper spheres and one lower one touching the Earth, where the same previous cartridge can be seen. Kircher is a master of image and symbol. We present here the entire triptych.

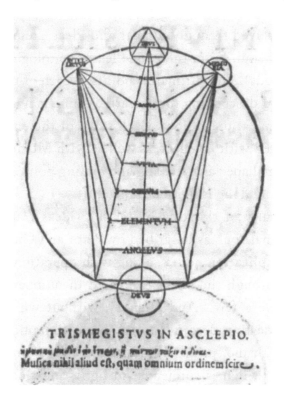

Figure i-3: cover of chapter. II Ars Magna of Consonance and Dissonance.

We have the upper triad, consisting of Memory, Intellect, and Divinity. It is worth considering that Memory is the mother of the Muses, who are responsible for channeling Inspiration, making it quite interesting to place Memory within this triad.

Intellect is where the musical operation takes place. The musical operation of the intellect itself causes the ratio; both ratio and memory belong to this soul here and are related to Pythagorean music and the play of proportions. When speaking of intervals - diapason, diapente, diatessaron, etc. - the intellectual operations with them take place physically in the head. They are not merely things one touches, but rather operations perceived through number and ideas, stemming from the rational soul. From there, one learns ontological realities (memory, gods). This ultimately points to each of the strata of this pyramid descending to the earth, which is nothing other than the emanation of light. Each stage of the emanation of light is linked with Intellect, as well as with Memory, serving as the original apex and starting and ending point in Divinity. This diagram alone is quite exquisite.

The faculty of thinking by relating ideas (ratio) resides in the rational soul, as described by Plato and Galen. This is where multiplication occurs, along with operations involving intervals, through the ratios expressed in numbers (2:1, 3:2, 5:3, to name a few). And memory, without which there is no map of destiny, descends to its abode. Simonides, Metrodorus, and Bruno, primarily, address memory linked to the image-idea, which is connected to light, and this in turn is linked to God, presented here as a pyramid mounted on the wave. And through the wave, the different layers of light finally reach the earth, passing through spheres and elements, and composing them as they go.

The large circle represents the Pythagorean animal, which is the All for the Pythagoreans, the great Leviathan of the Hebrews. As an animal, it identifies the anima mundi. There is another aspect, which is how the circle where Deus superior and the one where Deus inferior are placed split the circle in two, the Anima Mundi. Intervallically, this splitting in two is the octave, it is the creative lightning. This makes it quite interesting because there are diagrams in the musical speculator Cittara that have a lot to do with this. The student must see here a certain reference to the masculine-feminine duality that creates (created in Genesis terms) the wave itself. Imagine it as a sway: from high to low, tracing a circle to ascend and descend; a circle that is contour, that is limit. Only by moving in the circle can we understand the oscillation itself, and that ascent and descent are also wave processes.

3. The Hermetic Wave

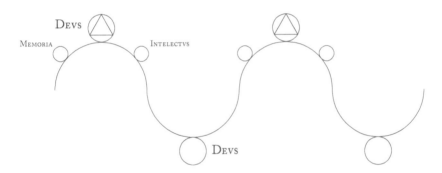

Figure i-4: the hermetic wave.

As a model extracted from the diagram on the back cover, we can construct a hermetic process based on wave movement (soul). Within it, the fundamental wave is depicted, to which its harmonics would need to be imagined. Given that the original diagram deals with the descent of light, the order will be one of descent and levorotatory, much like the life clock that gathers light. This is what we know as "ataxir". Thus, if we start from above, the intellect allows the light to descend into the World, into the dense, and it is Memory that serves as the center of gravity to carry the archetypes and images from man towards Divinity. Memory is the storehouse of ideas, of soul movements, providing the raw material for Inspiration, as we will see later on. The Intellect would be the one extracting all forms from the Light. This means that, for example, from the Sun, it extracts the reasons for things, from which their movements derive. For the ancients, referring all movement to the Sun (Zodiac, sidereal periods) was a way of linking the soul of light in motion, or of the body, to solar reference and thus obtaining its virtue. For Neoplatonists like Ficino, the Sun is *the* Good, it is the Truth, and they could articulate a hermetic thought path whereby the necessity of the solar reference link was recognized to properly position the mind. The center, the Sun, the reference for all reason, is marked by its rays, which are the vehicle through which humans resonate internally with the Universe. Linked with the Sun, and the stars with it, humans are able to connect with the harmony of the cosmos. This matter will lead to obtaining or tuning into it through Inspiration, and the diagram of the vessels later in the book explains it very well in terms of harmony. The process transforms the being from within outwards, making it capable of discernment. Hence the existence of harmonics, also in the original diagram.

The harmonics would represent precisely the hierarchical qualities illustrated by Kircher, (naming them as waves) O8 being the angels, O7 the elements, and so on with other names of the strata of the pyramid. Not without reason they all do emanate explicitly from the primordial wave O1 as indicated by the lines that start from the trinity Memory::G.od::Intellect. With that in mind, the harmonics will be:

O1: Primordial wave Trinity

O2: Man/Equal (homo)

O3: Reason (ratio)

O4: Feeling (sensus)

O5: Life (vita)

O6: Heaven (coelum)

O7: Element (elementum)

O8: Angel (angelus)

The numbering in the figure, however, is opposite: (1) angel, (2) element, etc. A certain path allows us to understand that, for example, the wave of the ratio O3 - disdiapente of the fundamental O1 - is the same one that undoubtedly shapes the musical universe, that is, the succession of all qualities (notes), one after another, like a circle of diapentes. The syncretic union diapente::ratio implies that each musical note is produced from the ratio when it constructs the quality as differentiated places. We see this when we observe 7 colors in the rainbow. There are many more colors, but there are 7 due to the division produced by the ratio, which is a divisive reason for the parts in terms of their quality. Just like the notes, it divides the light spectrum.

The Pythagorean musician, as he uses numerical ratios between sounds, necessarily tunes in with this third harmonic of the wave. Tuning each one and doing it in order up to the unity O1, the musician progresses, learning through the quality of sound. Undoubtedly, from this emerges a system of understanding based on the memory and intellect of the quality (note). Because memory is what we derive from our initiatory experience towards the divine, from our position in matter, as 'sculptors', and towards divine providence as the depository of our action. In the wave, we see that the cycle culminates in G.od, having passed through that. And therefore, through it, one goes to G.od. And God is *extracted* from the intellect.

In the wave we see that the cycle flows into God after passing through the wave. And for that, for her, he goes to God. And God is drawn from the Intellect.

What is memory? It's important to remember that we refer to the proper framework of our action, and that a framework is necessary for it to become golden (adhering to the symbol) and act as a divinizing agent. With that framework of memory, we pay homage to the art of subtlety, which the musician exercises when playing those temples of notes, within that framework. The state or mental environment in which music takes place is spiritual, absorbing, but above all, it is structural. Everything inherent to memory is so from the outset, as it sets the stage as context for the rite (enactment).

That archetype to which the act is later ascribed serves as a guide to reach divinity. It represents the content itself, the movement of the soul, the music with musical resonance in the chamber of memory in question. Therefore, the creation of a memory is so necessary, for we would indeed need to speak of the creation of a memory. Of ascribing to a memory that already exists. But what else is the adjustment in that memory if not the gods and the rites? Is not the rite that? When one enacts a rite, is it not the same as entering one of the locurum of the memory mundi? It's a way to elevate the chant, to bring the prayer upwards. Pico della Mirandola, with his truly theatricalized musical liturgies, or the baroque opera onwards, offer a clear physical example of the metaphysical realm inhabited by the hermetic musician.

And then there's the intellect, which is the way or formulation to bring down the divine archetype that memory has previously precognized. Where does it come from? Where is it born? From understanding, from reason. Hence the Pythagoreans, hence it's also about the environment as a manifestation of G.od. Hence a generation of memory and hence also an extraction of intellect. Everything that is divided by light would equally be operable by reason, so the musician could understand it from that point, from that intervallic action, and from its apex (head). And thus, divide it, in the numerical sense. Extract the wave dynamics and understand that everything manifests in cycles and their harmonics. That would be the intellect.

Let's then say this: from G.od emerges the Intellect; and from the intellect, all the waves arise, the harmonics of that main wave. From the beginning you have that main wave and then the others as secondary waves: second, third, fourth wave, and so on; already delving deep into the multiplicity (interval imperfection) of the smaller intervals.

All these secondary waves would already constitute tenuous relations with the tetraktys (echoes and shadows, very far from the original light), but until the fourth wave O4 we would be talking about the tetraktys as a repository of the idea, that is, memory. It is the task of the Intellect to unravel the light, separate the wheat from the chaff, and operate with perfection the tetraktys sine qua non to ensure the perfection of all numerical opera, since the tetraktys is the perfect decade. What's been differentiated, separated? Numbers-Idea. They are carried out as processes that occur between levels (ratios between integers). Hence the existence of musical intervals.

4. Music *Magnifica*

Musurgia Mirificae pars prima. Musurgia combinatoria.
Wonderful Music, part one. Combinatory Music. Here lies a
significant crux. The inquiry in Kircher's writing (we return
to it) is how many melodies are possible. It seems a question
worth pausing to ponder, doesn't it? Well, Kircher has already done so. How many melodies are conceivable in music,
altogether. Let us see how he frames it.

We've already studied his arithmological tool. Combinatorics is a part of mathematics -formerly called arithmolo-
gy- and has always played an interesting role for scholars in
contexts of any kind, even in the theological and philosophical spheres, as is our case. We will begin with the question
of "what letter combinations generate what words and how
many there are".

Our German friend could have taken any letters, but he
chose those of the word **ora** (to pray): the O, the R and the
A. In his first exemplum, he writes the six possible combinations: 1. ORA, 2. OAR, 3. ROA, 4 RAO, 5. AOR, 6. ARO.
The result is six combinations that start from the word ORA,
also implying a wider idea of praying.

Let's delve into another word, 'Amen'. Here, Kircher ex-
plores the importance of the word, together with that of the
number. This not only imbues the word with a special significance but also correlates it with the number of permutations
generated by rearranging its letters. It's not solely the number
linked to each letter, but a number linked to the combinatorics and likewise in the name there is a meaning per se, since
'ora' or 'amen' relate to the fiat 'as be it' of Creation. He deals
with the Logos at the end, it's an ancient idea. Well, so with
the word AMEN he gets 24 combinations:

A 1.	M 2.	E 3.	N 4.
1 AMEN	7 MAEN	13 EAMN	19 NAME
2 AMNE	8 MANE	14 EANM	20 NAEM
3 AEMN	9 MEMN	15 EMAN	21 NMAE
4 AENM	10 MENM	16 EMNA	22 NMEA
5 ANEM	11 MNAE	17 ENAM	23 NEMA
6 ANME	12 MNEA	18 ENMA	24 NEAM

Figure i-5: combinations of the sacred word AMEN.

He then proceeds to extrapolate and find the general formula, choosing nothing in vain and using the 5 vowels as 5 elements. Three elements yield 6 possibilities; with 4 elements, 24; with 5, 120. Although he doesn't outline the formula, since it is something that was common in his time, he took care to put all the numbers resulting from said combinations. The formula would be, for N letters of a word, the possible combinations are their factorial, N!. To illustrate, with 3 elements, the possibilities amount to $3 \cdot 2 = 6$ possibilities; for 4 elements, it expands to $4 \cdot 3 \cdot 2 = 24$, and so forth. Suffice it to say that for 24 elements (letters), there are 620,448,401,733,239,439,360,000 possible words...

Kircher employs this profoundly transcendent idea, which is that the language of the soul lays in the image. We already avoided it in the Musical Body (Mirror). If we look at the pyramid inside the circle and superimpose the combinatorial triangle, we can marvel at the combined forces of these two. How could it be otherwise? There will be unity and first waves at the top, a message that we take to mean that increases the intellect, referring to the combinatorics itself as an exercise.

In the superimposed image of the circle (undeployed hermetic wave) and the arithmological pyramid of combinatorics, we can see how the music that will end up being written (cartridge of the crow and the score, below) will have not just one (Devs), but the total possible combinations that are to be considered. In the image, 24 elements represented. He eloquently emphasizes that each stratum, each level of divine light - which is thus determined both by Memory and by Intellect - will contain three words and their combinations. This significantly advances the discussion, moving it to a more intricate level. To give an example, from Elements to Angels there is room for the words of 19, 20 and 21 elements, and before Memory and Intellect unite, that is, even in the sphere of Go.d, there are a total of 1+2+6=9 possible combinations. These 9 combinations are the first natural numbers, but this is another story that we are not going to discuss now.

Combinatorics with Music Notes

So Kircher moves on to the next level of complexity. Combinations of notes, what we could actually define as melodies if we assume a hierarchical nature. Let's think of three notes: DO, RE and MI (C, D and E). And let's combine:

(1)   DO RE MI
(2) MI RE DO
(3) MI DO RE
(4) DO MI RE
(5) RE MI DO
(6) RE DO MI

They are in fact 3 elements and they generate up to 6 combinations, just like the word ORA. Take the four possible notes: DO, RE, MI, FA (C, D, E, F).

(7) DO RE MI FA

(8) DO RE FA MI

(9) DO FA MI RE

(10) DO MI RE FA

(11) DO MI FA RE

(12) DO FA RE MI

Kircher shows only these combinations but specifies, erroneously, that it is the key of major G (*incipiunt à G*), when it is in fact major C. What is clear to us is that of the 24 possible combinations of four elements, it takes only six, which is its fourth part, to select only those that begin in the tonic C. We can repeat the process starting from D, from E, and from F, in each of them with six possible combinations. Finally, we have those 24. It assigns tonality to the notes; the order dictates that what will be played is tonal. The start on the tonic is fundamental and is the foundation of musical coherence. Musical coherence is based on there being a center, and this discriminates the number of combinations. The formula for this would be N!/N = (N-1)!, and there wouldn't be much more to say.

In the context of this prism, the key has its origin in a combination of letters, that is, in the Creation of the World (mysticism and kabbalah). Then the tonality comes from the word: what can be more related to the Logos than this? The ranges of notes, expressed in intervals, are also contemplated in Kircher's study, the maximum of which is a 22nd, that is,4 and a half octaves.

This actually constitutes an environment that grants space for all possible melodies. If we put together the entire range of the human voice from basses to sopranos, it is then all that can be sung, which makes it really interesting, since it gathers the framework of all the melodies that the set of human voices can emit, or all the possible melodies, that will be audible from the human timbre, in contrast with all the notes that an instrument can produce, which we would consider an artifact as soon as it transgresses the scope of the voice.

Let's remember that, although Kircher does not refer to this, the voice is represented by the Sun, corresponding to the heart. And it is Love, which is the force that unites all beings in the World: *Hic amor Harmonia est, hoc Mundus amore ligatur*. Thus, the magic number, with all the possible melodies that can exist, is unveiled:

$$\Sigma = 1\ 124\ 000\ 727\ 777\ 607\ 680\ 000$$

Et voilà. This represents, indeed, a colossal number. As a consequence we can see that, without words, there is no tonality. The word is the combination of letters anointed to give meaning. These games of qualities necessitate the existence of a tonality or radiant center (as exemplified by the hand model) that articulates the melody. The letters forming words necessitate a unique language, which is the pitch, the tonality, mode, or image, and this is the idea of a center-note, a Solar note, from which the others unfold up to a total of Σ times.

C:.II:. INSPIRATION IN KIRCHER AND HIS MUSURGIA UNIVERSALIS
II

And about how the strings we play in our memory enclose the circle that inspiration uses

Figure ii-1: Orpheus. Plate from Kircher's Musurgia Universalis.

This depicts **Orpheus**, playing his lyre and accompanied by Cerberus, the three-headed dog, who happens to evoke the inspiration of the present moment at another representation: the frontispiece of Franchino Gaffurio's Practica Musicae. There, a three-headed snake signifies that inspiration occurs only when the focus is at the present, neither future nor past, when the person is in a state of absence of focal moment towards temporal divergence (retrogradation or fantasy), uniquely and fully focused at the moment of living.

Figure ii-2: detail of the frontispiece of Practical Music by F. Gaffurio.

The meaning it has lies in the link between Inspiration and being in the present moment. Inspiration is a fire that storms in by communicating or causing the person to communicate internally with the ideas that lie within oneself, the inner presence of Divinity. Let's first define what it means to be **in the present moment.**

To guide our understanding, a series of guidelines responds to our call. All those issues of the body that can make us focus (awareness of the present moment) are the first to go through, as the physical body is the reference and starting point of the human experience. After it, all the others will come, as long as the person acquires goods, communicates, establishes a home, a circle of friends, and consequently a life cycle. I am not referring to activities alien to the spiritual dimension, even though they are done with the body. We will therefore focus on the body as an object.

The first disposition would be to breath. Through breathing we connect with the moment. The awareness of breathing, precisely, implicates our entire body, including our own heartbeat in the pulse that gives us life. That cadence, which endows us with vital spirit, is the receptor of the light from which we draw inspiration if we are well disposed of, and it is located near the heart. If our activity is of whatever nature, but it involves an artistic act, the minute we find ourselves upon inspiration we become infused by that idea, the inner gods, that lie within us. In other words, it is very important (conditio sine qua non) to "enter" through that door.

The suitable revolutions on the attention of the present moment are measured and worked through *pranayama*, as an entire science for the consciousness of the 'momentum fertile', as opposed to the wasteland. As a result, when we focus on a musical, artistic object, we necessarily have to work on breathing adequately to achieve concern about the prana.

Returning to the figure and after taking a timid look at Orpheus, the question about the Can Cerberus arises. In the myth, Orpheus calms the beast with his lyre, in order to pass through Tartarus and rescue Eurydice. And the answer to that, perhaps a sole initiation -given what we know-, must be plain simple: inspiration is linked to musical operations. As Orpheus operates with his nine-stringed lyre over natural things, embeds the seven qualities of these. This is how we see him in the myth when he moves the trees away from their place, or rules the wills of animals with his lyre, comprising the soul of All Beings. It does not point out to the mere made of playing an instrument, but to the fact that ideas dialogue with each other through musical operations. We will see how the stars are moving in the sky with a series of relationships among themselves that Kepler deduced and sort of captured (Harmonices Mundi), which are musical. When we take a look to these relationships, the intervals themselves, we realize that there exist ratios (rational soul) that measure them.

With this we know that the consequence is their movements, and their cause is the idea, those ratios. When we talk about music, we concern about managing those ratios, about the relationships between ideas. The dear reader should not be frightened or abandon the quest now, because this will be addressed, and perhaps the intellect will result soaked like dew does on the grass that so desires; just throughout the careful hours of this book.

The perfect allegory, or mystical conclusion and, therefore, comprehensive result on the musical operations of the internal instrument is in 'La Lira de Hermes'; like a turtle that serves as a base (resonant shell) for the light (strings). The skull of a person is seen as the celestial vault, a sphere in this whole theory of the ancient **macrocosm** and **microcosm**, which is the hermetic interrelation of the *above* and *below*. Within this vault is the light, and the soul is the movement of all lights. In this vault, which as said is the skull, there is a representation of the macrocosm. On a musical level, every domed instrument (bowed string family, the ud, to name a few), like the original lyre, wields this example of the macrocosm. If that shell that serves as a sounding board has an idea resonance with the celestial vault, the strings are what move within that celestial vault. And what is it that moves within the celestial vault? The planets. And more specifically, the light of the stars.

In other words: there is the fixed and the mobile. The body is the fixed, the mobile is contained within the strings, for when modulated by the musician's movements, they convey a sound resembling the light emitted by the stars. Thus, we see that Orpheus's lyre, being Hermes's plus two strings, is a representation of nine vibrations, speaking to us of Inspiration and the light emanating from G.od. 1+2+6=9 possible[32] divine words before

---

32 The union of the perfect number 6, which is perfect for the Pythagoreans

Memory and Intellect first merge. Hence, Inspiration (9 Muses) arises from Love (God, circle), which, as previously stated, is what binds the world together (see subsequent lecture on the total number of melodies). How is this related to the present moment? Do the Muses appear in it, or do the Muses generate it? The question is open.

At the feet of the statue lies a sistrum, an ancient Egyptian instrument with funerary connotations of a psychopomp guide. Let us not forget the Orphic myth of the descent into Hell, whose guardian is in fact the Can Cerberus.

Mother of the Muses

In light of the above, the circle that Kircher represents in the figure that we already saw in the Total Number of Melodies, is this Macrocosm, that shell. The entire Universe would be in this circle. The visible part of the shell is what corresponds to our Fixed Stars, to see the analogy. It is not only this vault, but this is its visible part. It will represent everything and the sky of the fixed stars. The vault that moves powered by the lever of the First Mobile.

The Intellect and Memory, alongside G.od, form a triad that refers to the three upper Sefirot of the Tree of Life, and the lower sphere would represent G.od on Earth, which is the Holy Spirit, the Hebrew Shekhinah[33]. This grace that comes directly from G.od and in relation to the Intellect and Memory passes through the unique moment when the initiate participates in the created, the

---

because it is both 1+2+3 and 123; and the divine unity and duality as the principle of undulation (1 and 2, respectively).

33   This is the name used to designate the presence of Adonai Elokim in the sublunar realm of Malkut, according to the Kabbalists.

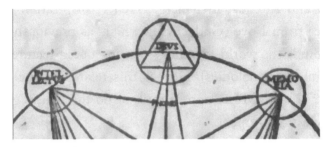

*Figure ii-3: detail of the figure from the Ars Magna
(chap II, Musurgia Universalis).*

only moment that truly exists. The perception we have of the future and the past is thus given by our inner selves. An experience is interpreted one way or another depending on our internal configuration (imprint). A person may contemplate the emptiness or the vividness of their memories, but reality can only be perfectly - or aim for it - lived and inferred from the present moment. The future is a union of elements that has to do with internal clocks (internal light) and the magnitude of these internal lights. These lights can be more or less bright, and they are based on the weight of our hearts.

Hence the relationship between the heart and the Sun, as a source of light, a source of life; blood flow::light flow,... and therefore link with the present moment. What happens? That the heart **stores** memory and that the mind receives intellect. So we have that these two elements harmonize in the divinity that is what is above them, that is, it is an attunement that harmonizes these "contraries".

This attunement links to the present moment. If we think about a projection into the future, this will be linked to Memory, as if we were predictive machines; and the Intellect linked to the Image and as much as it can dissociate that image from the Memory. There is one type for Intellect and another for Memory, and the harmony between both is precisely the consequence of that ray coming from divinity as an attunement of the triple (triangle of the Spirit). There are 7 elements, like 7 notes along the octave that represents the ray that divides the circle in two.

Memory: Mnemosyne, mother of the Muses
Intellect: Apollo

[1] If we have both, we have the Muses and the light that permeates through. Hence, there are 9 strings in Orpheus' lyre. The concept is that in the 9 concepts (Muses) the Intellect and Memory are ranked and unified in God, and that allows for the present moment's union, the inspired moment, the Divine Presence.

[2] Nine ideas aimed to construct a hierarchy of light, channeling the light from Apollo to Man. The circle with a triangle is on top and also in the set (large circle and lumen triangle). G.od is at the limit of the waters, belonging to above and below. Thus it perches on the waters and divides them.

[3] The idea that may be familiar to us is that of the brain with its two hemispheres. The intellect is a masculine part, it is Apollo; memory is feminine, it is Mnemosyne. This is identical to what is assumed about the hemispheres of the brain, so the union ends up determined according to the number 7 (hierarchies of the Intellect-Memory union) and through that link is that G.od comes down to His kingdom.

[4] If both hemispheres are interconnected, the light is produced inside the mind and this is the Mind of G.od or the Mens Apollineae. From there the Muses make descend the liquid or liquid light that is the caris or karis[34]. However, even though the left hemisphere is attributed to Reason and the right to Intuition (according to material science), it is more correct to express it as

---

34   In Classic Greek, Χάρις.

Intellect and Memory; from the former the ratio or reasons that relate the ideas; from the latter the capabilities of the deep record of experiences which, given as receptions of light, generate memory. When the memory is remote, it is Intuition. When not, what we commonly call memory.

In the present moment, the two hemispheres come together. With his illustration, Kircher places the 7 connections between both poles, one need only to imagine these consequent layers of the pyramid as phases of entry into the same inspiration, resulting in more localized brain activity. These connections have their names; if they have names it's because they have degrees, and if they have degrees it's because they have an above and a below. Above there is G.od; and below is our life experience, as if indicating gradations that allow for the connection of the hemispheres. It's like bringing G.od from within and placing Him on Earth, somewhat the Christic idea (karis::Kristos). And that hierarchy of entry into that depth is given by the Angel (*Angelus*), Element (*Elementum*), Heaven (*Coelum*), Life (*Vita*), Feeling (*Sensus*), Reason (*Ratio*), Equality (*Homo*). We must read it from the top down, that is, the last link of this connection with the Presence would be the angelic.

The hermetic motto of the image caption is, as it has been said, *"Music is nothing other than knowing the order of all things"* - Hermes (Asclepius). It is the mental, archetypal, numerical seat, where the idea of music rests. The octave is where the idea of duality and unity rests, and thus they order the world, plus they order it in a hierarchy.

And it reads above the diagram, *Quae bene disposuit, Spiritus unit Amor. Amor harmonia factus est, hoc mundus amore ligatur; Aut maror hunc mundum Numinis esse negas?* What we translate as "When it is well arranged, love unites the spirit. Love has become harmony, thus this world is bound by love; Or do you deny that this world is the very margin of the deity?". The idea is a reminiscent of Ficino, with Love equivalent to the Sun, which is the one who administers the light in Harmony, thus generating Good. The world is linked through love, from which we will conclude that the circle is that representation of Love, in addition to Anima Mundi, both concepts being assimilated to each other. G.od, Memory and Intellect are united and are in harmony, and they are through the Circle, that is why this is Love. The geometric representation of love It will be the circle, and that of the Spirit, the triangle.

Every part that exists within the circle will unite to the others harmoniously with all the other parts, like a kind of love that is geometric and that allows the support of the whole. Essentially, light is born from the Spirit; and the former is in the circle at the superior sphere and the second is circumscribed to the whole and is influenced by the graduation of Intellect and Memory.

Circle that encircles the soul

If we consider that the circumference represents the loving and harmonious union that links the entirety (spirit) of the parts, then it must be present in the division into twelve parts of the celestial vault. The geometry of the triangle and the square shapes this dozen (the minimum space between them). We are talking about geometry because it connects the parts in relation, whether through ligaments close to the origin of the harmonic series (consonant intervals), or through more distant intervals (semiconsonant and dissonant). These bonds are the manifestation of the lumen through its aspects.

The geometry represents the visual organization of light. Visual because it becomes perceptible through imagination; organization because it quantifies the empty space, and of light because we operate with light when imagining (mentis apollineae). By superimposing triangles and squares, and by a sort of effect, different shapes are generated in the mind as one fixes their gaze at the center of the inscribed circle. Some individuals perceive them moving, witnessing the figure mutate - either modally or antimodally - from its original perception. Everything operates within the mind (observer). This serves us for music. It's a kind of soundless meditation (internal music or geometry).

All that movement, so reliant on where we focus, being movement, engages the soul. Different shapes are generated in the mind by the marvel of this. There is one figure, then another, and another, ... Everything operates within the ratio, and thus serves us for music as it is an operation of light in the upper part of the body. This is how we work in the Intellect, while in the heart we find the realm of Memory, the other sphere in question. This union allows for its equidistance from the center (circle) of Being, defining the cohesion of the parts through love. The soul is our internal movement on this journey around the circle (Spirit). Of one kind or another, higher or lower (vegetative, to rational).

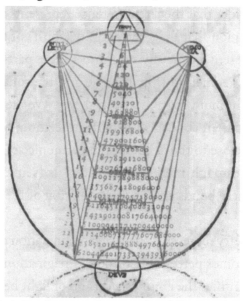

Figure i-6: Combinatorial pyramid and Heaven-Earth circle.

C:.III:. Inspiration as
THE SELECTOR OF OPTIONS,
DISCERNMENT

*And how inspiration transcends the illusion of the elective in
the free will of the human being*

Discernment

It is undeniable that inspiration not only allows for a biological consequence like the interconnection of the hemispheres, but that this occurs harmoniously, so that everything happens in accordance with nature. It is convenient to say this since modern science is very capable of observing a natural phenomenon, analyzing its operation in the realm of matter, and guessing a cause that produces these effects; which is by no means the way Nature operates on the individual. To begin with, there is no distinction between the individual and the "outside." It's all one, and what we are inside we experience as manna from outside, and vice-versa; the Hermetic axiom. What hermetic music actually teaches is the broad pantheon of sound-symbols that operate within us. The path of learning has been more than suggested in the ratio, the reason of the ancients; and the memory, both intertwined in the image. Hence we study geometry, hence we study the idea.

But a myriad of not only ideas but gods can be found encapsulated in a note, and from there give birth to ideas and attributes; since the note is Number, and this governs over the rest. This hierarchy would be: **Number → Word → Idea.** The combination that produces the number generates the word, and this is what designates the attribute of the god in question. The deities have multiple names, although it is more correct to say attributes. Hence the 72 attributes of God in Judaism, and many others depending on the context. The Greek gods also enjoy multiplicity, and although they may retain the same root, it is their "surname " that directly produces the attribute in the mind and hence the function it performs (ie: Hermes Psychopomp). Music underlies each of these attributes as a number that, of course, could remain

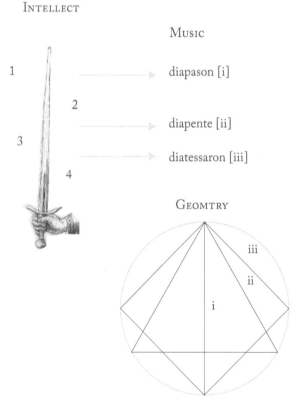

INTELLECT

MUSIC

1   diapason [i]

2

     diapente [ii]

3

     diatessaron [iii]

4

GEOMTRY

iii

ii

i

Figure iii-1: The attribution of intellect is the idea-intervals.

in the gematry or isopsephy (counts with pebbles), that is, the undulation of this or that god's word (thus the worshipping).

From this principia, existence would be moved by the attributes of the gods, whose visual representations would come from the idea of each one of them. From the Idea we therefore gather an Image, and here we can find the statues or talismans as images precisely of the same ideas that collect the attributes of the gods: **Number → Word → Idea → Image.**

What remains to be seen (sensible world, or 'olam ha asiah') is how number organizes itself, and for this, we have to delve into the concept of Chaos. Order precedes chaos (Kosmos, Khaos), and from there, it displays its myriad of possibilities, its sons and daughters, in the face of which chaos can only harbor a longing for destruction[35]. Order is perceived by the human being through the organization of light. A beam penetrating a disordered room evokes this idea: if the beam persists, the space will eventually be organized by the individual who has observed the beam, by unconscious will, by the influence of light. Therefore, light is the agent of order, and its absence allows chaos. We say allows, not generates. To find the cause of chaos, one must do the same, reach where there are no more causes, and take one more step. Then everything is darkness and void (*Tohu veBohu* in the Torah) and in turn awaits to be ordered.

The idea of a religious or chivalric order has always been the same: to produce the ordering of the individual to get out of chaos. Chaos of the psyche, chaos of the social place, chaos at the short and at the broadest stratum, of the cosmic underlying order. Therefore, chaos is not the same as destruction, but destruction can occur with order and chaos can be a builder. To

---

35 Such consideration of longing measures its strength in conjunction with light, giving rise to the cosmogenetic myth that later unfolds in the essay.

build, yes, but obscuring the endurance of what is built. That is why those who built the great cathedrals ("eternal" duration) were initiates (order/ ordered) in the likeness of those who built the megaliths or the Egyptian temples,... it is always the idea of the order of heaven produced on earth through the mechanics of the hermeticism.

Overall, Chaos will precede every cause; and for this reason, given that order comes through number, it will prioritize this: Chaos → Number → Word → Idea → Image.

As the Word orders this chaos, the Number must be its origin, grouping itself randomly and not randomly, and forming a consistency out of it. Now, it is in the Number, once it is grouped, that we have Music. The notes are complex vibrations given by the numbers, and the music is the union, the join, the alliance of these notes. Then, all together are meshes of numbers in constant movement, weaving an order from chaos and ending in god-words when become perfectly complex and shaped (Form). Hence symbolizing it with the sword (sword = s+word). We must take into consideration that music is therefore the main actress in the process of shaping the world.

To discern is to divide by the *s-word* of judgement what is chaotically united. Once the music makes its appearance, discernment occurs, which allows each idea to be made clear. In short, music frees order from chaos. If we return to the question of inspiration, as an energy that plays the role of vitalizing the act of man, of providing it with life, light, essence, we can conclude that inspiration and therefore Apollo and the Muses produce this insight.

Now we are going to argue, with brief sentences, why inspiration *equals* discernment. For this we are going to use the Table of Uses (*usus tabulae*) on page 7, book 8 of Musurgia Mirifica, by A. Kircher.

Tabula II

tas , fed quædam funt fimiles.

	I	II	III	IV	V	VI	VII	VIII	IX
I	0								
II	2	0							
III	6	3	0						
IV	24	12	4	0					
V	120	60	20	5	0				
VI	720	360	120	25	6	0			
VII	5040	2520	840	210	42	7	0		
VIII	40320	20160	6720	1663	336	56	8	0	
IX	362880	181440	60480	15953	3024	504	72	8	0
X	3628800	1804400	604800	159530	30240	5040	720	90	10

VSVS TABVLAE.

Figure iii-2: Usage table, A. Kircher I.

From the total elements listed in the left-hand column (Roman numerals), sets with both equal and different elements are taken. Once all possible combinations are generated, this serves to extrapolate towards potential melodies given by elements such as notes. We will also compute combinations for repeating elements. In practice, this is the case, as identical notes will repeat due to the tonal system, for example, the tonic, whose incidence, its frequency, is always markedly higher than others - discounting the dominant - and the dominant, slightly less frequent than the tonic.

The upper number in the table enumerates the following cases:

171

[1] Number of elements to combine
[2] Sets (when) all elements are different;
[3] (when) there are two identical;
[4] (when) there are 3 identical in the set. &c.

For example, for V elements, if all are different, there are 120 combinations; if there are two identical, 60; if there are 3 different elements, results in 20; and so on.

COMBINATORY CHART

TOTAL NUMBER OF ELEMENTS TO BE COMBINED	NUMBER OF COMBINATIONS THERE ARE WHEN:								
	ALL THE ELEMENTS ARE DIFFERENT	2 OF THE ELEMENTS ARE EQUAL	3 OF THE ELEMENTS ARE EQUAL	4 OF THE ELEMENTS ARE EQUAL	5 OF THE ELEMENTS ARE EQUAL	6 OF THE ELEMENTS ARE EQUAL	7 OF THE ELEMENTS ARE EQUAL	8 OF THE ELEMENTS ARE EQUAL	9 OF THE ELEMENTS ARE EQUAL
I	0								
II	2	0							
III	6	3	0						
IV	24	12	4	0					
V	120	60	20	5	0				
VI	720	360	120	25	6	0			
VII	5040	2520	840	210	42	7	0		
VIII	40320	20160	6720	1663	336	56	8	0	
IX	362880	181440	60480	15953	3024	504	72	8	0
X	3628800	1804400	604800	159530	30240	5040	720	90	10

Figure iii-3: chart of uses, A. Kircher II (translated).

Combinatory Table

I deemed it expedient to provide a "translation" of the table, wherein it becomes apparent that if we have V elements {a, b, c, d, e}, they can conjure a total of 120 combinations. If each element represents a distinct note, then there are 120 different melodies.

I: {a}
II: {a, b}
III: {a, b, c}
IV: {a, b, c, d, e}
V: {a, b, c, d, e, f}
VI: {a, b, c, d, e, f, g}
VII: {a, b, c, d, e, f, g, h}
VIII: {a, b, c, d, e, f, g, h, i}
IX: {a, b, c, d, e, f, g, h, i, j}
X: {a, b, c, d, e, f, g, h, i, j, k}

Figure iii-4: Elements of the combinatorial table.

We will then have, for instance:

{a, b, c, d, e} = {DO, RE, MI, FA#, SOL} → i.e: DO SOL FA# RE MI → 1 out of 120 possible melodies.

And this melody does not repeat notes, which means that to make it more organic, at least it will start and end on the same note. Because of this, an element should be repeated, and if we continue with V different elements, now we find: {a, b, c, d, e} = {DO, RE, MI, FA#, SOL} → ie: DO SOL FA# RE DO → 1 out of 60 possible melodies.

Sixty combinations are not that many, but if we think that we can only express five sounds, it is indeed a number worthy of consideration. We are talking about the fact that just the 7 notes of the scale, starting and ending on the tonic, would yield 5040 combinations. The general formula for the table is the following: $N!/M!$, where N = possible notes and M = equal notes. If I am inspired, thus subject to inspiration, a single melody is being derived, purified, from this total set of possibilities. Just one melody of a huge set. Let's say that a melody with 10 notes is going to be very repetitive and will use the tonic 3 times. There will be (expressed as a sum) a total of $\Sigma = 10!/3!=604,800$ possible melodies[36].

One of those 604,800 would be the simple melody we have here: DO (C) RE (D) MI (E) SOL (G) FA (F) MI (E) DO (C) RE (D) MI (E) DO (C). Where we repeat 3 notes (C, D, E) out of the 10 elements. This is nothing short of fascinating. A musician, that is, someone who, inspired, with an instrument, makes music audible, is refining, not creating, a single melody from an impressive total of possibilities. Creation would be what we think we do when we discern, and to discern would automatically be a creative act. Paying close attention to this deserves an extra effort from us, as we discern - like a sword cutting through the air - always between existing options (does one create the air?). By existing previously, they occur before and after discernment, and it is in discernment that they become present. The musician creates nothing. The musician can only first give himself internal order through the Pythagorean-Hermetic teachings themselves. Let's summarize the following:

---

36   To adapt it to a tonal scheme, meaning it starts with a note in all its possible combinations, we need to divide the previous number by N. Therefore, we would have:

$\Sigma = (N-1)!/M!$

So, the result for $N=10$ and $M=3$ would be 60480.

[1] Only one melody is discerned from an enormous set.

Music presents us with all these possibilities. If we were to consider painting, it would be more complex. How many color possibilities exist? We can't quantify them. While there are Pantone colors that establish the range of chroma, that number is artificial, and if we could discern more, it would be even greater. What's unique about music is that we can determine the possible melodies in conjunction with arithmetic, as we are doing here. We can visualize the possible melodies in a tabulated form.

This gives us an idea, as selecting one from that total provides insight into the power of inspiration in an individual. Let's extrapolate this concept of inspiration beyond music: our everyday lives are filled with moments of varying significance. It's evident that we experience some moments with less intensity and others with greater intensity. When we are fully present, that is, our consciousness is not dwelling on the past or the future, we are knocking on the doors of inspiration. We discern when we realize what future concerns lie ahead and which past pains subtly enslave us, even when they appear in a gentle manner.

The present moment is intimately related to breathing. It's no coincidence that life is generated through breath, and inspiration has that same act stored within its name. When we, not being musicians but going about our daily lives, inhabit a present moment, inspiration can appear in that moment. What is it like? How do the ancients describe it? Is it a flash? An idea? A solution to a problem?

In other words, **is inspiration - outside of music - akin to taking all the possibilities available and arriving at just one?**

If out of 604,800 possible melodies, an inspired moment bequeaths us only one on a whisper, the consequences of the hermetic-musical operation are clear:

[2] OF THE ENTIRE SET OF POSSIBILITIES THAT CAN OCCUR, THE (STATE OF THE) PRESENT MOMENT PRODUCES (DISCERNS) ONLY ONE.

And that's the crux of the matter, because the act of discerning is no longer ours, but rather that of Inspiration. This is the reality of the object. We are not the ones who discern. We'll get to that later. For now, we would have to think that inspiration produces the most appropriate of all possibilities, the optimal of melodies, since:

[3] IT RESONATES WITH THE PRESENT MOMENT AND WITH THE INDIVIDUAL AT THAT MOMENT. NO SPACE AND TIME IS ONGOING.

After we lay down 3 or 4 possibilities that we might be considering right now at the present moment in reference to a problem that we have in mind, and we all have dilemmas, can't a moment of inspiration help us discern?

Do you not perceive the profound significance of mastering Hermetic Music to grasp the essence of musical language? Joseph Campbell eloquently expounds on how we embark upon a journey where life unfolds—the heroic path. However, this journey is also arduous, demanding sacrifices. There exists a plethora of imagery across social media platforms depicting "the visage of spiritual awakening", yet there remains a stark contrast between perception and reality. While the idealised vision entails a rustic escape, communion with nature, and deep breaths, the actuality is often characterised by tears, trials, fractured relationships, familial estrangement, and illness. Such disparity underscores a profound complexity. Campbell asserts that once within this realm, *"doors will open"*, likening these portals to the muse of Inspiration.

This present moment is also generated by necessity in moments of crisis, where the individual does not really know what is going to happen next. From misfortune one goes to grace, depending on the hero type, of course. If we are able to receive inspiration leading to spiritual progress, and that allows us to make appropriate decisions, we set ourselves on that heroic path. I want to convey to you that inspiration as a way of understanding life experience is foundational. If out of 604800 total possible melodies in this very simple case of 10 notes, only one is selected unconsciously when playing inspired, when only we are presented with 3 or 4 options among the common problems, how come it will not purify the inspiration which option is the best?

Let's understand the life experience. [1] Why do we reason about the options to choose if logical reason has nothing to do with inspiration? [2] Why do we ignore the irrational? It is easier to take an instrument and reach a melody and feel very good when you arrive, but if it is an analytical decision, it is brainy and difficult. Why is it?

[a] The nature of inspiration is that of elementals **fire** and **air**. The air from inspiration, the inhalation of the present momentum; and the fire from the light that ignites within us, and produces warmth that is of Apollo (its cause) through the Muses.

[b] But a decision of ours in the world involves the **water** element, which points the emotions -the result of inspiration itself implies this- and also involves the **earth**, which is material (resignation, change), because we perform it on a physical object (clay, for the sculptor; instrument technique, for the musician).

The resistance arises from that which is denser (strong crystallization), yet it is not always the case. An idea may be more solid than a building. When we speak of inspiration, we may be delving into realms beyond music, beyond the ordinary notion of "I play and a melody I deem perfect emerges." Perhaps we are delving into life experience, into the optimal way we navigate our existence. Optimal with what? With the internal melody, with the notes composing that internal melody. With our key. Indeed, in English, tonality is termed "key," which signifies not merely an entry point to songs. A key unlocks a door, thus momentarily disrupting the status quo of the house – its atmosphere, its space, its form. Upon opening, something enters, something exits. Resonance operates in much the same way. If I manage to evoke resonance within myself, that something enters the house that is my identity, the temple I represent, thus acting as a key. It's a tonality, a certain pitch; we have a tonality, we have a note, and perhaps several, depending on the moment. As a concept, it is a singular idea.

This is the wondrous power of Music through Inspiration, enabling us to affirm that it unconsciously allows us to select from infinite options only the optimal one for us in resonance with our present moment. Living with inspiration at hand is living within a realm where one is guided, which aligns with the concept of divine presence, the immanent divinity within the mundane, the spirit nestled within matter.

The sense of spirituality

We talk about music; we talk about music indeed when we address spirituality. By that, it means we are discussing everything that encompasses music. Not only delving into the aspects of music that we are familiar with, for which there is an extensive literature, but also into the spiritual aspects of music, for which there is virtually nothing -conservatory wise. Therefore, this is dedicated to the spiritual aspect of music. To the hermetic part in the sense that hermeticism was an entire form of thought, we are not talking about abstract concepts in which to navigate and dissolve ourselves. They are not devoid of reason, of rationality, of coherence. Not at all. We are talking about tradition.

Many times, in classes, courses, on social media, I encounter people who are obviously drawn to these matters but have a foundation that is perhaps markedly "new age nosense". That is a term that refers to a way of being, a way of seeing reality in which one is completely detached from the tangible. It does not imply that these esoteric people frees their ego, but often they are consumers of the spiritual, of books, of courses. In this way, it still reflects a materialistic society of the spirit. It's like trying to escape from something that pursues you. What I aim for at all levels where Providence wishes to help is for these individuals to channel through intellect the matters that are of the spirit. For those who are too dismissive (the opposite pole), to approach the spiritual dimension and understand that it has been studied by other civilizations and sciences beyond what they may know. It is a mistake to detach ourselves from an entire tradition that supports us.

Kircher is a product of that tradition. Often, one finds oneself among those who seek a spiritual aspect of things that ends

179

up veering towards other cultures. For instance, a European may explore the Mayan zodiac or Jyotisa (Hindu astrology). A society shapes its own system; if we distance ourselves from our own lineage, we disconnect from our roots. Until this bond is lost, we forfeit a foundational seat within our civilization. We can adopt the form of something (a mirror), but not its substance and form outright.

Retrospectively, everything forms part of a genealogy. Europe, as a religious, socio-political, and territorial entity, birthed the tradition of Hermeticism. Though originating in Egypt, its zenith was reached during the Renaissance. Therefore, Europeans synthesize knowledge, yet always syncretize new insights within the framework of existing cultural sedimentation, rooted in classical culture. How many Europeans follow Buddhism? How many embrace diverse traditions from afar?

All "World Days of" are the new liturgical calendars artificially manufactured by a new religion to replace the previous one, the Catholic, that persisted under principles derived from the ancient, the Egyptian. This is quite interesting as we live in this world and time. It must be considered that every religion, including the one being established, will have its spiritual aspect. Spirituality has paved many paths for many individuals. It has led many people to take different paths in life, *calling* them to spirituality and manifesting in one way or another.

What has never led to anything is a person attached to material things who decides to buy ten spirituality books. That's what hasn't led to progress. You see, throughout life, some people have a marked external change, others internal, others a balance. But there is always a pull from life itself given by the course of the Sun. Listening to these movements is the foundation of vital progress, of one's path. If spiritual inclination comes from an external influence, it won't have an internal echo. If it has an internal origin, it will produce a spiritual process, attracting necessary things: a book, a channel, whatever is needed.

And here, we talk about music because music has this unique ability to convert, transform, transmute internal movements, that is, the anima/animus, the soul. It does so with a language that is universal, indicating that everything is composed of music, and this is plausible. Therefore, it's essential to steer clear of vague esotericisms, which don't delve deeper but merely deliver phrase after phrase, leaving you pondering as if it were a haiku, though it isn't. That won't contribute much because it doesn't emerge from the internal process. However, I don't want to offer criticism but rather to strike a balance between these two aspects, reflecting in people the realization that we all have a more rational part and a more irrational one. They may find that music, and more specifically the study of Hermeticism through Hermetic music, is the union of these two parts. It is the crossroads, the intersection of Heaven and Earth.

Man does not perform discernment

As a final note, I would like to deliver the final blow to the death of the ego that thinks, the ego that believes it creates. Inspiration comes as a result of discerning between the sensory elements captured by our nervous system, but our ability to discern is always separate from our ability to observe. We discern only when illuminated by the light of intellect, which is a mental point linked to the intention and will to discern. Our willingness to do so has led us to derive symbols from natural cycles and phenomena, which, when observed, enhance discernment.

Hence, in the diagram of the sword, it is not one who wields it, but the Divinity, and the blade is the word, the name, the Logos. By studying, hand in hand with Sophia, the truths of this logos through the word, then do we do discern; and from there, everything else follows.

As a consequence of these indisputable actions of the Muse on the Initiated Man, we encounter, without discontinuity and, moreover, head-on, the Pythagorean Y (ypsilon/ upsilon). The graphical representation of the letter (υ, Y) clearly

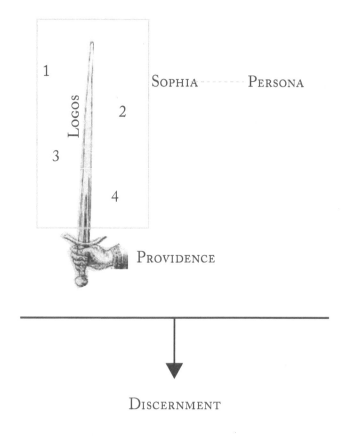

Figure iii-5: Discernment from the Logos.

expresses that there is a primordial division from a common trunk. Amid successive disjunctives, which are continuous in the vital journey, beneath every decision lies a principle of Justice, which is the virtue that moves into the decision (or not). Inspired, the Hermetic musician moves towards Justice; acting by inertia, lacking the divine spasm of the Muse, he acts contrary to it. With no middle ground, the imperative balance must reconcile man's stance in his world, whereby music becomes a highly useful tool.

As a consequence of these compelling performances of the Muse upon the Initiated Man, we encounter without interruption and, moreover, abruptly, the Pythagorean upsilon. The grapheme of the letter clearly expresses that there exists a primordial division from a common trunk. Besides successive disjunctives, which are continuous in the vital journey, beneath every decision lies a principle of Justice, which is the virtue that would guide that decision. Inspired, the hermetic musician moves towards Justice; acting by inertia and, lacking the divine spasm of the Muse, he acts contrary to it. With no middle ground, the imperative balance must reconcile man's stance in his world, whereupon music becomes a highly useful tool.

For the Pythagoreans, to discern is paramount, and we face an abyss if we fail to do so correctly. For this, there are moral, dietary, and labor codes on which groups, sects, religions, etc., have based their social cohesion. We could consider this as conscious or voluntary discernment, which implies sacrifice and balances rigor with mercy (Justice). Without sacrifices in one area or another, humans cannot access the gifts associated with Inspiration. The most direct sacrifice would be in diet, as practiced by the enigmatic master of Samos. If one is not vegetarian, they can always abstain from something that gratifies the senses. The premise revolves around the same center: depriving the body of something it explicitly desires.

Abstinence is necessary. It's true that little has been said about this so far, or that I have mentioned little in this or the previous work about the nobility of this attitude towards life. Let's put it this way: the temptations of the body, of the senses, mark a quick ascension path along one branch, while deprivations and rigors mark a slow one. Unlike the slow path, the fast one is immediately noticeable; its progress is evident. That's why it's fast. But that same speed is an illusion, as it's the body that perceives it without first passing through the intellect, which aligns with the numerical reasons of the cosmos and its cycles (the music of the spheres). Everything starts and ends in the stomach, as exemplified very well by some illustrations from the Middle Ages, with devils whose bellies house a face, or even devour people through them (carnal appetites), conveying the same message: the absence of subtle elements in the individual.

The progress that unfolds slowly solidifies on the path itself, and upon arrival and completion, it has constituted a seat of authority over oneself (inner 'autocritas'). The individual possesses his kingdom. But what does sacrifice have to do with discernment? Well, the reasons for a sacrifice can be external or self-imposed, and the latter are the only ones that, by definition, involve a decision. Decision-making starts with discernment to contemplate among several options and the paths that each one entails. Since this discernment can be vague or unconscious, the act by which it becomes conscious entails, like a backpack, sacrifice. And it's with this burden that the mind would gradually clarify itself in harmonic contribution with Memory.

Figure iii-6: Y (ípsilon).

Every path of sacrifice, once undertaken, requires strength, as temptation lives within that burden on the walker's
shoulder and can cause them to stumble over the precipice
(the archetype of the Fool in the Tarot). As such, the necessary virtue once on it is called the royal road, given that
strength-lion-king form an idea of Memory.

Temptations aside for the vital wayfarer (unnecessary to
explore here), one who cultivates the union of body and
mind through abstaining or sacrificing something unnecessary for vital functioning, is better poised for such ascent.
Otherwise, we can say Fortitude is cultivated through abs-
tentions. Returning to the symbol, the upsilon or Ypsilon
takes the shape of a club, Hercules's weapon and a suit in
the Spanish deck of cards, which tradition assimilates to

the element of Fire, the virtue enabling such ascent, as it pertains to the subtle versus the dense.

If one branch of the club-coarse-tree represents both Fire and reign, the other denotes Earth and sin. The great redeeming heroes possess this duality since they encompass the cognitive memory of the human ensemble, and they feel the need to redeem those on the fast route despite themselves employing the slow one. Such is the case of Hercules, wielding a club as a symbol that unites both branches into one thickened unity. His hand, where the ensemble gravitates, is Justice, for it upholds both branches unified. Another hero is Jesus Christ, of whom we possess clearer and closer echoes as a redeeming archetype.

Figure iii-7: Club, meaning Four element; Hercule's weapon (Sun's heat and light). Spanish deck edition.

C:.IV:.
THE MUSES OF GAFFURIO AND COMMENTARY.

*And how inspiration spills, vessel to vessel, through the
daughters of Memory and unto the willing hermetic musician*

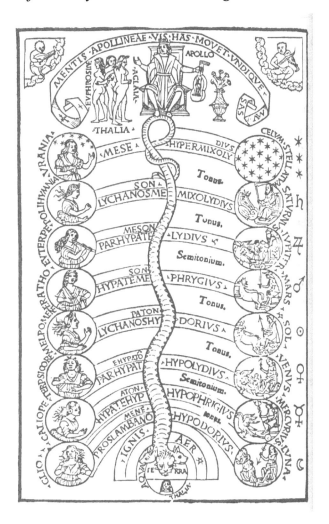

Figure iv-1: Frontispiece of Musica Practica by Gaffori.

Here I will say that what we have before us is Gafori's celebrated graph on muses, notes, music modes, and celestial spheres -and in more depth, Apollo, the Charites and the Lyre. What is it and what does it represent? Written in 1492 in Italy, it follows a diagram whose content belongs to Ramos de Pareja, a previous school on the same topics for there is a relationship between the notes, the spheres, the modes, and the muses that is present on the Spanish author's works. It is sure interesting to see the Greek names of the modes suffixed in Latin (mixolydi- us, phrygi- us, ...). In fact, these are the names that have transcended, although poorly adapted, until today. Concerning the names of the notes (mese, licanos meson, ...) we'll discuss in another part of the book; they have not transcended to our days. Today, we use the system that was founded by Gido d' Arezzo in the 9th century, and that grounded both musical writing and reading. Sure there is a lot of symbology at the diagram, and it is this side that is of interest to us.

Apollo

At the top of the image, there is a representation of Apollo and two representations of the feminine forces on the sides. We speak of Apollo, the god of light, music, arts, sudden death regent, in relation to musical inspiration in the image thanks to the figure of the lyre. Apollo, the patron of prophets and solar deity who adapts the ritual behavior of Egyptian solar temples to Greece. This, and it causes doctrines related to the light of then and later in the Arab world. Hermetic Apollo, as the religious reconnects with the Sun, playing truths with the lyre. The image shows, apart from a vase with five roses, he is accompanied by the Charites, the Graces, that show the purity of the three arcanes of life with their nudity.

Charites

What are the Charites? They stand for Divine Grace. Their names are Euphrosyne, Thalia and Aglaia. These three are the trinity of light, the *pyr vitae*. These three are the maximum expression of the form, of the spirit. They are the one (Apollo) become trine without passing through duality, without dividing, as only pure form can do. Similarity of the diapente creator of the musical note as an idea, the quantum quality of the sound that is revealed with the ratio of light between three and one. The division of light (Apollo) into pairs would involve matter. This division of light is when a wave and a body are generated, when it enters the material world (gnosticism). The 3 Charites represent the idea that the one divides into the triune, without dividing, continuing the light in this way due to its purity. This is exemplified as waves from O1 to O3, meaning the animic-formal part of the wave vs. the complete wave. Or what is the same: the soul stripped of the body that represents its energy; the pure, cyclical movement, without an associated body. And the feet of Apollo, purified by light, step on the serpent, through which the spheres of Heaven pass through. Spheres that are of the ancient order, collected by Ptolemy, several centuries before F. Gaffurio (1100 years) and that here relate inspiration with planetary influence. The spheres are those of the planets and luminaries as long as they can be seen by the human eye, that is, up to Saturn.

It strikes me powerfully that if tandem Apollo-Charites refers to pure spheres (waves without bodies), and at the same time he steps on the snake, he could be symbolizing an astronomical cycle without any associated body. It's a possibility. This, which deserves a separate study, exists as the complex harmony of the universe. In any case, and launching this hypothesis, the period to which it would refer could be, at least in nature, that of the lunar nodes which, in fact, are not a body, but a cycle, and which by Arab and Hindu influence could very well have been important in the Renaissance. It would be ruled out as a possibility since the period of the lunar nodes is 6800 days, which is 18 years, 7 months and 12 days; one more day, one day less. The problem with this hypothesis is that a single eon of this cycle covers periods only up to Jupiter (12 years), not Saturn, and not the sphere of stars (precession period). It is important to understand that we are dealing with celestial hierarchies.

Muses

In the left-hand column, we behold a series of circular medallions. They are spheres of muses, patrons of the arts and axioms of music. On the right-hand column rest the planetary spheres, representing the souls of the sky, that is, the cyclical movements that compose the cosmos. First of the muses (in descending order) is Urania, favoured in the order of light and linked to the impeccable pearly sky of the Fixed Stars. The next is Polymnia, linked to the sphere of Saturn. Euterpe finds pleasure in the company of Jupiter. Erato moves with Mars, Melpomene intones the voice of the Sun, singing in its rays. Terpsichore dances with Venus, adorned in its own harmony; Calliope, she of the beautiful voice, pairs with the eloquent Mercury; and Clio the glorious with the Moon.

To begin with **Urania** [Οὐρανία[37]], and in a starting point analysis complementary to that previously stated in 'La Lira de Hermes', we will say that it represents the first vessel where the light-water of Apollo-Charites is poured. This way of looking at it brings the reader closer to the idea behind the Muses (moys, humidity). The Urania vessel is not accessible to the uninitiated mortal in the other 8. The progression in the arts that the muses represent allows such ascent. Urania articulates the astronomical study, the substance that is born from the stars and produces the ecstasy or rapture of divinity. It is a high idea of universal harmony, of understanding, of silent and elevated listening. Gafori seems to suggest that it is accessible from the sphere of the Fixed Stars and through the hypermixolydian mode played from the note called "mese", equivalent in Ptolomy to LA-A.

Polyhymnia [Πολυμνία] represents the vessel of geometry and vibrations, harmonious among themselves. It is not difficult to observe the relationship between harmony and geometry, as we start from the divisions of the circle into parts to define intervals as harmonic waves of the whole. Saturn is the sphere of this Muse, as Saturn is a geometer, containing within it the science of delineating the spaces of matter, of which Saturn is the archetypal patron.

With **Euterpe** [Ευτέρπη] vessel of delight, comes what I think refers to the ecstatic pleasure of the musician. There is a concept, tarab طرب, specific to Arabic oud music, which I believe may be precisely associated with the effect of this muse. The reasons would lie in the deception, enjoyment, rapture,

---

37 That means 'from Heavens', or 'the uplifting one'.

that will occur in order to reach this state; and on the other hand, in its strangeness, it is an univocal sign of the spiritual elevation (sphere) that it is necessary to achieve. It is an enthusiastic voice, entheos, 'the divinity within'. And if Jupiter is the father of gods (Zeus, Deus, God), it is not entirely unreasonable to think that the muse Euterpe manifests in the abduction of the tarab, that is, occurs in this one.

Erato [Ερατώ] is the muse of poetic courtship, patroness of poets. Given that the qualities of each muse are widely discussed elsewhere within this book, I'll refrain from detailed elaboration here. It embodies love as a driving force, set in motion in individuals imprisoned in harmony, which is all of us. That is, it speaks about love in which the light of one individual is transferred to that of another, and vice-versa. In astrology, it is called synastry or simply transference. It is no small thing; Jung studied it, and prior to him, Ficino well treated the whole question of love as a divine axiom in his "De Amore." Mars, the associated sphere, makes the vasodilator blood flow for the sexual act, love's last destination.

Melpomene [Μελπομένη], the muse of melody, places the verticality of sound in a biological, physical, and material dimension. We are talking about harmony versus melody. The latter represents the individual's own movement, the unique one of the self, in contrast to the united multiplicity of the whole. Therefore, she became the muse of song, which in turn is the highest expression of the voice (Calliope). She manifests in singing when it is sincere with the person who sings. That is to say, the Muse attends not merely by singing, but rather when the singer sings with their own light. Linked to the Sun, she is discovered in the essence of the person when singing the melody that is their own. This question of one's own melody, as a sonic manifestation of what we are inside on an individual level, can perhaps be linked to Kircher's good stream where a single melody appears as the fruit of inspiration. I hope it is becoming understood.

On the next vessel, **Terpsichore** [Τερψιχόρη], we will say for now that she manifests during dance, then it is about how our body harmonizes with the music that is external to us. It is equivalent to moving 'following the waves', to take advantage of the astral moments of the sky to do one thing or another (elective astrology). We dance 'to the sound of', and that sound is what is heard, the macrocosm imitated, speculated with our physical body.

On **Calliope** [Καλλιόπη] we will state that she embellishes the voice of Clio, which has not been sifted by the arithmological aesthetics of music. Together with Mercury, it manifests itself when the mind participates in music. Mercury precisely illuminates the intellect, making it visible. Beautifying would be the effect produced by knowing the musical reasons, the numerical meanings, the musical scale (stairway::hermeticism), and in general everything that *moves* our mind during music. About Calliope, it is said in 'La Lira de Hermes':

> *"First of the Muses, door to the world were inspiration comes from, that is Calliope (Καλλιόπη), supreme among the nine muses for Hesiod. She is the muse of song, poetry and eloquence. It sets in motion the wheel of the flow of inspiration, or should we say the sphere. The first to move and whose gravitational effect acts as an invocation to the following, like a first domino piece."*

Clío [Κλειώ] is the emotion that music produces. Its raw, vegetative feeling is associated with the Moon and therefore acts on this system of the human being. It filters emotional experiences, whether sad or happy, but always in their raw form. Lacking the reason introduced by Calliope, they contain Memory in their first link/ stage. Depending on how we feel the music, and especially our inner light, the different muses weigh on each other.

Finally, **Thalia** [Θάλεια], the silent muse in earthly contact with the elements. She is the musician's gateway to the luminous-musical experience, to their journey into the depths of being and harmony. She appears when a person learns to listen, which is not just physical listening, but metaphysical. Listening is being attentive to the present moment, where signals or synchronicities occur.

To produce 'on Earth' a reflection of a cosmic harmony generates the serpent that intercommunicates and links the different spheres. The rope through which the blessing that the Charites extract from Apollo descends. That is why we speak of harmony as a vehicle between the 9 vessels. The presented graph can establish this clearly.

Perhaps the development of this diagram deserves a book alone. Anyway, my contribution comes from the conviction that the keys produce a sound on the instruments of the soul that I trust are my readers. It has not been easy at all to get to this point, but I suppose that life requires seamless connivance and unmitigated sacrifice many times. I have tried and do try to conjure my time, when I have had it, to make these issues known. I have made an allusion to the harmony in a concatenated and continuous way in every channel of inspiration in its descent. At each level the vessel receives and emits the previous and the subsequent, endowing or arrogating to itself the effect and the cause. Let us understand that harmony is the concept of the internal texture of the being, the cohesive composition that gives us coherence. Together, by all means, with the concept of light as the first cause of everything and

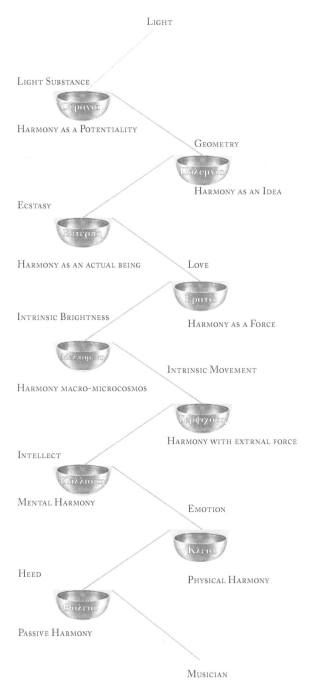

LIGHT

LIGHT SUBSTANCE

HARMONY AS A POTENTIALITY

GEOMETRY

HARMONY AS AN IDEA

ECSTASY

HARMONY AS AN ACTUAL BEING

LOVE

INTRINSIC BRIGHTNESS

HARMONY AS A FORCE

INTRINSIC MOVEMENT

HARMONY MACRO-MICROCOSMOS

HARMONY WITH EXTRNAL FORCE

INTELLECT

MENTAL HARMONY

EMOTION

HEED

PHYSICAL HARMONY

PASSIVE HARMONY

MUSICIAN

Figure iv-2: Diagram of Inspiration.

effect of nothing. Hence, light serves as an orchestrator of balanced order. In defining harmony, we must address an influential force that brings order to disorder within chaotic substances. It reconciles the dual principles of Apollo (representing light) and Dionysus (representing matter), aligning with order and disorder, respectively. Apollo symbolizes the idea while Dionysus embodies the imperfection inherent in matter.

Thus, when speaking of harmony, I prefer to speak in these terms. It is better understood that the vessels produce different qualities of it. Urania represents light as movement, and (1) **harmony as potency**; Polyhymnia represents (2) **harmony as an idea**, a prelude to (3) **harmony as an act** of Euterpe. The Musician receives (9) **passive harmony**, which alludes to synchronicities and sound outbursts, from which arises the interest and vocation for music. With (8) **physical harmony**, the vocation is externalized in a study of the effect based on emotions. The Pythagorean, accepted as mathematical, begins with the third one, (7) **mental harmony**. &c.

The gradations of light constitute a very interesting subject of discussion, which I will continue discussing here with good judgment and willingness. I hope there will be well-founded debate.

About the musical modes

It appears evident to point out that there is a synthesis of eras in Gaffurio's chart. The right half refers to the medieval system of eight modes (referred to as tones or sounds), as well as to the Neoplatonic conception of the Spheres, which is also medieval. We're talking about a thousand-year-old tradition by the time Gaffurio and Ramos discuss this. On the other hand, the left side, the reference to the classical world is direct. The notes and their names correspond to the beginnings of the medieval modes, and their theory is found in Ptolemy's Harmonics. The Muses are also a classical conception. It's as if the author wanted to establish a bridge, to synthesize, and thereby continue the spiritual tradition linked to music, bridging the eon of Antiquity with that of his own time, the Medieval-Renaissance period. Or if we refine periods, as we will do in another volume —G.d willing—, Gafori syncs the end (synthesis) of the period comprising the years 769 to[38] 1603 with the previous one from 225 BC to 729 AD. The date 225 BC comes from the Imago Mundi of Pierre D'Ailly, which states:

> *"About this time we have pointed out the sixth maximum conjunction, which we said occurred in the year 5120 of the world, (...), approximately in the year 225 of the incarnation of Christ."*[39]

As it refers to the maximum conjunction, namely the first in the fire sign, which is thus the first of all triplicities (elements), we must infer that it refers to the sought date. The span between the two dates is 954 years, adding up to a slightly higher number than the nominal 940. With this, we know that a colour similar to that of late Antiquity or the early Middle Ages imbues, quite rightly, his work. Hence, the

---

38 In 769, the first conjunction of the aeon occurs in the sign of Leo, marking the beginning of the cycle, which nominally is a millennium but de facto is smaller in this case. In 1603, the first of the following cycle (current) occurs in the sign of Sagittarius.

39 Page 528 of the mentioned book. Edition by Antonio Ramírez de Verger.

inclusion of references to Macrobius and Boethius[40]. Returning now to the musicological character of the treatise, the correlation between Greek notes and their 'modern' equivalents aligns the whole, derived from the Ptolemaic theory of his Harmonics, which assures us that the notes are in their correct equivalence:

> *prosambalomenon* = LA
> *hypate hypaton* = SI
> *parhypate hypaton* = DO
> *lycanos hypaton* = RE
> *hypate meson* = MI
> *parhypate meson* = FA
> *lycanos meson* = SOL
> *mese* = LA' (high)

Before continuing, I must mention that although this entire organization of musical memory unfolds throughout the book, the determining notes of each Greek mode lead me to establish a certain preliminary comparison with something that, on the other hand, will be studied in greater detail later on. Speaking of notes associated with planets will adhere to an ontological or archetypal knowledge, on one hand, and syncretism, on the other.

Divine and speculative is their nature, as they seek to bring the immutable closer to humanity, and this from hierarchical bases, facilitating a path where otherwise there is an abyss. This sheds light on this doctrine, since it is always easier to contemplate an order of penetration into the depths of one-self (heaven/hell) that allows one to name each step, than

---

40 IVth and VIth centuries AD, respectively, belonging thus to the previous complete cycle of elements.

to do so in a manner subject to complete ignorance, feeding what institutions-religion have done and will do. Perhaps that is why Gnosticism and Hermetic currents were the object of persecution and ridicule. Furthermore, this vision of the notes is syncretic, as they are associated with spheres, which are also hierarchical, and because there are seven planets. I believe, if I am not mistaken, that this accounts well for how the human mind operates and that undoubtedly in the creative memory of man these processes of uniting different arts into one take place. There may be different notes associated with stars in history, but they will always adhere to the septenary number-framework or ontological number. In this example, the sequence of notes is descending, as the ascent through the ontologies of the spheres corresponds to the natural order that the Greek modes (and even those from other places) have had, that is, descending.

In 'La Lira de Hermes', the order of the notes is similar, and each is justified therein. Here, as will be seen, and translating the previous to the notes of that, the order would be: LA (Moon), SOL (Mercury), FA# (Venus), MI (Sun), RE (Mars), DO (Jupiter), and SI (Saturn). The difference lies only in the FA.

Apollo's Cycle

It is interesting to observe this relationship it has with the serpent. Apollo Pythian, we have a god and an attribute, as we were discussing earlier. Apollo and the serpent. What is the serpent? What does the symbolism of the serpent imply? This is much older and implies an idea of **eternal recurrence**, a concept of transmutation, an idea that it revives once it sheds its previous skin: it dies and is born again, a celestial act

elevated to the idea. Expulsion of the old matter and generation of the new matter (as a product of inspiration, as its consequence). This links with the idea of immortality through
the cycle, both in its form and in the event of renewal, which
connects with immortality and therefore divinity. Perhaps it
is a symbolism of the greatest of cycles. If we are that little
thing that looks at time with a vague hope of a life span of
80-100 years, then the 4,320,000 years, something that could
be represented in the serpent as Maha-yuga, would be eterni-
ty from our point of view. This largest of cycles would point
from here.

Apollo is portrayed, in any case, as the embodiment of a
cycle of light, akin to the cycle of the Sun around the Galaxy.
Apollo represents the galactic transit of the Sun, and unques-
tionably, this cycle surpasses that of any human being. If the
serpent were to symbolize a cycle, it would be that galactic
year. It forms a wave-body reminiscent of the spheres, where
the wave resides in the sphere and the body comprises each
of the planets, animated by each muse within the wave of the
sphere. We can conceive of wave-body dualities in some manner.

We have not yet mentioned the Cherubs, symbols of the
harmony produced by love. We saw this in Kircher, in the
motto: "When well arranged, love unites the spirit." Symbols
of the driving force, harmony, from a markedly Neoplatonic
viewpoint. So we have as a framework love, light, and music. All within a Renaissance framework (from "De Amore"
by Ficino). As an attractive force, of union and cohesion of
divine and human elements, subtle and dense, luminous and
material, it will refer on a macrocosmic scale to movements
of great significance in the universe. The greater the love, the
stronger the cohesion and the wider the revolution, the cycle.

Thus, could Apollo represent the galactic year? Institutional science suggests that this galactic year lasts 225 million years, longer than the age of Man but shorter than that of the Earth. Returning to the Mahayugas, the year of Brahma consists of 1000 Mahayugas, hence 4,320,000,000 years. How many revolutions of the Sun in the Galaxy make up this immense period? 19.2 times. This figure closely approximates the cycle of the Chronocrators, Saturn and Jupiter, their synodic period, which is 19.8 years. Perhaps Apollo represents this figure, this year of Brahma, which would equate him with the same Hindu god. In an ideal sense, that is, in the Idea and not in the material "accident," the cycle of the Sun around the galaxy would be 1000 Mahayugas divided by 20 (in reference to the ideal Chronocrators cycle), that is, 216,000,000 years, undoubtedly a monumental cycle. Also similar to that of the lunar nodes -serpent cycle of 19 years.

Going to another point, or addressing it in such a way that the vision of the possible cycle of Apollo (and its significance) becomes clear, we have the system of the central fire. Apollo was the main god (along with Zeus) revered by the Pythagoreans, with Pythagoras himself claiming to be his son and paying homage[41]. Although we know that Pythagorean teaching barely escaped with two of his disciples, over time it seems that part of it was able to be preserved. Assuming adherence to this, Philolaus the Pythagorean and others spoke of a cosmological system where the Earth revolved around a **central fire**, showing a hidden side to it that would be uninhabited. The Sun, in an orbit of one year, would rotate in it in

---

41 *Lives of Pythagoras:* "And when he arrived at Delphi, on his journey by sea, he inscribed upon the tomb of Apollo the elegy by which he proved that he was the son of Silenus ..."

a wider one than that of the Earth, and in another smaller and inner one, the antiearth or Antichthon would do the same. Of this, Pythagoras himself says:

"(...) on the other hand, anti-earth, he had assured that they were the nine muses."

With all this context, the Muses would revolve around Apollo, with him being identified in that physically invisible internal fire. From here, two options branch out, in my opinion: one, taking the idea as such, would lead to Apollo being indeed the cycle of the solar system around the Galaxy; and another, which would be more peculiar, that the invisible central fire is nothing other than the galactic center itself, made unobservable to us by the arms of the Milky Way. If this latter case were true, Apollo's cycle would still be pending calculation, although, if we consider that the entire Galaxy moves (rotates) like a disk - not as bodies in solar systems do - the period of an object near its center would be identical to that at its edge, yielding the same cycle for Apollo of 225 million years.

All this underscores the immutability of Apollo and the notion of a distant and fixed nature (spirit) associated with light. Regardless of the period, the idea eventually permeates between the physical and the metaphysical. It is not necessary, in a first approach to all this, to know the exactitude of what moves at such a long period, since humans generally conceive cycles of time mundane, close to their lifetime or, perhaps, triple of it (parents, individual, children). Apollo, as the Sun revolving around the galactic center, is the interstellar traveler, and perhaps with his archetype we will come across in the future, when interstellar travels broaden our notion of light cycles.

C:.V:. ROBERT FLUDD I

Study of the lux cohesiveness

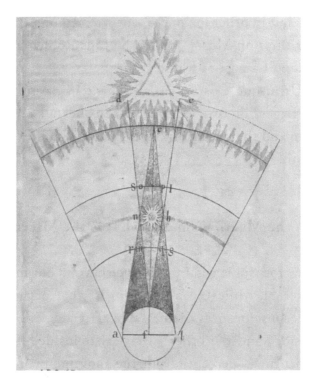

Figure v-1: page 81 of Utriusque Cosmi Maioris Silicet et Minoris Meta-
physica, Physica atque technica Historia. R. Fludd.

If previously we saw Gafori's chart, and prior to that, Kircher's "Musurgia Universalis," now we are going to examine
another exponent of all these matters of hermeticism and music, which is Robert Fludd. For this, we will work with this
document, which is none other than the "Utriusque Cosmi
Maioris," book three. We will discuss hermeticism and music.

It's curious because many of you may wonder what we
do with so many Latin texts where the extensive work done

towards all knowledge is referenced. We are addressing issues that have been humanity's wisdom at different times, and the interest in this lies in the fact that we have access to original documents. It's a pity that most of them are not translated, but in other instances, they are. Among these cases is the "Writings on Music," edited by Luis Robledo, which is a translation of a part of Fludd's work.

The "Utriusque Cosmi," in all its extent, is more than a thousand pages, in two volumes, where he talks about the macrocosm and the microcosm, so to put it in context, we will discuss both.

What is the Macrocosm and what is the Microcosm?

The macrocosm is what takes place beyond our initial idea of the external, while the microcosm is what occurs within our initial consciousness of the same. Trivially, one is "what exists outside" and the other "what exists inside." Primarily, the macrocosm is perceptible in the movement of the planets, the behavior of light, and other celestial phenomena, while the microcosm is evident in our body and its processes. The essence of music lies in its ability to resonate with these elements in mutual harmony. For example, in astrology, when organs and biology in general are related to celestial movements, a bodily zone (microcosm) is being attributed to a celestial one (macrocosm) in order to bring a unified understanding of the subject closer.

This issue connects to a union of two halves of the created. We recall that in Gafori, there is no transition through duality; it goes directly from unity to trinity. The same occurred with the *hermetic wave* derived from Kircher's theses, except that in the latter case, there is only a direct triad in this manner. When analyzed in depth, it is evident that it follows the natural harmonic order of the wave. Both halves of the created would indeed refer to two distinguishable concepts, but not to generate a divisive element of reality, but to make it cohesive through mutual inclusion (yin-yang). Essentially, it is a whole Cosmos, only with divided waters, as explained in the Bereshit or Genesis (I.6-7).

The numerical framework underpins the ontological reality upon which the distinction between the two "halves" of the cosmos unfolds. To elucidate, let us briefly explore the significance of the number seven. Seven symbolizes the seven celestial spheres: the Moon, Mercury, Venus, Sun, Mars, Jupiter, and Saturn. These spheres constitute the seven animas of the cosmos, emitting an ontological resonance and collectively harmonizing to create the celestial music of the spheres. The profound essence of each archetype is encapsulated in Plato's myth of Er, where the hero's journey traverses these spheres upon death. This vertical ascent signifies the hero's transcendence of each sphere, reminiscent of the initiatory rites practiced in ancient Egyptian temples and by Pythagoras. These initiations serve to liberate individuals from the astral and biological influences exerted by the macrocosm upon the microcosm.

By transcending external influences, one achieves freedom, allowing the spirit to move towards free will. Complex hierarchies are alluded to in lodges with the aim of attaining emancipation from external influences intertwined with earthly sway. An internal deity is nurtured through these impacts on the unconscious via symbols, empowering the initiate to develop an awareness of archetypes and a mental framework for each influencing idea. Understanding them enables transcendence, limiting their influence. This principle is also evident in cave art, where painting figures meant entering the animal's psyche through the stroke, a symbiotic connection leading to hunting success. Thus, referring to the animal as animated is fitting, not just because it's alive, but because to the primitive mind, it embodied a soul object, moving them internally. Mastering by delving into the animal's essence, its own will, and making it serve (as food, aid, watch, or companion) was a consequence, rooted in a profound unity between the micro and macrocosmic realms.

There is a principle that if not followed, one would act against natural law, and this precept that allows the union of souls is broken: *ananké*, necessity. This is linked to the Moirai, the enforcers of Destiny. It holds immense importance because this destiny ends when necessity governs the act, thus when intruding into the Anima Mundi to obtain something, if there is no necessity for it, it will not occur in accordance with divine justice, whose projection is that natural law which permits abundance. If achieved, it is enormously detrimental to the one who carries it out. Hence, this practice dismisses anything born from an impure heart.

Certainly, it's natural to wonder: what constitutes a pure heart?[42] It's one inclined towards goodness. Within our free will, we hold the power - whether great or small - to determine the direction of our hearts, towards the principles of love or hatred. The former undoubtedly embodies an understanding of the interaction between opposing entities, while the latter leads to a fast-paced pursuit, often resulting

---

42 Another, perhaps more esoteric, meaning may be found in the lightness of the heart, weighed against the feather of Ma'at, in the judgment of Osiris, a good analogy for the memory and its weight upon present actions.

in frustration if objectives aren't met, both internally and externally.

Through love, we cultivate qualities like optimism, patience, perseverance, and, most importantly, we align ourselves with tools that have served humanity since ancient times. These tools stem from love, firmly rooted in the classical notion of universal connection and compassionately structured within the natural order of things. The four classical cardinal virtues - **Fortitude, Justice, Temperance**, and **Prudence** - resonate from the realm of love, representing both emancipation from ego and the growth of compassion for all beings.

In conclusion, there are two paths: the slow and the fast. The latter, driven by immediate gratification, often leads to frustration, which then breeds resentment, hatred, and destruction. While it may temporarily alleviate common vital needs, satisfaction through this path burdens the heart with malicious judgment. Interestingly, long-term processes bring about transformation and learning. Even if the objective is not achieved, the journey of striving for improvement, giving our best, shining with love, fosters personal growth. Whether success is attained or not, there's a transformation towards goodness that enriches the individual (Sun = Good, a Neoplatonic concept, benign judgment).

This holds paramount importance for the vital progress of any individual, particularly within a collective context in our globalized world where relationships with neighbors, partners, and others play a significant role. From our perspective, we alone discern whether our actions stem from love or hatred, and we do not deceive ourselves in this regard. Hence arises the concept of the omnipresent Divine when Catholicism equates G.od with Love. If we position ourselves as a particle within the vector of love, which is a universal force, we would observe from this standpoint whether our emotions embody this love or not. In essence, we cannot deceive oursel- ves, and that is what truly matters. Someone who outwardly appears to act for the benefit of another but lacks this inten- tion internally does not act out of love. Consequently, if they fail to achieve the desired outcome with that person, they will harbor resentment and hatred, leading to a desire for reta- liation. This approach to the everyday must be extrapolated to understand the foundations of love and how our selfless actions in the realm of passions yield benevolent judgments and extract wisdom from experience.

The fourteenth Dalai Lama once said: *'People are like mountains, very difficult to change'*. This notion is fundamen- tally tied to love, which is inseparable from Hermeticism. Hence, we speak of love and motion. When one attempts to change another person, they are projecting their own self onto them and must deeply examine whether they do so out of love or out of a lack of self-acceptance, which is contrary to self-love and the concept of the Good. Someone who does not love themselves cannot, and will not, do good, nor will they accept it from others because they cannot distinguish it from evil. The confusion that arises from such individuals spreads like fear, easily engulfing even the most fulfilled indi- viduals in self-destructive spirals.

The blessing of inspiration is like a rope thrown to us from above, precisely guiding us on how to imagine what we should imagine by natural law. Receiving such inspiration is nature's way of showing compassion towards beings, like a friendly nudge from the universe. Every evolutionary leap must be inspired by this love, providing insights that even the smartest animal couldn't conjure up on its own and adjusting its internal clock to a new, adapted version of itself. So, I do believe that inspiration affects all beings, much like how the light from every star reflects on every blade of grass, as the Kabbalists say. Nature, personified as Geb, Gaia, or Gea, is indeed alive and allows individuals to receive inspiration as a form of redemption or blessing for the natural, physical, and psychological transformative creative process.

Love, the Sun, the heart, the Good, ... the Light. The cohesion of ideas through the blissful memory and around the light sets the mental context of the creative process, infusing it with life. Let's associate ideas: the heart, the Sun, the lion; the heart, the Sun, the lion, the roar; (...) the roar, the present momentum, inspiration, discernment. Out of the approximately 600,000 possibilities for an event to manifest, only one will transcend the physical layer, and that one will be suitable for both the macrocosm and microcosm, like a child of two worlds, born from two waters. Love predestines the artistic process towards embodied discernment in a musical work, idea, or movement. Discerning from what surrounds us (macrocosm), what resonates within us (union of macro-microcosms), exemplifies a function of the natural (adaptive survival). Resonance, roar, rudra (divinity), beginning; resonance, roar, rudra, beginning, vibration. It all stems from love, which is what binds the light of ideas.

The Macrocosmic pyramids

In the centre of Robert Fludd's macrocosmic universe lies the Sun, just as in the microcosmic centre lies the heart. The heart, the blood, the vitality, the Sun, the light, the motion. The Sun instills in the mind the forms in motion, much like its attributed force, both as a body and as a virtue, generates the cause of the planetary motion. The rocks of light formed around its galactic journey would never have existed without it. It centres a system of representation of order, of the cosmos, and Fludd represents it in the midpoint of the spheres' universe to endow it with equity and gravity. He bypasses a hermetic heliocentrism, or what we might find as such. Equidistant lie the Empyrean and the material Earth, so that the two opposing pyramids of light and darkness graduate their parts, and from the quantities of form and matter, the spheres emerge.

"(...) However, since the rays of natural light that extend downwards have not yet penetrated into the depths of the earth with the cone of their pyramid, it is necessary for the inner parts of it, being composed of four quarters, to possess four degrees of coldness due to their total lack of light."[43]

There are three heavens in the macrocosm: the supreme region of creation, the middle, and the lowest. [1] Above the supreme is pure light, the source, with "4 parts of heat." [2] In the middle, where half of it is occupied by the Sun, there are two parts of matter and two degrees of thickness, and 1 part of light. This is the lower heaven. I employ the different synonymous terms used by the author, which undoubtedly contribute to the conjectural image.

Below the lower heaven lies pure matter, earth, with its four degrees of coldness due to the absence of light (four parts of matter per zero of light). Let's pay attention to this relationship: coldness = matter = absence of light = absence of heat. One represents death, and the other life, bypassing a

---

43   Robert Fludd. 'Escritos sobre Música'. (Spanish ed.) Ed. Luis Robledo.

somewhat distressing dichotomy since beings inhabit beneath the lowest heaven.

The lower sky will harbor the elements in decreasing order of their heat proportions: fire-air-water. The latter will contain one part of heat for every three of cold; air will have two parts of heat and fire three to one part of cold. The intermediate sky will house the seven spheres (Moon, Mercury, Venus, Sun, Mars, Jupiter, and Saturn), and the upper one will determine the celestial hierarchies (Angels, Archangels, ... Seraphim).

As mentioned, the heart corresponds to the Sun, the centers of both micro and macrocosms, thus translating the entire diagram onto the human body. As I always emphasize, we must recall from the classics that imagery is the language of the Soul. Analyzing the pyramids, we see in the shadow, on one side, a projection emerging from the Earth's material body, tapering towards the apex of the sky. Similarly, light emanates from the Divinity. The center of everything is the Sun. It's intriguing not to perceive the Sun as a source of light but rather as a receptor of this light, which it then concentrates, serving as the central idea of the entire diagram, the entire scheme. The apex of the sky corresponds to human reason in the microcosm, which Fludd places in the head; the base, where there is the maximum amount of matter, is referred to by the author as the excretory and reproductive system. This identifies the first zone with ideas and serves as the anchor for receiving inspiration; the last zone is more associated with base passions and discarding unusable matter from the system (excretion).

Between each part, Fludd determines its musical proportions, recreating in the mind a silent listening of the "aerial" interval, and this is pure Pythagoreanism. To accomplish this, Fludd's mental and imaginative effort is remarkable. The pyramid of matter unfolds as follows:

> "Since the first (the earth) has four degrees of thickness and on the other hand the second (lowest region of the sky) has only three, so that they are in sesquitertia proportion, because the earth with respect to to the region of the elements and transparent in relation to 4 to 3. In turn, the 3 parts of this lowest region (...) 3 to 2 with respect to the two of the air region. (...) if they are placed with the only one there is (form part) in the highest or empyrean region, they are found in double proportion, that is: 2 to 1".

Similarly, the pyramid of light unfolds from the source with four degrees of heat in an identical process. Altogether, we will have two pyramids that will eventually merge, and from that union will arise the harmonies of the spheres and the divine monochord.

Moreover, the relationship between the macrocosmic system of the pyramids does have a musical development, and to highlight this, I'd like to draw a comparison: the lyre, Orpheus' instrument; the lute, Hermes' instrument; or the guitar, its contemporary equivalent. The right hand - in the case of a right-handed person - plucks the strings, which vibrate to produce sound, while the left hand adjusts the pitch by pressing different frets. By doing this, we replicate a system that we can see here, where the Sun is the source of that light, and the musical intervals[44] provide the gradation. This serves

---

44   The pyramids are divided, from the base to the apex, into 4 parts of matter per 0 of form; 3 parts of matter per 1 of form; 2 parts of matter per 2 of form; 1 part of matter per 3 of form; and finally 0 parts of matter per 4 of form.

as an initial concept, an approximation, where our hand is like the Sun, making the strings vibrate, which represent the different stages of the cosmic soul, namely, the Spheres. This is why the diagram is so intriguing. According to this reasoning, a guitar should have seven or nine strings.

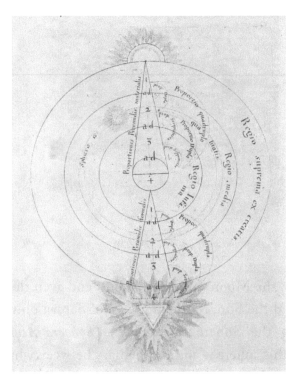

Figure v-2: diagram of the pyramids with the parts of light and darkness. Page 84 of 'Utriusque'.

The diagram of the spheres in the pyramids previously expands into this one. It reflects the same mutual mixture of light and darkness, only in detail, where the spheres are initially represented with those of the elements. Then come the pla-

This results in pure matter at the base and pure form (light) at the apex, where light and darkness do not reach, respectively. This leads to deducing the intervals of 3:1, 2:2 = 1:1, 1:3, as the musical structure of the whole.

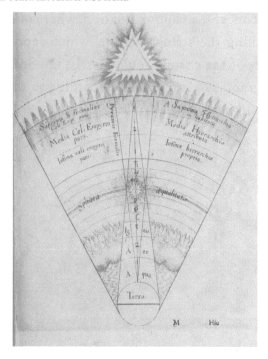

Figure v-3: Diagram of the pyramids with spheres. Page 89 of 'Utriusque'.

netary ones: the Moon, Mercury, Venus, and even the Sun, on one side; and the Sun, Mars, Jupiter, and Saturn on the other, surrounding the Sphere of Equality (*Sphaera Aequalitatis*). Therefore, this sphere is an intermediary between what is above and what is below. Above the Fixed Stars, we have things we cannot see, because manifestly we cannot see them (physically, and according to the classical conception of a dome). Neither above these, nor below the elements, beneath the spheres of the planets. The closest part to space is Fire, which is a semitone for Fludd, then Air (Whole tone), Water (Whole tone), and Earth (Whole tone). Does this refer to that part that is already a transition with space? That thin layer? Air would be the atmosphere, Water the lower atmosphere, its humidity, and finally, Earth would be the firm. There is no doubt that water penetrates the earth to reflect the same sea. As we have

214

seen, they form the lower sky, then the same fire is the atmosphere.

All that we have seen serves to tune a string, and it is the Divine Monochord. Divine because it descends from the highest, from the supersubstantial; monochord because it is a single string, an allegory of:

[1] *The sword, which divides the waters in the Bereshit (Genesis).*

[2] *The creative and fecundating lightning, which acts upon the first substance.*

[3] *The universal vibration underlying everything.*

It is unnecessary in the character of the book to fill the symbol with more than is necessary. The sword is the agent that *necessarily* divides the waters in two at the beginning of Creation. It has a connotation of intellectual division of the universe itself, a *conditio sine qua non* for the constitution of memory. In this division, which later leads to the spheres (with their criteria for it), the three empyreal heavens are previously delimited, so named to house the supreme hierarchy (Seraphim, Cherubim, and Thrones), the hierarchy of middle attributes (dominations, principalities, and powers); and the lower levels of the hierarchy (Virtues, Angels, and Archangels). All this at the top of the pyramid of form (light).

The form, the light, is the very allegory of the *light of the intellct*, the creative ray, or the purity and immanence (degrees of) universal vibration, which as it descends the pyramid loses the ease of becoming evident to man. The initiated man is the one who can ascend (Hermes) through the tunings of the Monochord and perceive the refined nature. Therefore, everything begins in matter itself, with the four elements, which thus allow the first exercise of discernment. It seems unbelievable, but it is not, that in our time we do not know how to distinguish what is from which element in Nature. And although Natural Philosophy is founded on the discernment of these things, few follow it. I will mention for the reader's assistance Agrippa, Heinrich Cornelius, and probably Enri for the very good friends. Who knows. In any case, his Occult Philosophy delights in this knowledge.

For those who do not yield to the authors (Gaspar de Morales, Giordano Bruno, and the longest &c. that exists), let them observe. If observed, it must be done knowingly that the qualities of warmth and dryness define fire; warmth and wetness define air; wetness and coldness define water; and coldness and dryness define earth. What we observe can be understood through these faculties and initiate discernment at this point.

The seven spheres, powerful in their number and elevated to form by their quality, follow in progression the increase of light. To move from 4 to 7 signifies the transition from matter (O4 of the tetractys) to the union of both matter and form of the third wave (then O4 and O3). Go forth, extrapolate, gentleman or lady, for in the mentioned *caelum empyreum*, the sum of waves O4, O3, and O2 is perpetrated with treachery in the 3 times 3 angelic hierarchical orders. Here is where the image of number resides in greater purity than all the connected zones, even in their decreasing connection to darkness (matter). The three parts that both, the pyramid of light and of darkness, divide (intellect), cause a tuning as analyzed with waves O4 in the sky of the elements; O7 and O12 in that of the spheres; and O9 and O144. They result from direct sums (same dimension) and geometric calculations. Namely: waves O3 and O4 give rise to a triangle and square, whose intersection is the twelfth part of the universal circle (chord): O12. The intersection of three waves transcends the past dimension (O12) in the same way that 3+4 remains in the linear dimension (of 3 and of 4) and 3x4 moves to the matrix dimension (12). In this case, 12 must be squared, resulting in O144. In 'La Lira de Hermes', we saw how Apollo corresponded to that number, which is equivalent to the transcendence of the sphere of the fixed stars (O12).

Thus, the *third heaven*, just transcendent from this sphere by its division, therefore resonates with O9 and O144. The former, a veiled reference to the nine Muses, and the latter to Apollo. Very well, one might ask, why are the Muses linked to planetary spheres? It is due to affection for memory, by necessity, and by the intrinsic fractal singularity of light: we must not forget that the three Charites represented to the right of Apollo could well correspond to these empyrean heavens, and that being one of them a Muse, it evokes a reminiscence of the entire nine, echoing in the seven spheres, the fixed stars, and the earth. Therefore, while we have delved into the high heavens, the tuning has been duly justified.

The quantity of light and the direction of the pyramid

The idea of the pyramid is well illustrated by the concept of flaring. Any opening whose width gradually increases or decreases manages to alter the flow of light, concentrating it at the geometric apex of the flare with its maximum density (quantity).

The bases of the pyramids represent the concentration of density, the victory or defeat of light: it is the defeat of light (misery) when there are maximal parts of shadow (darkness) -

exterior of the flare - and the victory of light (glory) when the opposite prevails - apex of the flare.

The Creator bestows the greatest glory upon the created. Let us note that we are talking about a duality of constant correlation between darkness and light, and light and darkness; and glory and misery are correlated. Doesn't this recall the hero's journey? It even recalls the semi-divine condition as an attribute of one who resonates on the monochord, of the Hermetic disciple. That mortal subject to darkness is miserable; that initiate on the path of lightning, the one initiated in the unique sound, is equivalent to the hero, who is the child of a **god** (glory) and of a **mortal** (misery). Knowing that the concentration of light, similar to the beam that a lens also produces, creates a physical effect of refinement, we understand that the liturgical buildings aimed to elevate with the mere entrance of the faithful into the temple. Fludd enters a highly appreciable symbolic terrain, even though everything said is also something physical. And it is precisely the delineation between the symbol and the physical within the same boundary that is an art of great skill. Choosing the pyramid reflects that skill.

Figure v-4: Church of the Monastery of Villanueva de Sijena, Huesca, with 14 archivolts of widening.

Passage leading into temple, in its musical idiom, advances in resonance with musical disdiapason (profound depth of gateway) which serves, in essence, as conduit between dense (mundane concerns) and subtle (celestial or shamanic path), facilitating nothing short of absolute clarity. Dual diapason also alludes to dual divine and human nature, while archivolts symbolize spheres that traverse between them.

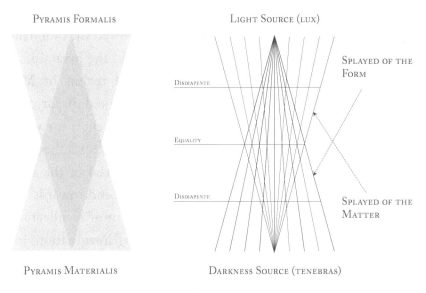

PYRAMIS FORMALIS   LIGHT SOURCE (LUX)

DISDIAPENTE   SPLAYED OF THE FORM

EQUALITY

DISDIAPENTE   SPLAYED OF THE MATTER

PYRAMIS MATERIALIS   DARKNESS SOURCE (TENEBRAS)

Figure v-5: Concentration of Light.

The Philosophical Hero

The Hermetic Wave presented here (derived from the Egyptian diagram, almost an obelisk, by Kircher), and Fludd's pyramids, represent two perspectives on the same constitution of light. The undulating figure presents the Hermetic principle of rhythm, providing a clear notion of the divine-human interrelation that underpins tradition. This can be understood as an approach or influence, alternating between withdrawal and surrender, to appetites. The dual animal-divine nature, or human and divine if you will, possessed by the human being as a perennial inclination towards study.

Much like the Nestorian idea of Jesus Christ, the center of the pyramids and the wave is pointed to as the axial point of both natures. The central Sun would vindicate for itself the veritable image of the Christian solar hero, as well as other solar heroes throughout history. This center, which is the heart, is the point of equilibrium between the divine above and the mundane below. It is clearly visible in both the wave and the pyramid.

Above the Solar Orb reign the ethereal realms of Memory and Intellect, realms which exhibit a marked disparity in their conceptualization between Fludd and Kircher; for while the former eschews a linear progression, the latter adheres to it. Allow me to elucidate. Following the traversal of the solar plexus, the corporeal energies of humanity ascend towards the cranial sphere, wherein they forge the sanctum of recollection. This ascension, facilitated by the faculties of imagination, incantation, or melody, heralds the soul's pilgrimage to celestial spheres. From thence, it descends anew, adorned with the luminous mantle of divine cognition. Such a descent signifies an epoch of spiritual reawakening, wherein the soul traverses the cosmic singularity, the ineffable godhead, only to return. This sacred homeward journey is engendered by the fount of inspiration. In light of these insights, our discourse transcends the realm of ordinary mortals to contemplate the Initiated Man, as envisioned by Fludd, Kircher, and even in the corpus of this treatise. Indeed, we eschew the pedestrian sphere of common humanity, ensnared as it is by base desires and worldly ambitions, and instead aspire to attain the pristine clarity of philosophical contemplation.

C:.VI:. ROBERT FLUDD II

Or how music represents an allegory of everything created,
with intervals and tuning that is its own

Figure vi–1: Temple of Music . Utriusque Cosmi. Robert Fludd.

With the blessing of the Muses, let's proceed. This is Robert Fludd's Temple of Music. It belongs to the Utriusque Cosmi, book 3, which discusses music. The tradition we're delving into leads us to Pythagoras and beyond, wherein music establishes the language of order for everything. Within this language of all, the expectation is that the student is capable of interpreting their surroundings based on the intervallic nature shown by each being, for to understand what something is, one must first discover those relationships, correspondences, those intervals.

On the left side of the temple, we have the monochord resembling that of Pythagoras, a single string, tuned by the hand of G.od. The taut string descends until it strikes the earth, and it is regulated from the most acute particle to the gravest with the tones and semitones of the spheres. This will symbolize the hierarchy, the seat of the divine empire of **memory**.

As the musician plays lower notes on the monochord, the pitch becomes sharper. However, Fludd's hierarchy operates contrarily: the pitch becomes sharper as it ascends. The spheres have their own speeds, and the higher a planet's orbit, the longer its period, thus the lower its frequency. But Fludd does not see it this way; instead, he sees it in communion with the amplitude of light (greater number, greater light), contrary to Kepler's physics. When *Robertus* delves into these matters, it is even late for his time and his worldview, given that he is an heir to the hermeticisms of the Renaissance. Kircher, on the other hand, is a formidable and sharp scholar, capable of exhaustively documenting things. He is a great enthusiast of all, but Fludd's mystical aspect is a paradigm given by him. The former is mixed with the Rosicrucians, the latter has different tunings, so to speak, within the spiritual realm.

Without delving into specific details such as the root note's origin, the overall concept of what we're observing resembles that of an instrument with its divisions, much like the
strings on a guitar. These divisions aim to signify the hierarchical arrangement of elements across various spheres.

Tuning

The tracing of intervals is that of the hermetist and star
sailor, who observes thereby the sonic evolution of the sky.
The octave that resonates with the Sun resonates with the
divine hand that, in turn, moves the monocord that traverses
it. Its tuning ascends from the low G note (gamma) in the
following manner: G A B C D E F G' A' C' D' E' F' G'', or SOL LA
SI DO RE MI FA SOL' LA' SI' DO' RE' MI' FA' SOL''.

Below, we have the four elements. Each element corresponds to an interval, with the Earth element lacking an interval; the water element represents a tone; the air element another, and finally, the fire element represents a semitone. These
divisions thus form the notes. An interval consists of two differentiated ideas within the same ontology. In this case, it
involves the 9 and the 8 (9/8, tone, whole step) or the 256 to
234 (256/243, semitone, half). Water, therefore, separates G
from A, serving as the origin of the scale, while Earth is akin
to the silent note. Air separates A from B, and fire separates
B from C. Of the four, fire is the least dense and borders with
the next layer, which is that of the spheres. This semitone
aligns with the concept of transition: the C scale, reaching
B, and then there's a semitone to start over. This transition is
marked by the smallest of intervals, signifying a phase transition, which undoubtedly characterizes the semitone.

Moving on to the next stage, we encounter the spheres: the Moon's sphere represents a tone; similarly, Mercury's too; Venus as well; and then there are two halves that divide the celestial realm from the spheres in what is called the sphere of equality. In the first half, the Sun ☉ represents a semitone; in the second half, another; Mars = T; Jupiter = T; Saturn = T. And in order, we would have:

TTS:TTTS ☉ STTT:STT

In other words, a symmetrical disdiapason is generated, that is a double octave. The representation of intervals, translated into letter-notes, is as follows:

Γ A B C D E F G a b c d e f g

The sphere of the Sun perfectly divides the disdiapason into two parts, with the faster cycles below the G note and the rulers of time and angelic hierarchies above it. There's a hint of Gnostic reminiscence here, which is Christian but with primitive roots and a subtle esoteric path. From here, the interval provides a particular vibration to those who study it, akin to a door that is passed through with the right key in the right hand, and pushed open with the left.

[perfect octave] diapason (double proportio)
[perfect fifth] diapente (sesquialtera p.)
[perfect fourth] diatessaron (sesquitertia p.)

Among intervals, the diapason reigns supreme, followed by the perfect fifth, and then the major fourth. This sequence delineates the descent from perfect consonance to the realm of imperfection. They serve as symbolic representations of numerical relationships. But what, one might ask, does an interval signify? It is the harmonious interplay of ideas in motion, a dance of movement intertwined with the very essence of the celestial sphere. From Earth to the Moon, the diapason resonates. Transitioning from the note G (Earth) to C (Moon) unveils a diatessaron, a perfect fourth, the preferred interval for final cadences, a sort of "that's it" or "that's a wrap" marking the culmination. Yet, should our musical journey ascend to the radiant Sun, whose note shares its name, a perfect diapason emerges. Thus, the Sun bestows upon Earth an interval of superior perfection than the Moon. Through the heart, we attune ourselves to the microcosmic octave, a symphony that awakens the soul nestled within, irrespective of whether its melodic resonance enhances auditory comprehension.

With the Moon, we can contemplate the realm of the soul's desires, while through the major fourth, we attune ourselves to the vegetal essence within humanity, harmonizing with the lunar cycles. Moving onward, let us explore the interval from the Moon to the Sun, known as the perfect fifth, followed by the interval from the Sun to the realm of the Fixed Stars, another perfect fifth. Two perfect fifths encompass the eight spheres, totaling seven tones. There exists a consonant relationship between Earth and the Moon, a stronger bond between the Moon and the Sun, and the most perfect union between Earth and the Sun. This, in essence, encapsulates the celestial harmony.

One may partake in the delightful pastime of observing the Moon and conjuring the appropriate intervals and notes in one's mind. Likewise, gazing upon the planets in the night sky, one may recite the previously imagined intervals, distilled to the octave, or the relevant notes, thereby imprinting them upon the memory.

As the discerning reader will note, we clothe the memoria mundi in the language of music, both nodal and intervallic. The natural is whispered into the attentive ear, thereby prompting a deeper attunement to nature itself. Thus did Pythagoras instruct with a monocord, imparting ideas that would nourish this memory, endowing the mathematically inclined listener with the radiant clarity (splendor) that each interval evokes in the inner movement of the individual (soul).

Derivative: the number π and the wonder of musical coordinates

The repercussion stemming from the Earth-Sun diapason lends itself to representation as a wave. The quality of the *earthly sound* is mirrored in the Sun. We could speak of replication and adjust the purpose of the meaning. If the sound replicates in its octave, it does so again in the next octave, and so forth. Fludd does not employ a single analysis, but in the case of the double diapason, simplicity allows for depth. Let us imagine the aforementioned binomial as the ray that cuts the circumference into two parts, from zenith to nadir. The interval reflected by this geometry, extensively studied in 'La Lira de Hermes', completes the cycle with another identical diapason, so that the disdiapason returns to its origin (a 360-degree turn). It is interesting to note this journey, as the entire monochord must be found within the complete circumference, both serving as archetypes of totality.

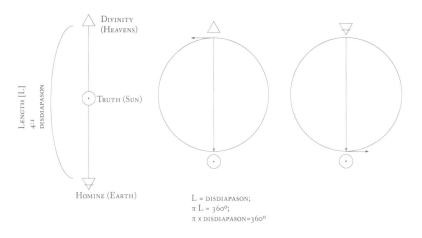

L = DISDIAPASON;
π L = 360°;
π X DISDIAPASON=360°

Figure vi-2: study of the number π in Fludd's Monochord.

The rope unfolds along 360° and both representations, circle (wave) and line (rope), will necessarily lead to the number π. In a hidden way, the monochord hides, with its double octave, the return to the circle necessary to build 2π R in length, in the vibration, that is, the monochord measures two diapasons and the wave two diapasons times π.

If we bring together all that has been said, we find that between divinity and man (Earth) lies the perfection of the number PI. Once again, the Hermetic wave that we saw in my analysis following Kircher's work becomes apparent. In both cases, the perfection of the number underlies, deciphered through the Hermetic dialectic of the musical interval.

As I mentioned, the parallels with the Hermetic wave from the study derived from Kircher lead to the same conclusion, except that this time, at the zero crossing of the Hermetic wave, we encounter the Sun. The lower 'Deus' of the same, which is the Divine Presence, would be incarnated in man. Hence, it is not about the biological man as such, but about the initiated man. This is the one who is placed at the bottom of the wave.

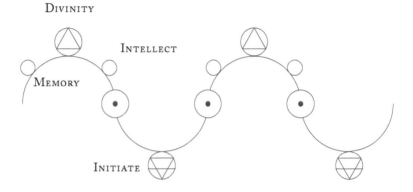

Figure vi-3: present proposal of The Hermetic Wave.

But the most striking thing comes from deducing, from the formula disdiapason times π = 360°, the following:

[1] diapason = 360/2 π
[2] diapente = 360/2 π · 2/3
[3] diatessaron = 360/2 π · 1/4

With the conversion factor from radians to degrees, precisely none other than 360/2π, the diapason establishes the intermediate factor between linear and angular dimensions, just as we have deduced before. Invariably, the mentioned intervals are degrees that divide the circle as their proportions divide the string. The marvel of musical coordinates confirms that music itself is a tangle of great arithmological quality and first-level physical and metaphysical transcendence. In reality, a symbolic language could be articulated solely with music; indeed, this and the previous work encompass all of this.

On the Nature of the Musician

Very much in the style of Boethius, Robert Fludd says[45] *"the musician is either perfect or imperfect"*. Perfect: who does not compose the parts of the music but can show the true reason for them, therefore the following are required for perfection:

[a] Natural philosophy
[b] Arithmetic
[c] Geometry
[d] Astronomy
[e] Metaphysics

Or imperfect, who only deals with harmonic music, namely:

[f] Who only plays the instruments.
[g] He only sings.
[h] He only plays the fiddle and sings at the same time.
[i] Or from rhythmic music or.
[j] From music metric physics (who dances well, &c...).

When we read this our modern schemes are thrown into time and space because the teaching we absorbed was mainly that of the conservatory and derivatives, in which that musical that plays and instruments is worked on, all this is the only thing we observe. There is no more. The true reasons for the music to which it refers remain hinted at or nurtured by:

[k] Natural philosophy, so that he can judge perfectly about harmonic music and show its perfect reason.

---

45 The following paragraphs are partially derived from "Writings on Music, Robert Fludd; ed. by Luis Robledo Estaire."

[l] Arithmetic, so that he can clearly perceive the rhythmic nature of music.

[m] Geometry, so that he can explain the metric essence of music and determine the proportion of intervals.

[n] Astronomy, so that he does not ignore worldly music (worldly music is that of the Worlds, that is, the spheres).

[o] Metaphysics, so that he can judge about human music.

[p] In other words, to understand what the Music of the Spheres refers to. That means to listen to it, because to speak of hearing that music of the spheres is to grasp that metaphysical understanding. What surrounds us are all imperfect musicians, basically. According to Fludd. The training we undergo is precisely to make this work as a perfect musician.

Philosophy remains inherent to the musician, and to define it, one must favor Sophia, without which music cannot be articulated in any way. It is impossible to attend to the definition without perplexity for any modern academic. And those who are not must at least marvel at the circumstance, for they find in this classification a certain good logic. Namely: the musician must know music and know themselves, and from there they will articulate a dignity as a gift from heaven, for it is a fruit of perennial Sophia.

Without knowledge, there is no access to the driving force that activates the reminiscent shamanic background of the composer, performer, or whatever it may be. Hence, the path begins and continues from study, from the search. In Philosophy, only the definitive course (truth) of what is studied fits.

The time at which Fludd formulates this coincides with the dawn of natural science, the observation of a natural model that challenges the old way because things are no longer fixed as they should be (for example, the observation of the supernova

SN1604 by Kepler, which challenged the immutability of the sphere of fixed stars). However, one thing is the natural model and another is how long it takes for this model to assimilate any novelty. This will be addressed in another volume, but undoubtedly Fludd belongs to those guardians of the old model, and when he speaks of natural philosophy, he refers to the model of light. In his time, as I mentioned, this model encountered no small disruption, but he was still able to synthesize it and apply it to the musician. Its consequence is what we have just read. The musician we know today is of type (f) to (h), mainly (ca. 80% of music enlisted in streaming services). If knowledge is the path to truth, it will pass through the perfect musician in the form of (a) to (e), issues that must be known. It is a model, so the aspiration towards it, when completed, constitutes a vector, not an end. These are disciplines never fully graspable; therefore, they must serve as guides for the musician at all times, like guides in the blinded darkness of the world.

C:.VII:.
The necessary Presence and nature of the archetypes

And of the musical loci to promote a musical art in accordance with natural law

About the quest for each sphere: musical heaven

In another section, we explored how inspiration acts as a discerning agent. All possible notes to form a melody serve as the basis for combinations, the discerned outcome being the inspired melody. The resulting possibilities are confined within the realms of entity, necessity, goodness, principle, means, end, and perfection. When one opts for a tonality, it gives rise to a distinctive melody, adorned with variations and diverse textures throughout the piece, yet fundamentally grounded in a motif as enduring as one carved in stone. This marks the moment when the melody resonating throughout the entire piece is encapsulated. Thus, the act of discernment sifts through myriad potential combinations to arrive at a single one. Naturally, this process is inherent to nature. When inspired, the creation by man becomes an act of nature, as it sifts through all possibilities to birth something from another: it sifts through all and selects one (multiplicity-unity). This singular creation emerges as if one were to birth a single creature among countless possibilities, the one destined for development.

It remains somehow interesting that it acts as a mechanism with its peculiarities. In Gaffurio, we see the serpent with the triple head. There are 3 heads, and J. Campbell speaks very clearly about this in relation to time. If the serpent represents the cycle of time, the three faces are the three possible synchronizations with time, or rather, the only possible synchronization, with the other two being past and future entelechies. It does provide the texture of three states of attention for man, that is, it is linked to the Earth and has three possible states of attention, and only one of them - in line with the serpent itself - is the one that synchronizes with it, thus with the cycles. Or with the grand cycle. Assuming the idea that being a great cycle of years, it refers to the total set of possibilities within that entire cycle at a moment. On one hand, the gigantic cycle of time converges in an instant, and on the other hand, the total of possibilities and universes converge into one possibility at the present moment through Inspiration.

The present moment synchronizes with that grand cycle of time and can access something that we will set aside here. There is undoubtedly an ellipsis towards topics more focused on a resonance of the spheres, more of the myth of Er and matters that slide towards the esoteric. This grand cycle is also the great repeated internal memory stored in species (reptile brain), and that triggering intuition is linked to the memory Plato speaks of, which is recovered in life and lost in living, by the passage of Λήθη (Lethe). Before Plato, the Pythagoreans, with Mnemosyne, another way of calling the Tetraktys, seem to conceive the sky as a musical world related to the serpent-dragon (between the Great and Little *Ursae*), conjuring the cycle-idea that resonates in the kundalini, which we must not forget may be related to Pythagoras (Pit=Python, serpent). If the Pythagoreans, Plato, &c. are making a reference to memory, and that memory is intuition, imagined in that great serpent, inspiration is bequeathed to us through prudence (classical virtue), whose modern name is the experience of the present moment. This is of great relevance at a musical level since inspiration will only occur in that disposition and moment.

Here is the proof or rather the teaching. The triple head is a symbol of a wolf, a dog, and a lion. The wolf howls at the past, according to Campbell, a past that cannot return; the dog sniffs towards the future, trying to guess it; and only the lion roars in the present. Only he has entity and body (Lion, Heart, Sun, Roar, Rudra, Resonance). Only the lion has a time and a space that he himself defines. He is also Apollo, but on earth. Hence, he is the first sound (rudra) produced by the effect of that perfect tuning of the present moment, converged Horos-Stauros. That perfect placement, and at the

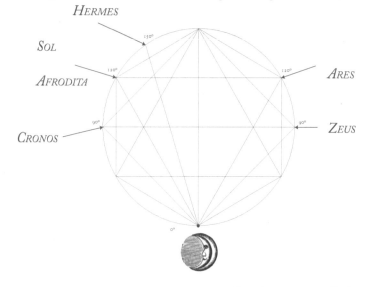

HERMES' MAX ELONGATION = 27°, AFRODITA'S = 47°

Figure vii-1: geometry of musical quests in an example of a song.

same time the Sun itself is giving us the clue of the passage of time for the tuning of the present. That is to say, inspiration will depend on it, inspiration will depend firstly on what man can do to receive it and secondly on Providence, undoubtedly, whether it happens or not.

Here is the proof or rather the teaching. The triple head is a symbol of a wolf, a dog, and a lion. The wolf howls at the past, according to Campbell, a past that cannot return; the dog sniffs towards the future, trying to guess it; and only the lion roars in the present. Only he has entity and body (Lion, Heart, Sun, Roar, Rudra, Resonance). Only the lion has a time and a space that he himself defines. He is also Apollo, but on earth. Hence, he is the first sound (rudra) produced by the effect of that perfect tuning of the present moment, converged Ho- ros-Stauros. That perfect placement, and at the same time the Sun itself is giving us the clue of the passage of time for the tuning of the present. That is to say, inspiration will depend on it, inspiration will depend firstly on what man can do to receive it and secondly on Providence, undoubtedly, whether it happens or not.

So we would be talking about a dual cause for inspiration. It's that instant that requires the adept's work to be executed, and at the same time, without the assistance of Providence (Apollo), it doesn't occur. That's why hymns to the Muses are employed, to reach Apollo-Providence-Cause. All these things serve to gradually lower this tuning since they always involve internal powers and are only accessible in the present moment.

It dresses entirely in utility, as it involves constant work from the musician, which is nothing less than the slow path we talked about, one endowed with love and following the unquestionable path of harmony. Why not think that even the qualities of the seven spheres have to be perfectly crafted? In Gaffurio, we have the clue in the note, mode, and muse, which ultimately connect Apollo with the earth, with the person. Whoever wants to be inspired must pass through the spheres of the Moon, Mercury, Venus, Sun, Mars, Jupiter, Saturn. They have to go through a series of stages, spheres, places, pitchers, where the poured light is taken as if it were a fluid, and it is a grace, a mercy of truth. A wondrous water that eventually flows into the person, who is about to reflect one of the Ideas of Heaven in a work of Earth.

What could each of these spheres symbolize, and how does humanity dignify each archetype to, precisely, dignify itself when receiving inspiration? From this inquiry arise the seven quests, conditions of Prudence (the sphere that comprehends them all), to attract inspiration.

[quest 7] Saturn's sphere implies perseverance in work, a steadfast **pulse in creation.**

[quest 6] Jupiter's quest involves the **expansion** of one's being in their art.

[quest 5] Mars' pursuit is to radiate a blooded and **passionate movement.**

[quest 4] The Sun's quest is to radiate with splendor the **beauty** and the Good, to be its champion and enhancer of love.

[quest 3] Venus' quest is a pursuit of the sensuality of beauty.

[quest 2] Mercury's quest is to **transmit**, to penetrate the nervous system.

[quest 1] The Moon's quest is to evoke **emotion.**

These seven quests serve as the gateway to receiving inspiration, each requiring a blend with the others for assimilation. Constant pursuit of beauty, expansion, action, projection

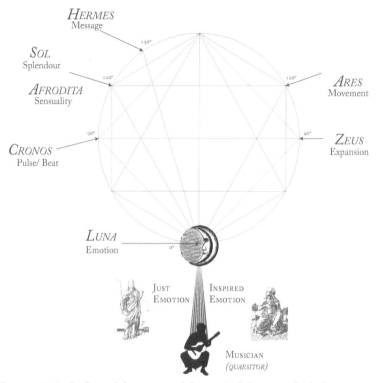

Figure vii-2: the flow of the waters of the musical sky towards the lower waters.

of beauty, transmission, and stirring emotions intertwine. The consistency, bearing the rhythm of Saturn, sets the framework for the sonic expansion of Jupiter. Subsequently, constant practice precipitates its expansion, with the light of Saturn permeating that of Jupiter, and so forth: Mars' action must be allowed to shine, exuding beauty and goodness, igniting passion, and being transmitted in the ecosystem where music resounds. The Moon collects and amalgamates the emerging practical music natures from each sphere, infusing emotions with the myriad of aspects proposed by the spheres in their combinations. One must understand music that energizes us for exercise as that which harmoniously aligns emotion with the blood's movement; a sensual one as that which merges with beauty. Conversely, a lack of constancy will be noticeable

237

in music that appears disharmonious between its rhythm and emotion. Thus, all of this sketches maps in the sky, intended to exemplify the pleasure and delight of the musician, who will find geometric meaning in the explanation.

In the example, as in everything, the center where felt (audible) music gravitates is lunar, the emotion, which moves the lower waters. It receives, in the example, the light of a music with an inconsistent pulse, somewhat distant, manifest sensuality, energizing splendor, which ignites passions and permeates its message, which can be in the form of verse with the said music.

The explanation is straightforward: the aspect (astrology) of the square is disharmonious, fitting Cronos within it, also Zeus, as it is not expansive but longing (distant). Splendour and sensuality stand out with harmonious aspects of a trine with the Moon (reception) for the Sun and Aphrodite. Igniting passions will involve an aspect of Aphrodite-Ares, either together or in triplicity; and the transmission of the message attributed to Hermes, the quincunx aspect, to exemplify a message that is harmonious with the music (i.e.: rhyme), but results in being unsympathetic. Again, I indicate, this is an example, and we can think of a song with the described passionate characteristics but with an ironic message regarding love. This would be perfectly portrayed in the aspect of 150° with the Moon. Using other aspects, the message, the voice, and the ensemble in general could more or less resonate with the nervous system. Or they could be completely ambiguous, as if suggesting disharmony, the system is not fully transmitted, or it does so with obstacles (Hermes-Moon square); or simply not understood (opposition), and alternative music is preferred. Hermes and the Moon must therefore be in harmony, after all, Tot is a lunar god[46].

---

46 The names of the spheres have been given their Greek gods, except for the

Quest 1, the quest of the Moon, becomes the recipient of all that came before, channeling it through its ethereal realm. It serves as a unifying force, drawing celestial insights into the musician's domain, one steeped in emotional resonance. Like a mystical conduit, it imbues the practitioner with cosmic knowledge, a torrent of divine inspiration cascading through the Hermetic gateways of the soul. While for some, this influx may manifest as raw physiological responses, akin to untamed chaos or a plaintive ballad, for those versed in its mysteries, it unfolds as a tapestry of profound meaning, akin to the mystical revelations of ancient Sefardic Kabbalists. As we present the following diagram, an expansion upon the preceding discourse, it's worth noting that when properly harnessed, this system can lead to transcendent experiences akin to the divine effluence described in esoteric texts.

The rays are carefully dosed by the gate of the Moon, perceptible through emotion, the trait without which we could not perceive music, the whisper of our destiny, or the wonders and dramas of life. Most importantly, we apply discernment to it as a means to dose the flow towards the lower waters (microcosmic soul). The same discernment we've spoken of, operating in emotions through inspiration, allows for self-awareness.

"Know yourself and know – the universe and the gods".
Γνώρισε τον εαυτό σου και θα γνωρίσεις το σύμπαν και τους θεούς.

In its proper measure, emotion is inspired by the Muse and allows for the expansion of internal knowledge. In this way,

---

Sun and the Moon, to prepare the idea of the necessary symbiosis between Mercury and the Moon for the musical aspect.

discernment and inspiration imbue the musical momentum that the seeker experiences as a journey beyond ordinary time and space, yet it is determined by the purest or purified light of physical creation (planets) or its reflection in memory (prior knowledge). This moment is most often encountered through the exercise of prudence, which is not far from the concept of 'fear of G.od' or petition-thanksgiving (end of volume two). Artistic work appears fortunate in individuals with and without musical knowledge because knowledge adheres very little to memory if it is not true. Hence, not only the question of the validity of the opus of artists with or without formal training, but also about the system that forms them (conservatories), which becomes clearly obsolete in light of these issues that rightly dimension the human being instead of merely technicalizing it. Natural judgment is not made on the body (technique, skill, admiration of talent), but on the soul (truth, sincerity, reflection of order), and the musician who tunes into this becomes a conscious mirror of such rightly inspired light. Hence the word itself, speculative.

A standout amidst the seven spheres would be another quest. The eighth classical sphere, the starry sky, gathers the light from behind this sphere and perhaps alludes to another pursuit: that of transcendence, of the Spirit, as it serves as a transition between what moves (planets) and what does not (prime mover/first cause). When I refer to transcendence in relation to the vault of the fixed stars, the explanation lies in their periods. It's helpful for the reader to associate rapid periods (Moon, Mercury) with rapid processes of the microcosm (emotion, thought), and consequently, the spiritual substrate (fixed or tending to fixed) will come from the longest periods of the observable cosmos: the distant surroundings.

"The influence of the Milky Way and the fixed stars responds to a very slow variation, and their position and movements change very little. Within this, the variable stars introduce alteration due to their own period (rotation, etc.) which, as we have seen, can be combined with that of the planets. The resonance of all of them in living beings therefore takes place on slowly evolving systems, that is, genetic and molecular"[47].

Thus, there would be eight quests, including the most complex one: the quest for the transcendent (sphere of the fixed stars). As we've referred to the sky with its lights, in no man's land are those we'll later see as astrological signifiers of music. And, more specifically, Neptune. As another example of musical translation between cosmos, a complex, mysterious music, of distant sensuality and lofty *phantasia*, with diffuse boundaries (molecular planes) and expansive in its breaths; of mystical yet certain message; of great strength:

[·] Sun in sextile with the Moon.
[·] Mercury in trine with the Moon, sextile with that Sun.
[·] Venus without aspect or weak aspect .
[·] Mars in sextile with the Moon.
[·] Jupiter conjunct Moon.
[·] Saturn opposite Moon.
[·] Neptune in trine with Moon.

I have no intention of a technical analysis, as it's futile, hence I won't delve into signs, moons, etc. Understanding the symbolism of each deity outlines the musical myth, an atemporal and a-spatial event that ultimately discerns the cosmological structure of the tangible in the physical and biological realms.

---

47   Astrología Física (Physical Astrology). Demetrio Santos. Ed. Barath. p. 60.

Nonetheless, I refer to 'complex music...' concerning its essence, whether or not it's translated into audible music. The Moon, its aggregated flow, the actions of the Muse and Justice; and the musician and their sounding instrument are not the same.

The persistent appeal to emotion acknowledges that it is primarily through emotion that subjects comprehend, allowing them to access the cosmic dance book that unfolds simultaneously with sensation. It's akin to peering through the lens of a telescope, gradually revealing even the faintest and deepest lights. In certain cases, we may correlate clairaudience—a mystical phenomenon—with the depth of one's gaze through emotion. Those adept at delving into mystery are naturally inclined to associated quests, which serve as attributes and connections, illuminating each deity from within through the practical awareness of their attributes (the quests).

On the Predominance of Lights and Nature of the Skies

On the other hand, regarding the celestial transfer of positions or constellations to the musician through light, other examples will include tense and disharmonious forms, which similarly permeate the biological ensemble with harsh aspects. If a celestial chart is dominated by Saturn, or by the combination of the Moon and Saturn, it will denote music with a melancholic influence, or distant from emotions. If Jupiter dominates the sky - among other things due to its rulership of the ascendant, midheaven, and domicile - the artistic result will reflect joy, jubilation, and a warm predisposition towards the divine.

Just as a melancholic work bears a predominance of Saturn, given its cold and dry nature, the same melancholy can be moved by the finest dignity and produce a work that renders sentiments sober, civilized, and sincere, while considering rhythm, pulse perfection, in the ensemble. This is how we encounter Bach's music, whose pulsating melancholy, albeit translucent, dignifies the listener with a polished rhythm and perfect pulse.

Education dignifies man, and even with the "positive" affections one can fall into defect if one does not possess it. Venus prominent in the sky can also generate music that we would describe as lascivious, destabilizing the spiritual balance of the Hermetic musician. Therefore, in the diagram, Justice is observed, which must be allowed by discernment, the ultimate conscious bastion, and if absent, leaves the musician at the mercy of defect and the inner beast. Proof of the latter is the madness that these forces have produced in many artists throughout history.

In an eminently solar sky, music can be, if the right distilled emotion is not present, proud, haughty, and tyrannical. However, something else is expected from the educated musician, who is not the one from the conservatory, to whom the following are characteristic: unlimited expansion of affections, melancholic repression of feelings, lasciviousness, and unhealthy competition, as undeniable and twisted attributes of Jupiter, Saturn, Venus, and Mars, respectively. One who is educated, as I say, through Hermetic music, will produce a splendid work that infuses warmth (vital force) into the hearts of those who listen to it.

However, the distance between sinking into sadness and emphasizing sobriety and decency lies not only in the education of the musician but also in both clocks, of the sky and of the earth, working simultaneously. Music has the power to generate dignity in the astral light. This is governed by the 3, the form, also the number of music (diapente, circle of diapentes). When resonating in the same idea (Pythagoreans), it constitutes the same numerical god. Therefore, it will be difficult for man to discern, even with great education, if the sky is "swirling" with bad spirits. As soon as the music prints that sky, it will create on earth the best possible dignity perceptible and equal for and to the education of the musician.

The purpose of this treatise is precisely that, education for the correct expulsion of harmful affection to man, to the human being. In man, properly, attention must be paid to the Sun and Mars; in women, to the Moon and Venus, with greater attention than to the other stars, which also, of course, will be important. What matters is what contributes to the vital energy or natural vitality of man, and to the generative energy or receptivity of women. At least, in this way, the biology of both is dignified, improving their lives from the body.

The *quests*, nothing more than sagittarius enterprises of ritual healing of man through Hermetic music, create in the musician's image the appropriate map of hierarchies imposed by cycles. It becomes a kind of mental map that fits with the natural. This map will include the beneficial attributes of each light.

Map of beneficial attributes:

1. The **Sun** gives the rule of the order of good, the worthy and evident truth, and frees all other celestial bodies from indignity.

2. The **Moon** gives in its greatest strength the unconditional home, sincere affections and simple love.

3. **Mercury** grants impartial friendship, diplomacy between antagonists, and lucid thinking.

4. **Venus**: the sweetness of the dance, the kiss of moist fidelity, the life-giving diva for the body.

5. **Mars**: the spirit of conquest, the strength of the pioneer, the quick movement.

6. **Jupiter**: the generous impulse, the full expansion of laughter and good humor, the measured intake, the abundant pantry.

7. **Saturn**: the sobriety of the vital zone, the structuring of the cycle (rhythm), the solitude of prolific study (music of the spheres).

They function as a tome, for each one engenders a symbol, which is a sphere, derived from the Hebrew 'sefer' (book), owing to its profound penetration into nature, identifiable through number. Being inherently natural and affecting the body, it naturally resonates with the number seven. When considering the journey of the soul, it aligns with nine. This embodies the hermetic-musical doctrine regarding how music operates within the material realm of the body and the ethereal realm of the soul, respectively. The eighth pursuit, intertwined with the fixed stars, emerges more as a consequence of the preceding seven quests rather than being an independent one. To illustrate the notion of boundaries or a gateway to the Spirit, understanding the essence of Uranus, the archetype representing the starry firmament, becomes imperative. We perceive it present within the wave and its polarities.

The musician remains a seeker, a quaesitor, his path aligning with the very air, ascending towards pure light, from the surface of his skin, his nostrils, his ocular retinas. This landscape is mirrored in the map, envisioned across varying planes. He must explore the dignities of these deities within his inner philosophy, laboring to temper the fluctuations of his thoughts and emotions, the most volatile aspects of the psychophysical composite (resonating with the short planetary cycle).

As it delineates the seven quests, archetypes, by their very virtue, he must tether their number and attributes to the descent of their flaws, their conquest, as elegantly proposed by Brunian thought. Thus, we must distance ourselves from the authoritarian dominance, the irrationality of base egotism, and the imposition of ideas onto others. Regarding the Moon, a quest tied to emotion, we confront stored resentment, akin to a well, stifling the ebb and flow of sentiment in cycles (phases), diminishing the lunar light's vigor. Moreover, there must be a reduction in the betrayal of emotions and the counterfeit love borne of guilt.

From Mercury comes the vice of a cycle of thought without fruition, the unworthy impartiality among friendships, and the separation of affection between siblings. From the Venusian quest within the internal archetype, and in order to overcome its flaw, we must identify the self-interested seduction, the indecent proposition, the prominent submission to the appetite of the lower abdomen. The artist is deeply afflicted by these flaws, which either hinder or obscure the preceding Truth (solar sphere). From the internal Ares, unrestrained anger, laziness, and careless technique are the adversaries to expel from the body. From Jupiter comes excessive eating, excessive generosity lacking discernment, such as giving to those who do not value the gift, serving as a witness to misdirected affection and misguided vital energy. From Saturn comes melancholy, heaviness, and pessimism, which repel life, sensuality, moisture, and abundant and merciful giving. An excess of these flaws also produces a flaw in its musical *uirtus*: rhythm. Hence the unredeemed melancholy of the romantic musician, whose rhythmic expression is subjugated to the service of excessive emotions (melancholic or saturnine Moon).

Once virtues and flaws have been studied from memory and practice, let us understand from each light its greatest musical dignity, acting as it has been said in perfecting heaven on earth. The solar provides the transfer of light and heat, infusing truth and goodness into the listener. The light is colored, filtered, and modulated by virtue, while the heat is allowed by the physical disposition of the individual, who, according to their texture, absorbs more or less than what they receive and radiates more or less than what they receive and absorb. From the Moon, its virtue is the generation of empathy, the listener's adherence to the sound flow, transforming into pure emotion. From Mercury comes the broad intelligence that inspires the listener and enables the understanding of proper resources, harmony, and above all, correct melody; from Venus, the sound when it attracts, enchants, and moistens the breathed air, producing pleasure in the body. From Mars, its virtue is a technique of agile and powerful movement, allowing for all kinds of paths to irrigate the air as blood circulates through the body. From Jupiter comes the breath full of energy, perceived as dignified as it revitalizes the instrumentalist's body and does the same for the listener. And from Saturn comes an exact metric, impeccable rhythm that allows its richness and abundance within the clear structure.

On the Timelessness of the Musical Experience. Thalia

Figure VII-3: Detail of the frontispiece of M. Practice.

At the end of Gaffurio's graph, we encounter the muse Thalia, residing on Earth (referred to as silent or deaf Thalia), absorbing the light of Apollo and the other Muses, acting as an interface with the inspired musician. The Kastalia fountain, which symbolizes this connection, pours forth, flooding the entrance to Parnassus with Apollo's light before descending to Earth, encapsulating the essence of this entire concept.

Kastalia and Thalia suggest a connection with the natural element within reach of the meditation that the initiate can undertake, both phonetically similar, both 'at the foot' of the mountain. Inspiration must descend (corollary) through the spheres and from the fixed stars, and this light can be wasted due to any distractions that arise, which is where our focus lies, our present, our bindu. Attention allows the critical point to emerge, separating us from the past and the future. What pertains to the past and what pertains to the future, well, that varies for each person based on their understanding. Neither one nor the other aids in descending inspiration. Probably because they induce movement.

The diversion of attention towards the future impairs the tuning of emotion because it sets a motion -after all- as an exit from one's own center, a movement towards something that has not yet happened, and implies an exit from the present: an exit from one's own center, an exit from the center, an exit from the sun. The center is that lion::-sun::roar::light. Or it can be understood in another way, according to which the energy of expansion, splendor, etc., (celestial bodies) shifts from being in the present moment to being imagined towards the future. And when imagined, they dissipate, as they cannot have occurred in matter and endured. Thinking about the past is three-quarters of the same: attention to something whose bodies are intangible and therefore belong to the realms of form. Just as what bears fruit in the future is intangible now. It's an incomplete system.

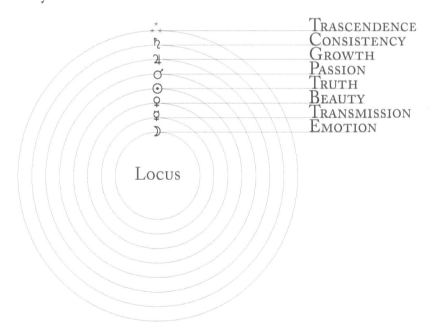

TRASCENDENCE
CONSISTENCY
GROWTH
PASSION
TRUTH
BEAUTY
TRANSMISSION
EMOTION

LOCUS

Figure vii-4: the eight quests for the place ('locus').

Let's think that the tetraktys or mnemosyne has a part that refers to stages of the formal and another that refers to the material[48]. When the material is absent and is absent both towards the past and the future, it is not imagined fully. And since it is not complete, inspiration cannot occur, because the sum of the first four natural numbers, which is what gives ten, which is what gives the complete and continuous (reiterated cycle), is coincident with the sum of Apollo plus the Muses. If we ignore the material part, there are four that are not added to the total, resulting in six. With which it does not achieve that fullness in resonance, it cannot function without the material:

[a] 10 = Apollo and Muses lead to inspiration

[b] 6 = inspiration is not allowed due to lack of the remaining quaternary (material) until the complete eon, then the purity cannot be imbibed in the matter (wisdom); The number 6 would therefore mean the past and future states, both formal (3 and 3).

We will recapitulate with a double condition and its counterpart (c3) for the inspired phenomenon:

[c1] Present state through any measures to settle therein.

[c2] The seven (or eight) quests (tuning with each of the spheres) through the tools given.

[c3] Having learned why looking to one side or the other does not complete the organization chart of the tetraktys and therefore the upper waters cannot descend through those ten points towards the lower ones.

---

48   Fourth level O4: material or sensible world; third, second, and first levels (O3-O1) refer to formal or spiritual worlds.

The 8 Spheres of the Eight Quests

It is necessary to connect the grace of inspiration with a moment and space on Earth, so that the cosmogonic model is presented in the musical act. With a slight variation, we can understand the 7 facets of musical creation and deduce from them an entire process protected by Heaven, with respective consecrations to each spherical archetype and, in the worst case, formulate a complete manual for the hermetic musician to perform his art.

Again, the eighth sphere will indicate a greater transcendence of physical action, which takes from each of the following seven. That is to say, the search for transcendence, the spiritual pulse of the hero, resides in the eighth sphere and every expert in the symbolic question will agree that it must preside over every process from there on. Thus, in the state of presence, and starting from the search for transcendence, all searches/quests unfold.

But the quest for transcendence, what is it if not servitude to Heaven? Or, if preferred, service, but one born of humility in the face of the ineffable and perfect that constitutes the universe. Music is suggested in that perfection that embraces chaos, and only those who know how to serve Heaven, Divinity, and listen to the Great Musician well can make use of all this. If the journey is completed, the emotion is palpable: as the aggregator[49] (Moon) of all previous

---

49 It is to be assumed that this unconscious and emotional bonding characteristic associated with the sphere of the Moon is behind its clear role as an object of inspiration or song for the musician, especially of a romantic nature or with a lack of female affection.

251

light: as ecstasy. This ecstasy is the makam[50], the musical ambrosia that the Graces pour forth. In the end, this is the Philosophy of music. The musician standing in their locus, place, makom, and making an obstacle for themselves of the inspired moment, becomes like a door between their world and the world beyond what they can understand, of emotions.

They constitute the door between the sublunar realm of the earthly and their place, and the supralunar realm of the god-spheres. And from there comes the transmission, the message, the becoming of the aesthetic force that leads towards truth, and all of this in turn places in pursuit of the certainty of one's own expression. All this proceeds to unfold. Simply, placing this hierarchy helps even in a practical sense to understand the paths through which the musician travels in a static state. So for that reason, I have considered this inclusion and link with the spheres, also of interest, to hermetic matters.

Little more can be said, save that one must learn the schema of these quests with utmost rigor in study and for years, so as not to have to think and deviate with the fluctuation of one's thought, in the inspired moment when it comes. In the seat, the musician who knows the order is an applicant of the right emotion and the inspired emotion, which they seek with the loving longing for understanding of the veritas. As just is the clarification of the immutability of the circles and of the amorous

---

50 This term refers to the musical enjoyment produced by the music of the ud, the lute. Its resemblance to the Hebrew word מקום (makom), meaning "place," is striking, from which we deduce that inspired music creates a spiritual place, a space of its own time and space, precisely characterized by musical ecstasy.

idiosyncrasy (Divine love) of the seeker's soul through the spheres, let these words of Ficino serve as a clue:

"If love does everything, it preserves all things equally, because the task of making and preserving always belongs to itself. Indeed, like are preserved by like. Love attracts like to like . parts of the earth one by one approach the other parts of the earth similar to them by this mutual love that unites them. And the whole earth eagerly descends to the center of the world as its similarity. Likewise, the parts of the water are attracted " They give to each other and with the entire mass of water they move towards the place that suits them. And the parts of air and fire do the same."[51]

As it cannot be otherwise, contemplation on the attraction between the similar leads to the study of the spheres for the seat of inspiration. Love also constitutes itself as a process of resemblance with the divine countenance, with light. Cultivating it within the bosom of virtue entails connecting with the current that allows the natural union of elements (earth with earth, water with water, etc.), and embarked upon the study, navigating through the quests.

The ultimate transcendence is assumed simultaneously as an artist's dissolution into their palpable ecstatic experience, and an integration towards a profound level of being whose experience is entirely intangible and non-sensory. Given that it represents a limen between the corporeal and the incorporeal, the visible lumen (from the constellations to the Moon) and the invisible (precessional equinoctial movements and even the timeless

---

51   De Amore. Marsilio Ficino. Duscurse 3, cap 2. Ed. Tecnos.

levels of the archetype), there can be no place for the musician beyond the eighth sphere. These certainly require various types of knowledge and initiation.

C:.VIII:. MUSICAL ECSTASY

On Inspiration and the Hermetic Wave that derives from Light

The conservatory does not validate the way of understanding music. If one wants to be an interpreter, that is, to
repeat works of others, it is suitable because they will be
instructed in the mechanics of works whose composers, in
some cases, technically were not so good. But if one wants to
understand, they should not even go to conservatories. Their
basis is the sum of tactile perfection (earth element) and its
causes. Thus, tendons, muscles, even nerves, everything is
aimed at the precision of the final movements, their scores
on the instrument. The posture matters little in terms of its
naturalness, as the technical end commands over the entire
musical process. Between music being sensitive to the intangible and music being sensitive to the tangible, the latter
wins out, as everything becomes objective even from the
subjectivity of the musician's mind.

What is analyzable, measurable, is the only thing that
exists in the *discourse of the method*, and even the transmission of sound is measured in terms of good or bad sound by
its waveform (envelope), identifying therein the pleasant-
ness of the sound. Once again, a physical variable. Another
approach is needed that sublimates the natural gift of the
musician (individual) from its subtle elements (focus on the
Spirit), which is where music truly works, by the grace of
the Muse and daughter of prana, the *humiditas* of air and
water, cascaded from the spirit of fire to our very era.

Light, Heat & Humudity

The symbol-note, symbol-interval, Muses, inspiration, the journey through the heroic path, ... are necessary studies to undertake. All these matters are archetypal and psychological patronage of Apollo and the Muse, on the one hand; and of Hermes, on the other. It is a path that restarts, for music is a symbol of our soul and our dynamics in general, an intangible engine synchronous with universal cycles. Everything that nourishes us, moistens us, impregnates us with divine spark. The basic (primordial) trinity is light, humidity and heat.

[1] Light, since source vibration issues are discussed.
[2] Humidity, because what it is about generates internal humidity, that is, it permeates the being with knowledge.
[3] Heat, because a burning is generated in the heart, a consequence of the internal resonance of the present moment, similar to the brave burning of the Sun in the sky.

The humidity that allows closing the circuit of the cosmic ray, which we discussed towards the end of 'La Lira de Hermes' is equivalent to inspiration. In the Hermetic Wave, to intellect. Inspiration is the light in act of union with the internal humidity of the inspired being, impregnating the work of Number, of Logos, and thus producing the divine opus on Earth. The Hermetic wave stages it by bringing it from God and towards the solar hero, who receives the inspiration. Apollo is the symbol of the union of the solar hero with God, through inspiration, represented in the nine Muses. Of course, the equivalence of Light is God Himself, although the ultimate meaning of the highest ontology is only linked to what lies beyond light itself, as the end of the book suggests. But, in this case, it is indeed about the vital process permeating the human being with *gratia*. The heat, which fundamentally proceeds from the conditions of the environment and light, especially solar and lunar, to another degree signifies the increasing vibration, up to the ardent ecstatic journey through the mnemonic palaces of the note-spheres. This heat, insofar as it is vibration in its physical energy, is linked to physical bodies that emit or reflect light, giving a characteristic warmth of their soul.

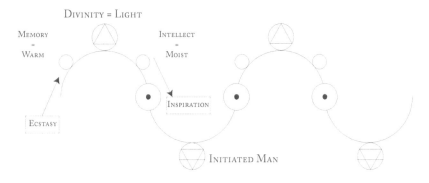

Figure: Hermetic wave as light, heat and humidity.

When we talk about the song of the sirens and refer to the waves of the planetary spheres with it, the effect of that song is heat, and this effect spreads among them (harmony) and combines in us its final geometric compendium. What happens in Heaven shall sound because the heat that crystallizes in the memory palaces that are composed by the notes, the intervals, the spheres, produces a resonance in the biological bodies here below. A prolonged inspiration over time will give rise to a well-conceived work, although for the work to be natural it will have to be governed by the cycles of nature (memory/water/wave).

The Opus of Chaos

We'll now attempt to reflect the cycles of the cosmos, what is called speculative music. A mirror where we place certain musical elements that will reflect the sky; sometimes reminiscent of Renaissance magic, where these correspondences are used to traverse a certain path, to achieve a particular resonance. All of this is presented in 'La Lira de Hermes' in a comprehensive and rigorous manner.

We proceed with the 'Utriusque Cosmi.' The divine monochord is crafted from consonant proportions, providing it with coherence. It comprises two diapasons (octaves), with the first half representing matter and the latter embodying form. However, within each lies a realm of additional subintervals. Form, typically perceived as contour and equated with matter, is, in reality, immaterial (linked to the number 3). As we embark here from the musical proportions of the earthly element ascending towards the realms of the Sun, Good, and Beauty, these proportions assume a material nature. Conversely, when our journey commences from the divine tuning hand—the super-sharp G—formal proportions, devoid of materiality, are engendered.

Natural Perfection

We observe in nature an inherent and emanated perfection only when we perceive its movements in a calm manner. In Space, the orbits of the stars occupy specific places. But at the same time, these places are not perfect translations of the idea-number. Not even tuning an instrument allows us to preserve the perfection of form. So then, what does imperfection lead us to? The space between the formal idea and the material object belongs to chaos; thus, chaos is present in everything as the glue between idea and final work, between light and matter, between Father-Uranus and Son-Saturnus. This chaos is super substantial to matter and at the same time resident in it, for we see its consequences and can with no doubt measure them with modern Astrophysics.

Therefore, chaos proves that the idea encounters something, that it encounters an element disharmonious to it, a necessary readjustment, a toll for tangible existence. This toll, taken as supersubstance, proposes the primordial existence of such chaos, as a deviation particle in the multiplicity of the unity of the idea that inevitably leads to the controlled randomness of the Cosmos when manifesting (degrees of inaccuracy of orbits, etc.). I hope to have the opportunity to present this in writings; but for now, let it serve as a placement of the idea of imperfection, and how we continue to be tied to the laws of the heavens even when we make mistakes.

The imperfection of nature refers us to something perfect. Since we are talking about the realm of forms when we consider perfect intervals, what we actually observe in the physical world will always be something else, a physical reality. Therefore, one cannot just take the distance to the planets and find intervallic correspondences because it will not work. It is within the idea that one works with the image and its projections; and that of the divine monochord is precisely that, an image of Creation. Like if it were a musical word, it precisely refers to the music-numbers of the chain that we've already studied, which serves as ontology and cosmogonic order.

Chaos → Number /Music (ie: Fludd monochord) → Word → Idea → Image.

Understanding this is essential, because throughout the same monochord, numbers are given that are indistinguishable from intervals and therefore from music. They are, upon reaching their harmony, the very word that triggers the idea of a string hierarchically measuring the levels of consciousness vibration from and to matter or from and to light. Hence the fact that, for the memory to assimilate it and for the idea to be interwoven, an image like this must be used.

Undoubtedly, Fludd was very different from what was beginning to thrive in his time; he preserved hermeticism in the face of a science that would ultimately relegate the true knowledge bestowed by natural philosophy not to complete oblivion, but indeed to outmost secrecy. One of the ideas we extract is that of diapason, diapente, and diatessaron characterized as *material*; a contrasting notion to diapason, diapente, and diatessaron as *formal*. In the Pythagorean tetractys, the material comes from the number four and the formal from three, although it is extendable to 3 plus 2 plus 1. The lower spheres of the Sun, Venus, Mercury, Moon, and the four elements are embedded in the scale of matter, perhaps following the logic on short cycles therefore density of vibration. This folds into the Sun or perhaps from the Sun, and from Mars onwards through the heavens beyond the Fixed Stars; everything moving to a higher degree of subtle.

Ecstasy would respond to a wave vector, the ascension of light experienced by the being when remembering (in the Platonic sense), which for many doctrines constitutes awakening itself; also graduated by the stages of both inspiration and the ones depicted in 'La Lira de Hermes'. Viewing it as a wave, it can be inferred that the individual synchronizes their phase with that of the wave in order to experience the cycle of wonder, which they will identify as their seat to receive inspiration. It is where the rapture or ecstasy takes place.

In relation to the initiated man, the nature of mystical study makes the notion of inspiration very delicate from now on, as the musician will naturally approach the creative powers of nature, not bound by the constraints of conservatories. But this does not imply ease, as it is indeed much more difficult (for is elevated), but the sound, the work, the study, the enjoyment, and the other earthly aspects of music are thus more real. Therefore, we shall provide ideas of what initiation consists of, and where we find its prelates.

C:.IX:. JACOB'S LADDER AND MUSICAL INITIATION

Pythagorean lambda and the new musical institution

Figure ix-1: The Radolt Scale / Der Allertreüsten, Verschwignesten und
nach so wohl Frolichen also Traurige[n] Humor sich richtenten Freundin
Zu ihren Affecten mit helffenten Gesbillinen, 1 7o r. Vienna.

The visual is not mere perception; it's an invocation that resonates within the soul's sanctum. Behold the eyes, not merely as recipients but as emissaries of cosmic light. Ancient wisdom attributed the Sun to one eye and the Moon to the other, as if signaling a profound dance between celestial forces. Echoes of this insight rippled through the wisdom of the Egyptians, pioneers in the science of perception. Their symbolic gaze placed the sovereign in the right eye and the queen of heaven in the left.

The image that graces our vision is born of light's caress, awakening the spectrum of visible vibrations within the eye's sacred theater. And so, it traverses into the cerebral microcosm, painting the inner celestial vault. Within this inner cosmos, every external cosmic source finds residence, knitting itself into the fabric of the individual's being. Let us embark on an exploration of an image that transcends the mundane and resonates within the depths of our soul through the portal of our eyes. Behold a painting, a cover gracing a treatise for the ud, that encapsulates the essence of the macrocosm in its intricate forms.

The painting is a cover of a treatise for the ud (lute). It has three main elements, which are the entire part where the close-up figures are represented (terrestrial) and the part that has less defined colors (remote) and then there is the celestial part. The figure in delta is directly the Pythagorean Lambda, which is a figure that with two arms clears the intervals (overtones and infratones) in a direct and inverse harmonic relationship, which takes us to the bijective nature of the sound, similar to the question of the eye and light.

The Pythagorean Lambda

Since the first reminiscence is that of the scale, since seeing the painting takes us to that, let us first sketch so as not to return and deal with the symbol that announces a journey into the esoteric richness of Pythagoreanism. We have two arms that house number paths. The first, the series $1 \to 2 \to 4 \to 8$, and the second $1 \to 3 \to 9 \to 27$. Musically, the first are octaves, and the second are fifths, so the lambda divides between the musical structure and its content or quality. If we take the numbers as vibration, DO appears as 1 and the series of octaves, while the sequence SOL RE LA configures the second arm. In total, four notes that encompass up to a ratio of 1:27. Pythagoras, with his numerical purity, greatly facilitates our understanding of other disciplines or arts of the number, even in the field of high esoteric culture, such as in Kabbalah. The 22 letters of the Hebrew alphabet, combined with the 5 final letters, make up the same number. A number that, as already expanded upon in other works, or hinted at in this one and stated in 'La Lira de Hermes', has connotations of deep symbolic roots.

Anyway, this is the lambda in its simplest version, and it allows us to deduce that ascent and descent are made by taking the structure and content of a whole. I would like to point out that in a good way it seems that the series of octaves and the diapente series configure the exoteric (diapason::structure) and esoteric (diapente::content) part of classical hermetic knowledge. That is why I have included it in the figure, intentionally.

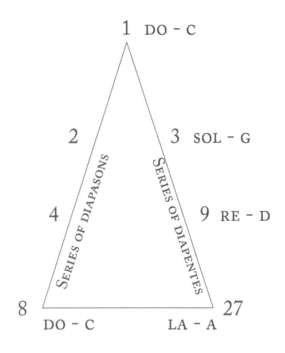

Figure ix-2: Pythagorean Lambda Explained.

Visual Analysis

Knowing the esoteric meaning of the Lambda, what is interesting here are the multitude of details. Let's list some:

[1] The two men on the right feed a fire, which has the same color as the intermediate and distant region between Heaven and Earth.

[2] The pythagorean lambda acts as a stairway made with sheet music.

[3] We can see a scale (hexachord[52]) written: DO RE MI FA SOL LA/ LA SOL FA MI RE DO. Or in other terms, D E F G A/ A G F E D C.

The interest that there was in the past in summarizing the content in it was sublime, just as paintings and art in general were done, it was sought that the works that served to disseminate a certain knowledge they could reflect. A kind of invocation prior to the work, sometimes represented by a deity.

[4] Athena, who is the goddess of wisdom and strategic warfare, which is not equal to Mars' worshipping of war.

The warlike impulse of Ares is not the same as what Athena embodies, which is the very geometry of movement, while

---

52 Just like in Robert Fludd's temple, and according to Guido of Arezzo, the hexachord symbolizes a music without the tritone, without the note B that creates the "forbidden" interval with F. In the context of a religious image, this makes sense.

Mars is the impetus of movement without an intercession of intellect, as occurs with Athena. It offers therefore a struggle between geometries, between movements, as a demiurgic allusion (lightning and prime matter), like the spirit entering the water and drawing the geometries of the circle.

This lute treatise is made in Austria, and its emblem ([5] the double-headed eagle) serves to mix the divine (Athena, patroness of Vienna) with the human (the kingdom itself). What for? For inspiration, to cause the breathe of the divine wind onto matter. Here Athena inspires wisdom to the composer and therefore creates the work. It's also important not to forget that the sacralization of the art of musical learning in this case has much to do with the meaning of music itself, which delves into why these matters always have a purpose. Now there is no such spiritual fervor, through which the student sublimates their dense essences into subtle ones when learning. The idolized conservatories are schools of gears and machinery in the service of preserving in formaldehyde the articulations of musicians who have long ceased to be anything more than dust. We continue enumerating with the fifth point.

[5] A fire is fueled by men carrying a substance.

The fire is the internal Sun, which produces the microcosmic movement, that is, an allusion to the heart. What does the heart feed on? Fuel for the spirit, the Grail. It matches the era. There are a few more details to pose our insights on:

[6] A motto in Latin that seems to say "Space of counterpoint".

[7] The material that is brought to the furnace (athanor) of the heart is mined in the intermediate region between Heaven and Earth. Whatever it may be, its nature is of light, and it can be taken as collected inspiration and brought to the soul of the body. The heart must be fed not based on earthy passions, but with the light of the intellect, that which is brought from the quarries of the spirit. That's what the detail seems to suggest to us.

[8] There is an archer who tries to hit an arrow at the initiate, the one who ascends the lambda.

This archer has drawn several arrows, hence striving for it never to arrive. Jacob's ladder, which symbolizes this ascent, shifts from being held by angels to being held by archers. The arrows are the rays of light, hence their malevolent power (arrow) can ruin the spiritual ascent if not done in order. Here, the archers are thus referred to as instruments of Apollo himself.

We may remember The Ninth Gate, a film based on the book 'El Club Dumas', by Arturo Pérez Reverte, where the main character "receives a threat from above" who is none other than an archer. One of the nine engravings from the Book described within (adapted to a film: The Ninth Gate) is depicted here: danger comes from above.

The archer tries to prevent our Jacob, this Radolt, from climbing the ladder without his permission. There is always a permit to grant for climbing the scale. Where is it? In the form of Athena, who watches the rise and guards the initiate. The work is therefore consecrated to Athena, as the musician's company attests, and this is a guarantee of promotion. There is no promotion in the work without consecration to the goddess. She is the patron of the work, and she is so with spiritual permission.

[9] The score that appears on the staircase is necessarily the same as that composed by the musician. Through the composition it creates the staircase itself. Up and down, and in that creation it has the goddess. The presence of this spiritualizes the musical matter, that is, the notes themselves, their sounds. Reason, the spear, fire, Athena, the triangle of Lambda,... All symbols of fire. If we project a man onto this lambda, we would have the heart on the ground and the head at the vertex. Concupiscible and rational souls.

VERB. D.SVM C.S.T ARCAN·

Figure ix-3: goalkeeper from one of the plates from El Club Dumas, A. Pé rez Reverte, a work of fiction with an esoteric basis (employee for educational purposes).

[10] Radolt's scale ends in a chorus given by the Muses and Apollo himself.

The passage of Jacob's ladder corresponds to Bereshit (Genesis) : 28; 11-19.

‫[11] יפגע במקום וילן שם כי אב השמש ויקח מאבני המקום וישם וישם‬
‫מראשתיו וישכב במקום ההוא:‬

Translation: (G.od) struck the place (lightning) and (Jacob) spent the night because the Sun had set. And he took one of the stones from the place and put it under his head, and he lay down to sleep.

‫[12] ויחלם והנה סלם מצב ארצה וראשו מגיע השמימה והנה מלאכי אלהים‬
‫עלים וירדים בו:‬

Translation: And he dreamed, and behold, a ladder set up on the earth, and the top of it reached to heaven. And behold, the angels of Elokim were ascending and descending on it.

‫[13]הנהו יהוה נצב עליו ויאמר אני יהוה אלהי אלהי אברהם אביך ואלהי יצחק‬
‫הארץ אשר אתה שכב עליה לך הננתא ולזרעך:‬

Translation: And behold, Adonai stood up and said, "I am Adonai, G.od of Abraham, your father, and G.od of Isaac. The land on which you stand is yours, and for your descendants."

‫[14] והיה זרעך כעפר הארץ ופרצת ימה וקדמה וצפנה ונגבה האדמה ובזרעך:‬

Translation: And behold, your offspring shall be like the dust of the earth; and it shall spread out to the west, the east, the north, and the south. And blessed be your family and all the descendants throughout the Earth.

[15] והנה אנכי עמך ושמרתיך בכל אשר תלך והשבתיך אל האדמה אעזבך כי לא אעזבך עד אשר אם עשיתי את אשר דברתי לך:

Translation: And behold, I am with you and will keep you wherever you go, and will bring you back to this land. For I will not leave you until I have done what I have promised you.

[16] וייקץ יעקב משנתו אכן יש יהוה במקום הזה ואנכי לא ידעתי:

Translation: And Jacob awoke and said, "Surely Adonai is in this place, and I did not know."

[17] וייִרא ויאמר מה נורא המקים הזה אין זה כי אם בית אלהים וזה שער השמים:

Translation: And with fear, he said, "How dreadful is this place! This is none other than the house of Elokim, and this is the gate of heaven."

[18] וישכם יעקב בבקר ויקח את האבן אשר שם מראשתיו וישם מצבה אתה ויצק שמן על ראשה:

Translation: And Jacob rose up early in the morning, and took the stone that he had put for his pillows, and set it up for a pillar, and poured oil upon the top of it.

[19] ויקרא את שם המקום ההוא בית אל ואולם לוז שם העיר לראשנה:

Traducción: And Adonai called the place Bait El, but Luz was the name of the city at the first.

We extract, not without persistent effort towards synthesis, that:

[a] Jacob went to Haran and fell asleep at sunset.

[b] He laid down placing the stones around him and fell asleep.

[c] He dreamed of a staircase whose top reached to heaven and the angels ascended and descended on it, symbols of transcendence of his physical planes.

[d] G.od would then have spoken to him and told him that the land where he slept would be given to him and his offspring, so he blessed the blood and seed (biological foundation of the lineage) of Jacob.

[e] Jacob waked up and assumed that G.od is in that place.

[f] He took the stone and blessed it by pouring oil over it; he then called it Bethel, or BaitEl.

[g] The name was Luz before Bethel, from which it is presumed that there was another settlement before. The similarity with the homophonous word seems almost a gift, but obviously this must not be what it seems. In fact, the word light in Hebrew refers to the hazelnut, which alludes to a response with a certain symbolic degree.

[h] He bowed saying that if G.od was with him, he would give him bread to eat, &c., and this stone that he had placed as a pillar would be the House of G.od.

Bethel is composed of two parts: Bait and El, meaning house and G.od respectively. Therefore, consecrating Bethel as the House of G.od is a tautology. This divine abode, where the mystical passage occurs, begins with the consecrated laying of the building's cornerstone. This helps us understand the place from which that internal Sun is born in the figure's furnace.

Figure ix-4: solar athanor.

The idea is that from a mystical vision, the foundation of something is reached. We have this in the founding of Mexico-Tenochtitlan. The sign is an eagle gripping a serpent. It can be something physical, or it can be something dreamt, allegorical of the eagle (air aeon) triumphing over the serpent (earth aeon), or rather the rational soul prevailing over instinct. It may have been a vision, it may have been a dream. Maybe. But in this case, it involves a dream with winged figures ascending and descending the ladder. A hermetic idea, that of ascending and descending the scale that rests upon the initiated. The *betyl*, on the other hand, a word derived from Bethel, has been in Spain a construction for communications with the divine, always in high places. There are many, although most are in ruins, vestiges of a time of communication with the divine, even in the most prosaic ways, yet no less precise for it.

The consecrated stone anchors the mystical experience to the earth; the dream itself leaves it as a trace of its reality, given that its ontology does exist, even if only dreamed. In fact, on the cover of the treatise, we see a temple to the left of the image, where Athena and the musician are located. The place is consecrated with a series of archetypes made symbols that propel music towards the spheres. The one climbing the ladder is a musician, as they ascend through the scores. It is also unnecessary to explain everything about this cover, as I neither know nor believe that other questions should not be imagined, not fantasised, by those who see it. Nevertheless, we provide some more.

[11] Radolt is adorned like a hero, thus consecrated by Athena and elevated in his listening. He experiences the function of angels in the score. He will ascend and descend like the angels, as the notes (DO-LA; LA-DO/ C-A; A-C) are written as a summary of the scale. These notes ascend and descend like the angels do.

They are a scale up to A[53], drawn at the base, indicating the idea of twelve eons (add up the notes) and with it the ascension

---

53 Same as the secret painting of Sta. Cecilia, in the church of Virgen de la Carrasca, Bordon, Teruel, Spain.

and descent of the year itself. The solar cycle links the musician with the heroic cycle (Hercules, 12 works)[54].

[12] What the miners undermine is within the earth even though this may be a celestial vision. It refers to the chthonic, the mother forces, the inner Titans, what moves beneath our earth... it is Jung's Shadow, which is sublimated in that furnace, while that hero ascends, sublimating his own matter, his own being.

Athenea and her counterpart, Apollo

Alright, then. We have a hero ascending a Jacob's ladder built by steps that are the score presented by the musician in this treatise, called the Radolt scale. And this allegory presents Athena as the patroness of everything that is happening, that is to say, she is the earthly equivalent to the celestial divinity (Apollo). She is the representation on earth of the god Apollo, akin to the orbs we saw in Kircher's triptych.

They are not considered counterparts in the pantheon, but here they are arranged as antitheses. Apollo and the Muses make the musician ascend. Athena gives him permission and guards the earth, anchoring him in life.

The Time of the Conservatoires comes to an end

The treaty, from 1701, is a son of its time, and reminiscences of what preceded the conservatories are still visible. According to

---

54 The suggstion is very attractive: half of the year corresponds to the scale from c to a; the other is the descent from a back to c.

the law of cycles, 240 years pass for each eon that affects reigns, dynasties, empires... and also institutions. This is an ancient law and little known to the common people, which measures time cycles based on the two lords of time: Jupiter and Saturn.

The period between their conjunctions is almost 20 years (see: Brief introduction and basic concepts), but extrapolated to the time they spend conjoining in each element (what is called triplicity) among the signs of Heaven (signs of Fire, Air, Water and Earth), this gives the figure of 240 years. That is, for 240 years (approximately), Jupiter and Saturn concatenate conjunctions in the signs of Fire, then in those of Earth, then in those of Air and finally in those of Water. Be careful with the order, because it is important, it is the same as that of the zodiac.

To establish the inception of the first conservatoire, we may consider various dates, but as such, the inaugural conservatoire (the model to be replicated) was established in 1795, in Paris. Therefore, it would be around 2035 when the next wave is expected to be established. Specifically, on December 21, 2020, the Hermetic-Musical School of CITTARA was founded, which can be deemed the premier institution, in the eyes of Heaven, which is what truly matters, in this regard.

Approximately 225 and a half years have passed, which intriguingly aligns with the cycle of chronocrators. However, it is the Royal School of Singing and Declamation, founded in 1784, that truly originated the conservatoire, as over the following years (1792 and 1793), elements were gradually added until configuring it as such. If we consider that solid foundation of the Royal School of Singing, we arrive at 2024 by calculation. In other words, it's evidently the end of the conservatoires and the commencement of a different form of education.

The Initiatic Music Education

This aspect is of paramount importance and is reiterated throughout the book. The preceding cycle of history, spanning approximately 220 years, aligns with the earth element through the cycle of the chronocrators in signs of the earth element. Since December 21, 2020, both Jupiter and Saturn have begun to continuously conjoin in the triplicity signs of the air element (Aquarius, Gemini, Libra, etc.). This trend will persist for the next 200 to 240 years, much like the previous cycle was associated with the earth element, and before that, the fire element.

If we trace back from 1784 to the inception of the Fire Cycle, we arrive at 1603, marking the end of the Renaissance era, characterized by Hermetic ideals and widespread religious influence in music. But beyond that, it was also a time that sparked significant scientific and theological debates. Most notably, in 1600, we witnessed the death, more akin to a sacrifice, of Giordano Bruno, the precursor of Freemasonry in England and Rosicrucianism in the Germanic world. Remarkable!

However, unlike other disciplines, music did not remain confined within the secretive confines of the lodges until now. Instead, there were only theorists discussing the philosophical current known as speculative music. Now, the landscape has changed. The established Speculatory now comprises both an exoteric and esoteric component, allowing it to perpetuate the Hermetic tradition, which essentially circumvents the earth cycle of the chronocrators. With the unique characteristics of the air, music now receives illumination in its purest form. It is the moment of reason, the very essence of music's breath.

In that aeon of fire, musical teaching was dispensed only (let's say music of culture or traditional standards) to the elite (the highest and most sublime of the elements, blood::fire::nobility). The following cicle (earth) progressively homogenizes the possibility of musical teaching to any social stratum, and bases it on economic resources and technical skills.

In the aeon to which the Musae of **Cittara Hermetic Music** give entrance, marking the beginning of the *Musical Speculatorium*, air reigns supreme, governing the realm of ideas. In terms of education, music is only taught to the most intelligent; emotion is not even the foundation (the water aeon), but rather the philosophy of music, ideas, discernment—qualities that will characterize musical instruction. Previously, one became a student if one belonged to the upper class (blood, light, fire); later, anyone could do so if they had money or great skill (earth, matter). Now, a music student will be selected for their intelligence, and their approach to justice will determine their capacity for study. A certain arcane aspect arises as a corollary to this, a virtue that comes to light. Of the four classical virtues— **fortitude, prudence, justice,** and **temperance**—the one corresponding to the air element is the latter. Its sword (instrument) is what discerns the parts, what is discriminative within the mental sphere. Thus, the first thing to be divided by this sword is the very circle of the whole, which begins its division by reason and does so, naturally, with the ratios of natural numbers—that is, intervals. Elitism will continue to exist, as it pertains to music (waves::hierarchy), but those who excel will be those with agile speech and mercurial intelligence, not those of emotion, liturgy, or great technical skill.

What happens when teaching music without a spiritual part? One may ask. And the answer is that Music is not taught. By definition, spiritual refers to matters of the soul and spirit. The latter is not sensed in conservatories, anywhere in that teaching or subject; and the former, easier to handle, could only be addressed in subjects like acoustics. The soul pertains to cycles, and the notion of what a wave is ties in with what the soul is, so without one there is no gateway to the other. Focused solely on practice, music fulfills its role as an amplifier of light without a direction for improvement, since the earth as an element remains absorbed in itself; if the vector is in the air element, there will be improvement alongside the amplification of that light. Here there is transformation. Without a spiritual component, therefore, there is only an amplification of one's own imperfections. The rock does not end up polished, does not end up with geometry. It does not end precisely as suggested on the aforementioned cover with Athena, that is, strategic, orderly, angular movement, forming a whole, and containing the wave. In other words, a polygon, a geometry, a soul. As a concise categorization to aid readers intrigued by the Speculatory, these traits would mirror each referenced eon:

Ignis (fire)....................liturgy/ praise of the spirit/counterpoint

Air (air).....................intellect/ interval/ idea- number/ melody

Aqua (water)................emotion/ fluctuation / density/ harmony

Terra (earth)..........practice/ technique/ resource/ speed/ quantity

I hereby beleive that the reader will be supported by the brief slogan below: as above, so below; so that the very teachings of hermetic music will also be subject to it, changing its subtle corpus depending on the element that moves in that eon. In fact, the characteristics of the Pythagorean school are of Air, and hence the interval, the idea and symbol of the number, and the pattern for the present cycle.

C:.X:. ASTROLOGICAL SIGNIFIERS OF MUSIC

And how to astrologically define Music adapts to the lights in a hierarchical way

Reasons for its Study

What grabs one's attention about symbols is their immediate resonance once employed. Of all, astrological symbols are the ones that captivate the public the most. The musical celestial creature moves through all the celestial spheres to convey and transport the hermetic prayer, and in its journey, in harmony with inner illumination, it distills the essence of the influence of the stars on the biology of beings. Various celestial archetypes govern different aspects of music. Here, we shall delve into which simple configurations, which constellations, define the musical idiosyncrasy from greater to lesser cognitive proximity.

Correspondences of the art of music and of heaven

Venus, the primary embodiment of music, earns this distinction due to its proximity to Earth and utilizes dance to express her essence, her quality. Recently a student mentioned, perhaps with intense problems regarding the exact definition, what the possible astrological significance of music could be. We shall now delve into an astrological correspondence pertaining to music, governing its essence or its celestial significance.

One endeavors to establish the rightful connections with music, turning to the Quadrivium for guidance. Within it lies a perfect square of arts, seeking to bring heaven down to earth, fostering mutual understanding among these disciplines. They are referred to as the "materiae," akin to the four elemental components of matter.

The domain of astronomy/astrology delineates correspondences with all else, employing arithmetic and geometry to complement music. Music possesses a language, alongside astrology, unequivocally conducive to comprehending cosmic order. Building on the previous example, a student was asked, "How is music signified in a natal chart?"

The student replied: Pisces, Jupiter, primarily. The student was correct in stating that Pisces is a sign indicating the abandonment of forms, and music has an aspect in which forms are abandoned, but it is not the only one, because music contains tempo and that is a formalization, a structure. But if we talk about music without rhythm, at the dawn of frenzy, emotion, ... and excluding musical mantras, whose repetitions imply a rhythm, if ultimately we aim at complete and thoroughly undefined music... it could be of Pisces-Neptune.

The music is indeed in the water, but I believe it's because the waves are visible in the water. The water makes them visible in the medium change from water to air. One mustn't forget that they are also waves in the air. Not just in the water. When one observes a wave in the water, they are simultaneously in the air and in the water. Therefore, music is also of both elements. It will be related to what pertains to Water, let's say the Moon, Venus, and Neptune; and what pertains to Air, let's say Mercury and Jupiter. And these would be the real significants of music. Music expressed through singing would be the Sun. The Sun sings in the old-fashioned way, as Goethe said, and the structures of music would always be endowed with the image or imago of Saturn. The faculty that music has to "bring back the dead" would be in Pluto. Of controlling the masses would also be in him. Of controlling. Its martial impulse would be in Mars; and that Apollonian power that seizes the will with the reason of a few chords or notes would be in Uranus. So, we have made the whole journey. But if we consider one meaning, it would be water, and it would be air. That's how straightforward it is.

With this, one would have to find the closest signifier within water and within air elements. Within water, we would have Venus and the signs of Cancer, Scorpio and Pisces. With Venus in Cancer, the music will be pleasant and that of the majority; aiming the tastes of the whol community rather than the margins of it. Venus in Scorpio would indeed satisfy the pleasures of the occult desires, and move the listener onto a dark athmosphere. A Venus in Pisces: the music would become intricate, losing certain -or absolutely all- structures and venturing into frenzy, where the will gets lost in that mystical trance, which is one of the significant meanings of music. But it's also air, and it travels in the intermediate of air and water. Just read Macrobius: "Harmony is in the intermediate of Water and Air." And in the intermediate realm, we always find Mercury, the herald. Mercury is a mediator. It communicates what is above with what is below, and viceversa. Thus, fundamentally, **Venus conjunct Mercury** would be a way of seeing this significance of music.

If the sign it is found in is of water, music will evoke emotions and do so deeply depending on the nature of the sign. If it's Cancer, it'll be commercial music; Scorpio, visceral, with hidden sounds; Pisces, complex and mystical. Or if it's in Air signs: in Gemini, it'll be intellectual; Libra lacking in ideas but using the other's to balance in style and nuances; and in Aquarius, it would be very atonal music. It wouldn't have a center and would assign the same value to all notes. It would be the opposite of tonality: equal importance to all notes. Notably, it's the opposite sign of Leo, heart, center (tone/ tonality).

Ultimately, music is the formulation of harmony between the parts, as an idea. And it does so through notes, intervals, sequences, ... all constituting the expression of the musician's soul. Thus, the union between these two parts is that of air and water. Hence, I mention Pisces, which is ruled by Jupiter and Neptune, respectively air and water, and would yield religious and mystical music; or the harmonious liaison of Venus and Mercury, symbolizing an erudite and emotionally resonant musical expression.

Additionally, there exists a significant aspect that aligns with the classical tradition, and that is the realm of the fixed stars, regarded in their essence as a celestial sphere. The subtle resonance of this element finds its parallel in the Muse Urania. From the stars emanates the visible wellspring of inspiration (the loftiest and most transcendent visible light), which then permeates through the subsequent spheres, irrespective of its manifestation. Thus, the radiance of Urania -"hear every music"- corresponds to the music that, in any instance, is inspired, contrasting with all that deviates from the natural and divine order, and consequently lacks permanence on Earth. Thus concludes the astrological significance attributed to music.

C:.XI:. QUADRIVIUM

Or how understanding subjects beyond numbers helps bring the student closer to the Ancient Wisdom

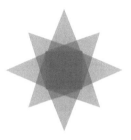

Introduction

The Arts of Number summarize the scholarly teachings of Late Antiquity and the Middle Ages. The notion that with four disciplines of the Sophia's study one comprehended the knowledge of number set the boundaries of that within the natural, for the observer. The aim was thus to achieve the perfection of a cultivated thought that communicated different approaches to number. In many respects, today the four facets of this polygon are necessary for a certain departure from the idea of specialization. Nowadays, post-academic education and training have taken these latter paths, but before it was advisable to nurture a person capable of understanding the interrelationship of things in their environment. Consequently, with the *heraldic* interrelations of Arithmetic with Geometry, with Music, with Astronomy/Astrology, they inherited the ideals of Egypt, or at least the aspiration to produce *trismegists* for contemplating the cosmos, much like the creature alluded to in Pythagorean tradition.

In the Material realm, there are the 4 constituent elements, signifying that they can encompass all that is manifested. Thus, the four disciplines of the natural art of number will observe the manifested from different perspectives of the number itself. The four studies will precisely engage in hermeticism by dedicating their study to complete presence and through the illumination of memory and structuring of the intellect.

The **Arithmetic** will regard the number as the distillation of **astronomical** cycles, interrelating them. **Music** will take these relationships and apply them to sound waves to create sound qualities (notes). Finally, **Geometry** will manifest in matter the reflections of the consonances and dissonances of music. This forms a chain from one discipline to another, a shared framework, as if each defined a unique quality or 'power' of number. The four branches, once their nature is discerned, will derive from the qualities of the same matter that concretizes them in the physical, and this lineage, in turn, arises from the intellectual, where the movement that shapes them originates. This implies that, concerning number and its principles, in one way or another, the four refer to the element of air. Nevertheless, we will first approach them through their projection, which admits no intermediaries, onto the constituent elements, and then we will do so from the reason that gives them origin and constitutes their trunk.

[1] Astronomy: fire corresponds to it, since it is the part closest to the Light.

[2] Arithmetic is of air, since philosophical reason operates with the numbers of light and does so in the realm of the idea.

[3] Music corresponds to water, because they are physical

waves and their effect and nature is water because of the soul that carries them.

[4] Geometry corresponds to the element earth, as this element is the crystallization of every idea of number and geometry to appear in every crystalline structure.

But the order can become complex. After all, the rule of memory that has just been outlined aids in an initial understanding of what is being discussed. On the other hand, we can further our understanding of the four arts by considering that they can also connect the four elements, serving as a transition between them.

The geometry is conceived amidst the primal *lux* (fire) and primordial seas (water), akin to the lightning that rends chaos to create order. This concept originates from Genesis and will be explored further with **commentary on the Timaeus** in the forthcoming volume. The harmonics of lightning are the geometric figures that ultimately generate the biologic metastructure of beings, known as "sacred Geometry," through the imposed order of light. Music, as a wave laden with the soul's moisture, resides between air and water, both humid elements. Astrology analyzes the effects of light (fire) on the biology (earth) of all beings, especially humans.

Arithmetic, as a discipline organizing the ideas contained within Number, and leading to praxis through its system (from which mathematics derives, a tool for putting advanced concepts into practice), links air (idea) to earth (praxis). Of all these, arithmetic governs the general element of the ensemble; music—sonorous—diverges from this to delve into the humors through water (emotion); geometry leads to the archetypal and singular idea behind every visible form in the world, thus directing towards fire; and astronomy shifts the imagination of light towards the biological realm. The imagination, therefore, is stirred in the student, and by the action of number, by these four disciplines, a movement that serves as exercise to memory and the habitation of intellect; contributing to the structured understanding of the interdisciplinarity of numbers.

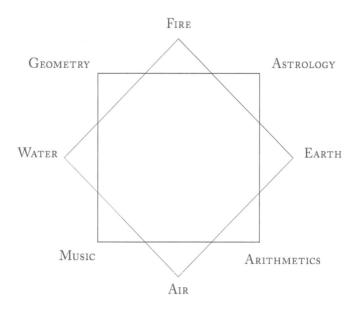

Figure xi-1: Quadrivium and the transition of the Four Elements.

From Heaven to Earth

When we discuss the notion of bringing the celestial realm down to earthly matters, it entails a profound movement of ideas nestled within the realm of numbers, whether within a particular discipline or another. This movement carries forth the experiential aspect of observing reality. Consequently, the sensible world discerns its influence upon the individual, differentiating between what is ordered and what remains unordered, thereby engaging the imagination within the very act of observation.

The imagination, in its essence, is akin to a fire that ignites the conceptual framework, the structure, the rationality, and the numerical underpinnings of intellect. This metaphysical Fire, projected towards the material realm through the conduit of number (Air), participates in the spiritual elevation of matter, embodying a masculine philosophical principle or immanent divine essence.

In this manner, a methodical approach to education serves as a means to expound upon more intricate concepts, paving the way for those who seek to traverse these intellectual landscapes. This pedagogical journey forms four crucial links. Amongst the realms of Air and Water lies music, for waves become perceptible only when the uniformity of both media's contours is disrupted. A wave, discernible and influential, impacts both the aqueous and aerial environments concurrently, at their boundary. Conversely, the manner in which geometry organizes light stands in stark contrast to arithmetic, as the latter embodies the relationship between abstract ideas.

The Earth prompts the necessity to relate numbers, facilitating the encounter between one idea and another. This interaction involves the idea belonging to the realm of Air, while its confrontation occurs within the domain of Earth. Consequently, Arithmetic bridges the two realms. Hence, the concept of three and two pertains to Earth when confronted but belongs to the Air when retained as ideas.

The imaginative force, acting as an agent of motion, manifests uniquely in the realm of music. It undertakes musical ratios, transitioning them from the warm and moist to the cold and moist. In a sense, it compels the musician to seek inspiration in the act of creating music, remedying this moisture, as will be elaborated upon towards the volume's conclusion. The collaborative operation of the 'imago' functions as a single organism with its own language: the language of number.

The ideas of music

To expound upon the aforementioned, considering the ideas, denoted as I_i, which belong to the realm of air; their confrontation and subsequent union, symbolized by the operations of division and multiplication, these ideas assume a similar dimension when confronted. The religious sphere engenders religious ideas that converge within its domain, akin to technological concepts. One cannot engage in a discourse regarding the price of grain with an individual who counters with religious apparitions (e.g.: I_3 vs. J_2, instead of I_3 vs. I_2). A common element (context), represented by the earth, becomes imperative in such interactions.

Assuming that by ideas we understand either concepts, symbolic images, numerical vibrations, or even planetary cycles (gnosticism), we call them "I" (generic ideas) and we assign them the element Air. If we confront, compare, relate and therefore bring to a field of observation for its delimitation two different ideas I_1 and I_2, we conceive the relationship in another dimension different from that of origin, since in it they can only occur and not confront each other. This element of context for their mutual relationship is the earth. For example, $I_1 / I_2 = 3/2$ are the ideas of the ternary or triune and the binary or dual, one in relation to the other. By themselves they reside in the air, but their confrontation brings them to earth and they cease to have a separate entity: one is understood in relation to the other and vice versa, which splits the absolute from the whole.

If the previous has been understood, it can be agreed that musical intervals suffer from this transformation: the note (idea) disappears when the relationship between notes, the interval, occurs. In fact, the listener perceives an interval as soon as it occurs, masking the first note. Let's imagine a monk meditating on Om: the sound of the monosyllabic mantra invades the mind of the listener and he perceives the concentration of the monk and his own as a consequence of the fact that the same sound is unaltered. If, on the other hand, we hear a note that jumps towards another, it is the leap that leaves an impression on us, not the source or destination note. At the first scenario, we talk about stillness, the absolute, the spirit; at the second, of movement, of the things relative to each other, of the soul. Spirit and soul manifest their sound idiosyncrasy respectively in the sustained note and the interval.

Obviously, when it comes to music, we do not talk about Air to Earth in the same terms as if we are comparing ideas. It would be more appropriate to assign Fire to the idea-note, and Water to the interval, or else the moisture quality with which Water and Air are irrigated[55].

A deserved continuation by succinct explanation is the equivalence spirit::note; soul::interval. In 'La Lira de Hermes', the path of the soul (hero's journey) was explored, and in this exploration, the interval defined each stage of the soul, its phases. This constructs a dynamic narrative. Towards the end

---

55 Reminder: the elements air and water both contain aspects of moisture; their difference lies in the air being moist and warm, while water is moist and cold.

of that book, there is mention of deity-notes, hence, notes in an absolute sense and archetypal ideas. Thus, ultimately, Soul and Spirit resonate as both interval and note.

Study from a new paradigm

We turn our attention towards a practical utility. I urge the student to review the relationships outlined here. They are simple, but upon repetition, one will notice a certain fabric forming in memory that should allow for extrapolation to other examples that the student may intuitively perceive to exist.

Firstly, let's imagine the progression of the four elements from a different perspective: fire-earth-air-water. This order, which will surely be familiar, is the one that nature follows with its zodiacal eons: Aries-Taurus-Gemini-Cancer, ... These are the succession of signs of these elements, which, extended three times, complete the solar year. Thus, the cross-reference refers us to form (number 3), movement, soul, and diapente. This is logical, as we are discussing the quality of philosophical matter, not its structure, in which case we would simply distinguish between the duality of light and shadow. Conversely, astronomy, geometry, music, and arithmetic are ways of imparting quality to light within the framework or embedded between light and shadow.

When the sky forms a trigon aspect between planets, lights up places that add that quality to the whole celestial movement, endowed with light and its effect on shadow (matter). Let's think about the light breaking through the darkness. The lightning bolt draws a straight line from one end to the other, thus creating light, as it contrasts with the darkness. In the circle of the sky, this is equivalent to dividing the sky in two. From this division arise the straight line and the 180-degree angle, transitioning from the astronomical to the geometric. According to classical knowledge, a celestial body at the zenith of the sky casts its rays straight toward the observer.

This straight line, by dividing the circle in two, produces a half on each side. This is arithmetic. Now, if we consider a sound and multiply it by 1/2, or by 2 if we reference one part (1) to the total (1/2), then said sound will respectively decrease or increase its vibration by an octave.

Let's say the sky depicts three stars separated by 120 degrees. Astrologically, they form a trigon (Grand Trine, in fact). The arrangement of the lights forms a triangle, and each part divided by this is in a ratio of 1 to 3 with the total. It holds true if we take one, but if we take its complement, the ratio is 2 to 3. In both cases, these arithmetic relationships produce a variation of an octave in any given sound.

To illustrate the last example with the final interval of the tetraktys, envisage four stars at 90 degrees each from the next and previous in the circumference (sky) of the zodiac. Geometrically, it forms a square, where its individual part in relation to the whole forms a ratio of 1 to 4, and its complement, 3 to 4. Musically, a note vibrating at a certain frequency, multiplied by the ratio 3 to 4, yields a lower diatessaron; and if it's 4/3, an upper diapente. As the square intersects with the line, which was the diapason, when multiplying a vibration by 4, I have a double diapason, not a diatessaron; and if I divide by 4, the same is true for lower. For this reason, the square is harmonically an octave of the line; the octagon of the square; &c.

Regarding the elements, fire comes first as it pertains to light, astronomy; earth follows as we discuss geometry, the order of mineral matter, which precedes vegetation and animal

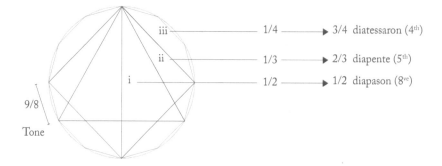

Figure xi- 2: the geometry of music.

and human matter hierarchically. Air follows these as the ratio of proportions is arithmetic. And finally, the undulatory and emotionally consonant aspect produced by Music. Et voilà, the interrelations of the quadrivium for the main intervals that give rise to the scale. Once the diapente and diatessaron are understood as triangle and square, trine and quadrature, it is observed that the sign of the sky corresponds to the tone of the earth.

The explanation is straightforward. The ratio between the diapente and the diatessaron, as seen, is 9/8, which is the Pythagorean tone of the scale. The geometric figure imbued between the triangle and the square would be the dodecagon, as there are 30 degrees between 90 degrees and 120 degrees, the basis of the 12-sided figure on the circumference of the sky. For this reason, the tone corresponds to the zodiac sign.

Each sign influences, if one wishes to see it that way, on the earth (geometry) measured according to the Pythagorean tone, and the year, summing them up, is of 12 tones, or a relationship if one wishes to see it as such, of two octaves. While arithmetically 4.10989 would be the precise factor[56], the two octaves calmly refer us to Fludd's monochord and other related allego-

---

56 Since the tone is 9/8, which stands as twelve times $(9/8)^{12} = 4{,}10989$.

ries of Heaven and Earth. It's of interest, as it exemplifies an intersection or syncretism between the numerical disciplines, something that necessarily and seemingly truthfully leads to the Truth. Here it does so from discernment, since the ratios that divide vibrating strings, in turn, divide the circle of the firmament, the visible monad of Uranus, which embeds spheres and earth.

I hope with this, there is a good establishment of the goodness of the quadrivium and the interest it derives in the student of natural philosophy.

C:.XII:. NUMBERS

Or the origin and causalities of these

א

Nature of number

No. This is not the 'chapter' *Bamidbar* from the Torah; there is no other similarity with the desert other than the wave of the dune being that of sound, that of number. Every wave, which are the parts of the universal vibration, have their harmonics, and from these, and given that their order is in whole parts (not decimals), the number is obtained. The so-called harmonic series is nothing more than the way in which nature manifests the idea in the context of the physical, and each harmonic is a number separated from unity. By uniting number 1 with the first wave O1, it begins to ground, to support the rest as harmonic replicas. Two comes from vibrating double (O2), three from vibrating triple (O3); four to fourfold (O4), and up to the final unlimited finite wave-number (ON). Therefore, they do not exist except in the idea that is subsequently formed. As explained in another section: from the physical, we go to Memory, from there to God; and from this, through the Intellect, we return to the physical. Well, Memory stores the waves of the physical, and after passing through the eye of Divinity, the intellect brings Number with it:

Waves → Memory → Divinity → Idea (Ratio) = Number
{O1-O2-O3-O4...-ON}   {1-2-3-4-...-N}

Without the binding power of memory, which is of the nature of water, one cannot understand the harmonic phenomenon and how it is transformed into numbers. The number exists, yes, and it expresses itself, but it does so only because the sound itself, or the vibration in the meta-sensible, exists in the sensible world too. The evocation of a 2 is traveled towards the diapason, the structure, the limit. With 4, 8, 16, and every power 2^N of two, the exact same thing happens. Not for naught, the light-dark duality that we can see in the binomial {1, 0} defines the digital storage structure whose scaling is in powers of two. Constituent structure of the binary artifact, it is a container (space) of a content (information), always structure vs. quality. Storage structure in digital, since it exists only in base two.

That these analogous conjectures leave clear imprints is important, since it conditions the way of seeing the environment. We know that numbers are a continuum, either in the hours we see or in the accounts we make. They are vibrations. In the same way that the eighth harmonic O9 (ninth wave) is further from the origin than the first (O2), the number 9 is more evolved than the 2, and that when we see a price that begins at 9, our reaction is different than if it starts at 2. The image is direct. Due to our brain configuration, seeing the high numbers on the right (for example, a price of 23.99) produces the effect of dominance over the distant harmonics, a natural succession, since the high numbers come after the bass and here they have a residual range. A price of 19.95 is no nicer than 23.99. Furthermore, our nature teaches us two things: achievement and completeness. If something covers up to 9, it is complete in its cycle, but only if the order is natural and that 9 is in the last instance. For that reason, also a price of 24.59 (1, 4, and 5 are almost consecutive) is more attractive than one of 23.99.

The mind demands order, for without order there is no memory, and without memory, the human connection to Divinity remains severed. Controlling numbers is as crucial as deciphering the grand cycles. Hence, elites are historically associated with symbols. However, there's a crucial consideration for humanity to grasp the essence of numbers: one must delve into their study from their very origin.

As observed, sounds exhibit O1, O2, O3, O4, O5, ... and from there emerge the numbers 1, 2, 3, 4, 5, ... Can one imagine a sound composed of its O5 as the fundamental, with octaves of the former as harmonics? It would be disordered. Chords accomplish this; when one inverts a chord and places the third above the fundamental, the sound ensemble is centered on O5. The effect differs from that centered on O1 or O3 (diapente). Similarly, with numbers, given the plethora we observe, it's no wonder numerology garners adherents, as it stems from a noble quest to restore order through intellect. The reader must note the vital distinction between the former and arithmology, the latter respecting natural order and law, with its inherent entitlement.

The musician, in performance, achieves precisely this. However, it's evident that the more one distorts, the more one perverts. Well-grounded music rooted in its fundamentals induces profound relaxation and tranquility when played. It organizes numbers, which serve as the basis for the motion (waves) propelled by the soul. Given these insights, the contemplation of numbers undergoes a significant transformation for the hermetic musician.

Numbers and their hierarchy: causes and consequences between them

"We typically tackle the product, from which stem the rationales operating on vibration. Addition is an operation that adds elements that can be added, namely those that share a realm. The number one can be the result of adding itself plus zero, as many times as we wish.

$$1 = 1+0 = 1+0+0 = 1+0+0+0; [\text{and derivatives}]$$

So, the numbers 1, 10, 100, 1000, and so forth, are equivalent in vibrational terms regarding their purity: the mind perceives no greater complexity in one than in another but does perceive greater vibration within the same quality. Therefore, 10 is the equivalent factor to the diapason, referred to in the decimal system, which is perfect concerning number for exercising the placement of objects in memory (tetractys-mnemosyne). The decimal system is suitable for memorization as it allows for the harmonic creation of memory spaces due to its perfection, as discussed by the Pythagoreans, since $1 + 2 + 3 + 4$ (the first four numbers) equals 10.

The one therefore derives from itself or from nothingness. And that makes it dependent on itself and the empty set or darkness. In the case of two, it's different. It can result from adding itself with nothingness, but also from the double sum of one.

$$2 = 1+1 = 2+0 = 1+0+1; [\text{and derivatives}]$$

From these dependencies we can extrapolate that:

[1] 1 is linked to 1, and 0, thus depending on 0 and 1.

[2] 2 depends on 0, 1 and 2.

[3] 3 depends on 0, 1, 2 and 3.

[4] 4 depends on 0,1,2,3,4.

[5] The 5 depends on 0,1,2,3,4,5.

And, taken to waves:

[1] O1 depends on O1 and *O0*.

[2] O2 depends on O2, O1, O0.

[3] O3 depends on O3, O2, O1, O0.

[4] O4 depends on O4, O3, O2, O1, O0.

[5] O5 depends on O5, O4, O3, O2, O1, O0.

With waves it looks perfect. The octave harmonic (O2) effectively depends on itself and the fundamental that precedes it. And so the rest. The zero wave O0 is the wave without vibration, a natural consequence to which the Intellect leads us with respect to the number. This is the set that becomes the silence of Thalia. The issue is more esoteric, but essentially *Surda Thalia* represents the reception of every wave on the earth from the rest of the vessels (Muses) and that comes from the Light (Apollo). As long as this moves, it has a reference that doesn't: a point of support that receives all influence from the waves. This is figured in this muse and in wave zero.

By no means should we remain here, for as seen in the wave derived from the study of Kircher, God is both above and below O1, precisely signifying that omnipresence of Divinity O1, and suggesting in the previous nothingness, O0, the same splendor, not in act, but in potential. Charting the path from the opposing point, the hierarchy imposed by Neoplatonism would place the First Cause of all movement in the number 0. In the first mover, which comes afterward, the succession of all sound would be found in the numbers: 1, 2, 3, 4, 5, 6, 7, 8, and 9.

Thus, the continuous possibilities of number, its own existence, unfold. Viewed as causes, one is the cause of itself and of the other numbers, as seen in the harmonic series; but zero is only the cause of itself. Hence, it is considered in communion with the First Cause. It must be seen as something unfolding. Zero is Nothing, and then comes the 1, which structures, like a ray, all existence in successive octaves. The octave is equivalent to multiplying by ten. What lies in between are the remaining numbers, the quality, the rest of the intervals:

0 = Nothing
1 = the Whole, creator of the structure = Octaves
2, 3, 4, 5, 6, 7, 8, 9 = qualities within the Whole

Grouping the numbers to form the arithmetic of the intervals and attracting to the Earth the idea that encapsulates the light (First Cause), that is, operating in the **image and likeness** of the <u>First Mobile</u>, we get:

$$\{1, 2, 3, 4, 5, ...\} \rightarrow \text{\textit{idio, diapason, diapente, diatessaron, dia-tria, ...}}$$

0 NOTHINGNESS

1 ALL/ FIRST CAUSE
2, 3, 4, 5, 6, 7, 8, 9 / FIRST MOVER

♄   FIXED STARS' SPHERE
♃   SATURN'S SPHERE
♂   JUPITER'S SPHERE
☉
♀   MARS'S SPHERE
☿
☽   SUN'S SPHERE

TIERRA   VENUS'S SPHERE

MOON'S SPHERE   MERCURY'S SPHERE

Figure xii-1: Neoplatonic diagram based on the number.

From this set, taking a subset that eliminates the 1, the intervals we form will exclude the identity (idio) and will be configured as:

{2/1, 3/2, 4/3, 5/4, ...} = *diapason, diapente, diatessaron, diatria, ...*

All intervals are inscribed in this set. Up to O9 we obtain the tone or epogda 9/8, which would mark the first important limit of the harmonic series and effectively equates to the limit of number, as the series of numbers repeats once it reaches 10. It is interesting that the last number of the series forms with the penultimate the precise basic unit of the scale, as is the tone. Remember that the semitone is considered a consequence of the tone due to how the scale is constructed, and not a basic unit and therefore the cause of the scale (see section *The Scale*, in the *Corpus Musicum*).

First, there is the Void, and from there, it generates, creating the structure and in an instant, the Whole (the octave of 1). The rest would be the qualities within that Whole (2, 3, 4, 5, 6, 7, 8, 9). The numbers themselves belong to the prime mover of the Universe, the first mobile sphere. They are not identified with the subsequent spheres as these are consequences created from these numbers as a cause. One only needs to observe the cycles of the planets, which embody or materialize the spheres, to see that they are subject to cycles derived from numbers as an idea. Jupiter, ideally completing its cycle in 12 years, but it takes 11.89 real years. It acts and derives its soul (movement) to Earth through the number, which in turn serves to define it and define its harmonies, such as Jupiter being harmonic with the zodiac itself (12 signs), and hence embodies Zeus for the classics.

The physical, therefore, derives, in the successive spheres, from the ontological ideas that the number constitutes based on the very nature of the physical (waves and harmonic series). Hence the question becomes so complex. In the duality of structure-quality, which we found in the 1 vs. the rest of the numbers, we obtain the Pythagorean idea that everything is number. **All is Number,** and you start to realize this, converge either in **structure** or in **quality**. And none converge in Nothing. That's why Nothing is unknowable. The First Cause is identified with Apollo, that's why Apollo is unknowable. That's why the Muses are necessary, they "water down" Apollo's wine. That's why Apollo strikes with lightning at the improper approach, because facing that, you die, you end up in nothingness, it's over.

First Cause = 0
First Mover = 1,2,3,4,5,6,7,8,9
Sphere of Fixed Stars, &c. = derived numbers (11.89, 1.9, ...)

Each celestial sphere, indeed, adopts, for its physical parameters, numerical values that exhibit a certain disjunction (chaos) from the ideal number they epitomize. Hence, the amalgamation of corporeal impurity and numerical fractionality becomes apparent. When decimal fractions reconstitute a semblance of order, it is attributable to the number's intrinsic representability as a fraction derived from the primal mover's numerical components. The transition from zero to unity encompasses the realm of integers (and consequently, alphabetic symbols), subsequently delving into fractional expressions (rational numbers), and culminating in the realm of irrational numbers. In the realm of music, the realm closest to purity is occupied by the inaudible, followed by the domain of pure frequencies (devoid of decimals and divisible by integers), succeeded by the emergence of intervals alongside the celestial spheres. This juxtaposition of intervals with spheres and

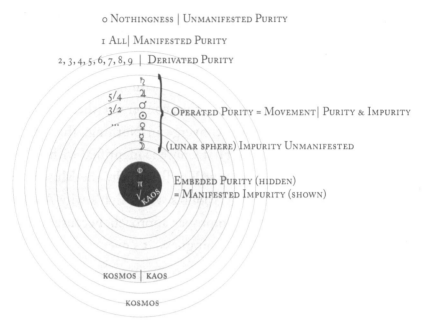

Figure xii-2: the number and its universal nature.

numbers with stars instills a profound sense of intrigue and fascination.

It's worth asking, as a corollary, whether the numbers π or φ were sacred, due to their irrationality, since they belonged to the Earth, and because each system encapsulates divinity, being the keepers of this in this the Kingdom of the Divine Presence. Whether it is nothingness, incapable of awaiting any dilemma about purity since it defines it; the unit then shows it; the harmonics, since they derive it; the intervals, since they operate with it to define movements; or apparent impurity, to encapsulate beauty itself in its number. The entire system is perfect.

There are many temples that follow the numbers of the canon and of the circumference; in Egypt, for example. But we can find it also in certain constructions around the 10th and even later on 14th-16th centuries in Spain and France.

Dressing the matter in these proportions seems to indicate, according to this study, that what it absorbs, that is, the air inside the temple, or the water in the container or container, has purity. The purity of lux.

The reader may also wonder about the gradation from cosmos to chaos and what significance I attribute to it in the figure. In reality, it represents the transition from order to disorder, correlated with the purity of number towards its impurity. This constitutes a unique study on a fundamental pillar of Pythagoreanism and Gnosticism, namely the number; and also of Hermeticism, as it deals with light within the number. And what is this concept? Well, it's a very ancient and difficult-to-decipher key. From it, the hierarchies of light are born, as we will soon see in the Tree of Life study.

Similar to a pathway traversing between realms via numerical constructs, transitioning from disorder to order or vice versa occurs with the discernible influence of numeric principles within each realm. Three distinct phases delineate the approach of the imago towards material existence: the pristine, static realm of numbers in their intrinsic form; the dynamic realm of imagery, embodied by celestial bodies and numerical relationships (depicting the movement of conceptual ideas). This intermediate stage embodies both purity and imperfection, mirroring the irregularities observed in orbital trajectories (such as elliptical paths). Finally, the ultimate stage signifies the pure chaos of material substance (earth), where these ethereal images navigate within confines deemed sacred, adhering to proportions rooted in fundamental irrational constants like ϕ and π. It's intriguing how Neoplatonists conceived of celestial spheres and the divine entities dwelling within them. The very essence of the sphere is derived from π, while the imagery of deities or melodious sirens encapsulates dynamic motion—an archetype instilled within the soul and integral to its essence, reflecting the luminous essence inherently embedded within the structural fabric.

From each end of the ladder or pathway, a numerical process sequences itself, and as it continues, it allows for delving into the depths of a broader knowledge that directly pertains to music—a more extensive and essential knowledge than the ordinary one concerning spheres or numbers in isolation. Absolute ideas must ascend to partake in sensible creation, for which 1, 2, 3, &c. will combine their ratios, engage in discourse within their ideas, syncretize their symbols, and thus form the intervals. Once these intervals are formed, we have the movements defined by them in Johannes Kepler's "Harmonices Mundi" or as he deciphers them from the Solar System. We will not dwell there (though we will later), and the ratios, which form the rational numbers of the global set, as they arbitrate ideas. We move on to the numbers not encompassed by reason, the irrationals, of which we have mentioned according to classical criteria the Egyptian canon φ, π, and the roots.

The intervals, as an intermediate world, are poised to revolutionize images and create gods, so that these ideas are encoded in the realm of matter, which therefore can only be understood clothed in physical dimensions, and thus are proportions that must be palpable. Like temples. Now perhaps a clearer understanding of what a musical interval is and where it leads emerges. The interregnum that rotates in successive spheres according to intervals, and which has been studied by hermeticists of the highest and lowest stature, offers the student of hermetic music an elevated view above the temples of the world. Music, when apprehended in its sounds, and these sounds subsequently imagined, allows for the recreation of the ratios of the spheres in the mental image, tuning into the gods of each sphere because they are substantiated in the movement of said image, in the musical interval.

This does not exclude that in temples, torches or the movement of the Sun with its carefully studied annual cycles, radiate light on statues and bas-reliefs, producing movement, an inner soul of the temple. The light acts as an engine and the figures seem to move (light-body-moving shadow::soul) within the Templar enclosure, thus offering the same thing as the imago towards the spheres: the encapsulated soul of the world. The number on Earth is therefore decipherable as a staircase to the next world, that of the spheres, and it is so through the use of music. Encountering a "Temple of Music" in Robert Fludd's writings is the quintessence of enjoyment for the Hermetic student, since, at least in the case of the writer, upon arriving there he understood the whole in its pure sense. And this, dear readers, is markedly ecstatic. In fact, the fine line of this sculpture of the number must amaze us, because through imagination and music we can go beyond the dense realities of matter and reach the gaze of the purest images of light.

Perhaps he has spoken about the so-called irrational numbers as if man had pulled them out of his wrinkled scientific sleeve, but that is not the case. The proportion called urea is in nature, just like π. We won't say much about the second number, but there is nothing more to it than observing galaxies, snail shells, plant growth, ... and music? And music. In this specific case I will paraphrase a part of 'La Lira de Hermes' that talks about how the musical intervals conjure the Egyptian canon. Look at the following: the diapason gives way to the diapente, and then diatessaron and harmonic ditono form a relationship of 5 to 3 when joined, which groups 5/4 and 4/3 (diatria and diatessaron). Up to this point there are 3 groups: of 1 interval; of 1; and of 2 intervals. Continuing with the Fibonacci series, and grouping them according to the harmonic order, the next term is 8 between 5, and groups the intervals 8/7, 7/6 and 6/5. One of them widely used (just intonation), and also along with the others present in Ptolemy's systems. The next term of Ptah[57] is 13/8, which groups 13/12, 12/11, 11/10, the small tone 10/9 and the Pythagorean 9/8. Numerically, this term is 1.625, very similar to the canon, to which each term of the Ptah series is brought closer and closer, until it is approached with minimal divergence to phi proportion.

And what does this result in? That music becomes imbued in the golden ratio, which in turn encapsulates the light of the Spirit in the animated. This directly implies that the intervals are in fact that Spirit which, subject to matter, is in turn subject to the interval rather than being given in its univocal form. Perhaps now the reader understands why the teachings of number were so important, and even more so, music, for the ancients. A sign of culture and of degrees of initiation into the mysteries of Nature.

As an exercise for the intellect: number-idea: 5 → it constitutes part of the 5/4 interval found between the diurnal movements of Saturn's perihelion and aphelion[58] → it is imbued in the third term of Ptah {5/3} in every canonical proportion and in every relationship in natural growth that involves 5 parts of 3 or 3 to 5. Conversely, when observing a pattern in a plant with 5 branches that in the next level are 3, we have the interval 5/3 → aphelion of Venus with aphelion of Saturn

---

57 Nomenclature given in the aforementioned volume.

58 Johannes Kepler. Harmonices Mundi.

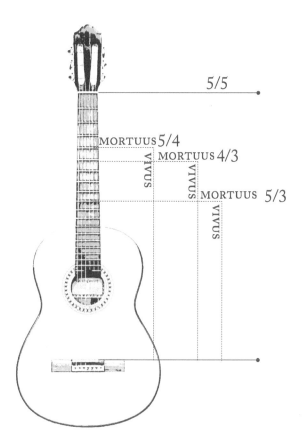

Figure xii-3: sound guide for the exercise.

(octave), on one hand, and if 5/4 and 4/3 → aphelion of Jupiter and perihelion of Mars (reduced to the same octave)[59].

Mentally, these processes of the imago must be sequenced according to sound. The intervals are heard. It is impossible for me to reproduce this sound in a book; for that, we have ears, but with a musical instrument, they can be reproduced. The figure indicates the part of the string that is vibrating or *alive* and the part that remains *dead* (vivus/mortuus), to assist

---

59 See the planetary displacements presented in the subsection "Models of the Spheres.

the student and with the purpose of describing the astronomical intervals.

Instrumental and comparative study of intervals

The strings shall reproduce an interval in their vital part, object of the total possible, which is the unity. From each string, which we identify with unity, we produce a ratio, which will always be the more or less perfect division of said unity. The essence of playing is to graduate the descent from unity into a natural hierarchy that produces sonic harmony. If the planets maintain among themselves relationships of such harmony as we will see conclusively in another section, the one who plays the instrument must master and understand them both in mind and body, to operate adequately in the language of the spirit. The first thing the cosmos shows are broad intervals; the second, that these intervals are of great perfection, for there is ample diapason, diapente, ditone, and there is no chaos as the inexperienced intellect might think if it doubts the musical order of the universe.

So, the one who plays the instrument will beforehand understand the lengths of living and dead string that emulate the rationality of the solar system, which is the animal in which we are immersed. The body that contains us 'is' the orbits of Jupiter, Saturn, Uranus, ... and those internal to them along with those internal to the Earth itself. To know anything beyond without the internalized cycles of the stars and the intervals they create is a symptom of lack of intelligence, for intelligence is defined by the dances of the planets among themselves, with the idiosyncrasy of their lights combining to create myths (aspects). If music is to reflect anything, on a mechanical level, it must be the essence or synthesis of all this. Thus, the Pythagoreans knew well the starting point, and the classics capture it with the same intention. The harmonic series, as we can study it today, which we can even see its numbers in the frequency spectrum, forms a Pythagorean synthesis that reflects the movement of the spheres.

In a string, since the unit taken is the string itself, the ratios will be derived from lesser lengths, meaning higher sound frequencies. The series will look like this:

1, 1/2, 1/3, 1/4, 1/5, 1/6, 1/7, 1/8, 1/9, 1/10, &c.

As the guitar loses the possibility after 1/3, we will work with partials:

1, 1/2, 1/3, 2/3, 3/4, 4/5, &c.

Thus they do not refer to origin, but to the preceding component, the living part of the string becoming wider and the dead part shorter, up to the semitone. With the persistent geometric representations it is perfectly understood, since the circle is equivalent to the rope, and what remains of taking one of the parts of each inscribed figure is the interval as such.

Through the triangle, we obtain 1/3 diapente divisions of the string, in accordance with the form, or astral force. Divisions by the square (by the diatessaron, four) produce a noticeable pitch intersection between frets 5 and 7. For a triangle and a half or two squares, we have half the string or diapason. Recalling the Musical Body, the seven stars would be syncretized through both sets of figures:

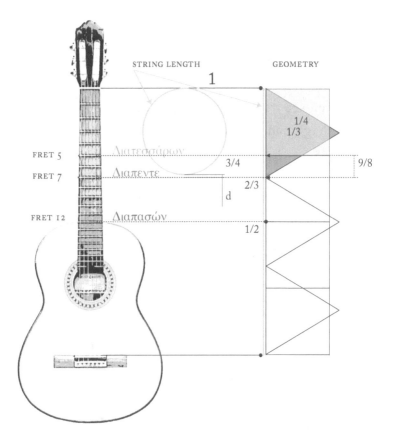

Figure: musical instrument geometry (1).

- [squares /diatessaron]: from the 0th to the 5th fret, Moon; from the 6th to the 12th, Mercury; from the 13th to the end, Venus; Sun in fretless regions.

- [triangles / diapente]: from the 0th to the 7th fret, Mars; from the 8th to the 19th, Jupiter; Saturn in the fretless regions.

In view of this, the emerging tone resulting from applying geometry to the guitar corresponds to Mercury and Mars. A conjunction of both, applied to the musical realm, signi-

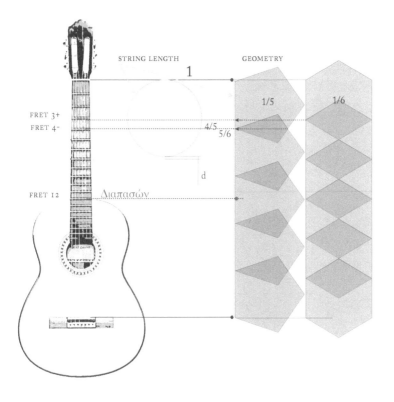

Figure: musical instrument geometry (2).

fies swift technique in melodies. It refers to the left hand; its symmetrical counterpart, not represented on frets, alludes to the right hand under the influence of Venus and Saturn. Another conjunction of this application signifies a cooled affection, a sober sound; or a sensual rhythm, on the other hand. This span practically covers the very soundhole of the guitar. Indeed, closer to the neck it sounds more like Venus (moist), and closer to the bridge like Saturn (dry). The guitar (and the instrument in general) is a natural model.

In the following case (already unrelated to planetary numbers), the intersection results in the difference between frets 3 and 4, signifying the transition from the semitone to the whole tone. The pentagon represents the former, and the hexagon the

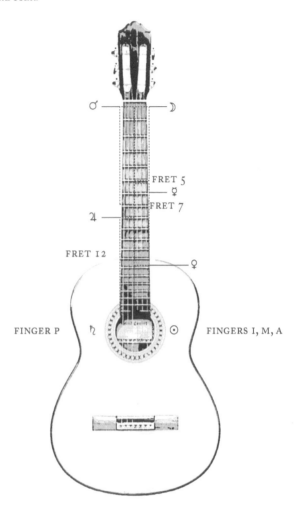

Figure: musical instrument geometry (3) [first depicted in this edition].

latter, just as the square represents the diatessaron and the triangle the diapente. In both cases, the string can be wound around a circle whose diameter lies a few millimeters from the 7th fret. It would be exact if π were 3, and it is precisely this minor yet significant difference (**d**) that holds a musical meaning. I wrote about this when I was studying the diagram.

$$d = \text{differential between } \pi \text{ and } 3$$
$$\pi/3 = 1.04719 = ca.\ 25/24\ (st\ Nyuna)$$
$$1/24 \cdot \pi + 3 = 3.13 = \pi$$
$$\text{Then: } \pi \cdot (2\text{-}Nyuna) = 3.01 == 3$$

The *nyuna* is one of the three Carnatic microtones, the others being *praman* 81/80 and *poorna* 256/243. That is the intermediate one, and if we multiply the other two by 3 we would have, respectively, 3.0375 and 3.16. The second is a good approximation of π, from which we conclude that the Pythagorean semitone or limma, coinciding with the poorna in Hindu music, measures the diapente in the perfection of the circle. So, constitutes the step of the linear to the circular, the material to the spiritual. Knowing that there are 13 *poornams* in a diapason, if we place the lunar scale on each of the 12 notes of the diapason circle, we will have a 12-year cycle symbolically represented (each year with 13 scale notes). lunar founded first on C, then on G, then on D, ...), which takes us to Jupiter. In reality, it intimately relates the Moon (13 lunar months) with Jupiter (12 years) and not with the Sun since the latter, by the number twelve, refers to months and not years. The notes of Jupiter and Moon are, respectively, C and A. Between the two there is a ratio of 27/16 = 1.6875, which is approximately Φ, the Egyptian canon. The **Zeus-Hera** tandem forms the backbone of the heroic cycles of the Greeks, which are movements. The Olympic marriage has its vibratory archetype in the do-la tandem, therefore, and in the golden number as a ratio.

In terms of sound, it can be seen (penthagon and hexagon) that the ditone is slightly smaller than the current major third. The difference is from 1.2566 to 1.25. In the case of the minor third with the semitone 5/4, it is smaller than the right interval. The difference is from 1.1892 to 1.2. This suggests a broader, more perfect "minor" interval that will produce a more natural effect on the listener than the slightly tempered one. I don't think it sounds any less sad, but it does represent a color definable not by this epithet. It is very simple to make the comparison. Tune a guitar as follows: 2nd string B = 243 Hz; the 1st string D = 6/5 · 243 = 291.6 Hz. Comparing the 2nd open string and 3rd fret, with the second and first open strings, we will have a sonic idea of the nuance of color that reigns in their difference. By tuning the 8th fret of the third string to 303.75 Hz, that is, 5/4·243, we will hear the bright third and by contrast we will be able to adjust the auditory perfection that is lost with equal temperament, although not as much. He does it in the diapente and the diatessaron.

As with all natural sounds, and also occurs with Pythagorean tuning, the body perceives it harmoniously, transcending the perhaps feigned dichotomy of the tonal era between cheerful and sad, and reaches the level of the seven parts (intervals, spheres). This transition from the binary to the qualitative is that of the opposed, polarized, the political; towards the natural system, the quality, the right living with both matter and form. The seven intervals that effectively naturalize hearing are:

$$2/1, \, 3/2, \, 4/3, \, 5/4 \, (\text{or } 81/64),$$
$$6/5 \, (\text{or } 32/27), \, 9/8, \, \text{and } 16/15 \, (\text{or } 256/243)$$

Seven intervals, viewed also as frequencies (1 Hz, ... 16 Hz) of a harmonic series with a fundamental of 1 Hz, reach the limit of the audible range (16-17 Hz) that was considered not long ago, and perhaps corresponds to that of healthy newborn babies. It's precious: music is configured as a preliminary program and enabler of the interpretation of the sensible world.

The four elements on the Classical Guitar
(and by due coherence of every other string instrument)

Attending to the timbre of the guitar, and applying what has been said, the equivalence for dry would be playing near the bridge, for the timbre is sharper; thus, 'the sharper' the sound (right hand), the drier the quality. Similarly, 'the rounder' the sound (also righ hand), the wetter the quality. All the previous respond on a higher and lower frequencies' energy enhancement, respectively.

Turning to the other two qualities of matter, it might be easier to comprehend that the higher the pitch, the hotter the quelity; thus, the lower the pitch, the colder. That being said, it's not hard to establish where to find the 4 elements in the art of playing the guitar. Now with an undoubtedly higher comprehension (next 4 figures).

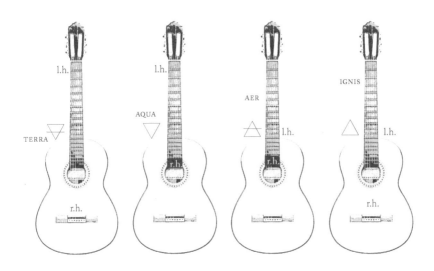

Figure: the four elements at their zones [first depicted in this edition].

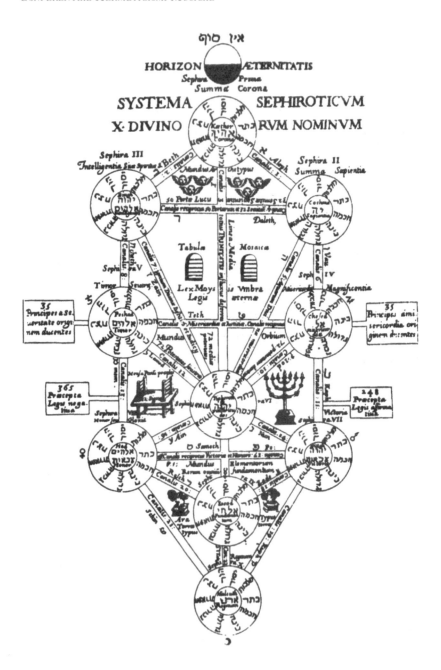

Figure xiii-1: Athanasius Kircher. Sephirotic tree. Oedipus Aegyptiacus III, p. 216.

C:. XIII:.
THE TREE OF LIFE AND MUSIC

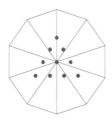

Introduction to the subject or transition to music

From the eons of Gnosticism, to the Neoplatonic spheres, we transition to the Sefirot. If one perceives, in all cases, they are at least figurative images of the vibration and quality thereof. The hierarchical characteristic of our texture and that of the universe induces these spheres to progressively elevate ideas in their ontological sonic continuum. These are Plato's sirens, and likewise, by continuity of tradition or perhaps historical linkage, the Sefirot of the Kabbalah.

Let's delve into Kabbalah in music. I keep it very much at arm's length when I speak, and I do so for many reasons, but there are elements emerging in the network that are dissecting the theme, not necessarily being convenient.

To commence, what **precisely** is the Tree of Life? One might posit it as the ontological framework of vibration, elucidating how we are fundamentally structured in accordance with its essence. It epitomizes a pathway to enlightenment, a conduit to such, as it descends and ascends in a specific sequence as mirrored in tradition. This sequence aligns with that of the spheres, yet beyond this, the structure interlinks the Sefirot through various avenues, furnishing diverse pathways for each aeon.

Hence, it holds a particular fascination, an added interest. The interrelation, for instance, between the sphere corresponding to Saturn and that of the Sun via a 'path' imparts insights absent in the Neoplatonic sphere diagram. This renders the tree a system of interconnection of vibrational realities and their attributes. The kabbalist, as evident in Kircher's works, attributes multiple names or attributes to each Sefirot, which could be perceived as its inherent qualities. These are its manner of rotation, movement, animation, both individually and collectively. They define the attributes or virtues of the light embodied by the sphere in question and also how it intermingles with others.

It consists of 10 interconnected archetypes linked by 22 pathways, totaling 32 abstract concepts, as both stages and transitions merge into a single ensemble to elucidate the creation of the universe. The sefirot represent these 10 archetypes. The word ספירות derives from "number" and "book" simultaneously. One can envision the scroll of papyrus, later the Torah scroll, as a reflection of the same archetype idea unfolding according to number and closing like a book. This evocative concept leads us to natural processes, the penetrating capacity of light, and the very formation of life. As for the set of 32 "paths of Wisdom," these are called netivot נתיבות. Kircher believed this diagram originated from Egypt as its tradition would originally be Egyptian. It is noteworthy that the 22 pathways are equivalent to the 22 Hebrew letters, and through them, vibration ascends and descends, harmonizes or disharmonizes, forms the intervals.

"According to the Kabbalists, these 32 paths are alluded to in the Torah by the 32 times the name of God, Elohim, appears in the first chapter of Genesis. In this regard, the expression "God said"

appears ten times, and these are the ten expressions through which
the world was created, in parallel to the 10 Sefirot.[60]

If we consider the vibration of the total number, 32, taken as a harmonic wave ensemble, we refer to a harmonic system (natural sound, yet metaphysical) with the waves O1, O2, O3, ... O10; and then O11, O12, ... up to O32. The relationship between O32 and O1 is 2 raised to the power of 5. Let's recall that in the Sefer Yetzirah, a cornerstone text for students of Hebrew mysticism and essential for any cultured individual, five dimensions are discussed, along with their connection to the 5 books of the Torah, albeit in a different manner. In Pythagoreanism, 5 is the number of man. Thus, there are 5 octaves encompassing the entire Creation, from O1 to O32. However, in its mystical aspect, this is discussed in The Lyre of Hermes, and here it is pertinent to approach the subject from the perspective of wave theory for its connection with the Idea, the foundation of Hermetic tradition. Five octaves that interconnect all ontology could very well allude to these different dimensions precisely delineated by the diapason. Here, we speak of a diapason as an idea, but as we have discussed, the diapason reflects the structure of something, its contour and boundary; hence, having it five times alludes to dimensions. As we can see, once again Pythagoreanism and Kabbalah intersect, and rightfully so, as nowadays this and the aforementioned book seek to embrace the common tradition of so many questions that are commonly thought to be related, but the strength of their connection is not well understood.

"Sefirotic system of ten divine names", is what Kircher's diagram says, although as has been said, the path of 32 elements

---

60 Aryeh Kaplan. Sefer Yetzirah.

must be contemplated to acquire the full potential of the ontology that lies within the diagram. This number, 32, is not only a harmonic series up to this number and continent of 5 octaves, but the value of this number yields the word heart. By gematric equality (value of its letters), the vibration of the word *heart* includes those 5 octaves, since *lev*, לב, heart in Hebrew, equals 32.

Relating to Music: second insights

In light of wave theory, or stemming from it, we derive that the note one might approximate to facilitate the musical diagram would originally be C. This we could validate in a preliminary instance - which is the intended one - as the vibration at 32 Hz (and that of 1 Hz) is a C.

When I came across this in 'La Lira de Hermes', I found it surprising, as it suggested that the symbolic organization of the mind, that nexus between all human beings, operated spontaneously in shaping the models. The musical model had begun through the Pythagorean path with an initial sound that would later be called C. However, that this is the vibrational origin (1 Hz) of the scale, harmonic (equivalence O1 = 1 Hz), and ontological (Tree of Life), would signify a vector towards the depths of the symbolic mind, and that music as such follows natural law and is confirmed as hermetic science through its scale.

Thus, by rescuing the scale here, we can contemplate up to 4 scales corresponding to the 5 octaves. Scales within this framework of diapasons (pentadiapason) resonate at different levels simultaneously. This, and no other, constitutes the starting example to relate music and the Tree of Life, as it partakes in the common nexus of undulation.

Anyone attempting to correspond the Sephirotic set linearly to the notes is bound to be disappointed. The two octaves presented by the ten sefirot lie within the realm of the tetraktys, leaving the other 3 for the 22 nexuses (letters) between the spheres. Meanwhile, by undulation, from O1 to O10, there are three octaves and a major third ($2^3 \cdot 5/4$), subtracting an octave and a small tone of 11/10 to complete the 32 nevitot. Returning to the tetraktys, which encompasses a disdiapason, we should recognize the remaining triple octave as a tripartite link with the soul, with the letters corresponding to each diapason: ten Sefirot :: tetraktys :: disdiapason = diapason 1 and 2:

Letters of value 1-9 :: diapason 3
Letters of value 10-90 :: diapason 4
Letters of value 100 -400 :: diapason 5

In this manner, albeit initial, it allows one to understand how each diapason operates in different dimensions of the soul and vibrational ranges. To clarify it and have it written down here without the reader needing to flee to know which letters they are, a first diapason, 'א, ב, ג, ד, ה, ו, ז, ח, ט'; the second, 'י, כ, ל, מ, נ, ס, ע, פ, צ'; and the third, 'ק, ר, ש, ת'. With this, the reader can understand that there is a way to correspond to them according to the musical sense. However, subsequent treatments and secret correspondences are only accessible through initiation and further study.

Let's take another example and analyze it. One that places the names of the notes on the tree. It is obvious that this is a way to urge criticism and construction of one's own path instead of accepting -nor should it be done with what is presented here- the path of others. If we briefly search for 'sefirot tree music' on the internet, we come across some curious things. As

I cannot reproduce something in this present book for which I do not have permission, I will refer to the book that the visited page mentions. There is a book from 1972 called 'The Tree of Life' by Z'ev Ben Shimon Halevi. The diagram shows an octave between Keter (crown) and Malkut (kingdom), and in between are the rest of the notes. From the top, in the direction of the ray (descending), it generates a scale by contra ascending:

DO RE MI *INTERVAL* FA SOL *SAME* LA SI *INTERVAL* DO.

As such, the interval is undefined. It corresponds to the sphere of Da'at, which we have not even considered, so we'll

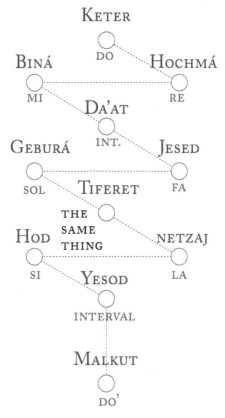

Figure xiii-2: Example notes and sefirot diagram (Z'ev Ben Shimon HaLevi).

skip it. What matters is the identity of the Sefirot corresponding to the Sun (Tiferet) and what it attributes to it, as if it
were a note that reflects the identity of the Sefirot from whichever angle you look at it. Quite a puzzle. It's better not to
continue in that direction. The notes are of interest.

[1] First we see that there is a scale, an octave.
[2] Follow the descending order: Keter → Hockmah → Binah
→ Hesed → Gevurah → Tiferet → Netzach → Hod → Yesod
→ Malkut.

Skipping Da'at, the sphere of knowledge, seems to pose no
problem whatsoever, as it's not a Sefirah in the strictest sense.
However, Tiferet and Yesod are, corresponding to the Sun and
the Moon respectively. In these, the commentator on the tree
places notes in a very logical manner. The only significant variation lies in the mysterious interval, perhaps, dare I say, referring
to said Sefirah as generating the interval between the two adja-
cent notes (B SI and C DO) or simply not knowing what to put.
As a brief foray into what one typically finds on the internet, I
believe it's been sufficient. The reader who begins to grasp the
sound being played in this book will have understood the inherent disruption in the model presented.

Structure of the Tree

The Tree of Life is formed by 10 sefirot or spheres, or lights
that are arranged in three pillars. On one side is the pillar of
mercy, and on the other, the pillar of severity, with justice in
the center. It is stratified into four levels, which are four worlds
(olamot):

Olam HaAtzilut, *the world of emanation.*
Olam HaBeriah, *the world of creation.*
Olam HaYetzirá, *the world of formation.*
Olam HaAshiyá, *the world of action.*

The first refers to the first three sefirot, the second to the next three, the next to the following three, and the last to Malkut. And each one can further expand into another tree, as many Kabbalistic authors or those related to the subject point out.

Consider, on the other hand, regarding the original note as a C is debatable without an argument to justify it. We have introduced this note before, solely mentioned in relation to the powers of 2 that the nevitot's sephirotic set possesses. But what if instead of notes, it refers to intervals? The origin of O1 would be a fundamental, but of what note? The original note of all Creation emerges before our eyes, but this and other questions must be respectfully considered. It's akin to Robert Fludd's monochord: why is Γ (G) the first note? These are matters that exceed the idea of explaining the assimilable part in this initial instance of musical hermeticism. There's no justification in the text, but C is the beginning of vibration, as we've seen. Everything starts in this breaking of silence, ex nihilo, from nothingness. From zero, we move to one, from the first cause to the primo mobile through the contraction of the first duality. The vibration at 1 Hz is, as a note, a C. So, should we consider it as both the beginning and the end? As alpha and omega?

The rest involves placing the octave: knowing the origin and knowing that everything must be framed within an octave, it's about how it's distributed. In reality, the descent of the lightning bolt must be orderly from high to low, so it would be DO, RE, MI, etc. The spheres of Tiferet and Yesod, if they do not have an associated note, would have to embody the entirety of the scale within themselves and share a basic characteristic of their idiosyncrasy as binders and emitters of the same spectrum of light. They are the active and passive principles of the heaven's radiance.

By our own decision and with external impetus, we must endeavour to define the structure as a process of the soul, linking the same intervals together, to delineate a complete structure and content of a vehicular system of the soul. For this, the 22 letters can be likened to the major arcana of the Tarot, and the 10 Sefirot to the points of memory (mnemosyne). In this manner, the hero's journey of the soul is that of memory recovery, and thereby the arrival at divinity (see again the diagram of the Hermetic Wave). Thus, the Neoplatonic and Gnostic cosmos is constructed (although for the latter, details are lacking) with clear instructional utility in the paths for the dynamics of the anima.

22 linkages :: heroic path; 10 sefirot :: memory.

The memory, as accessible through symbolism (Freemasonry, Rosicrucians, Brunians, Mnemeric), is constructed in each chamber through the attributes of each Sefirah. Thus, these, extensively studied by A. Gikatilla in Portae Lucis[61], may be the builders of boundaries in these spaces of memory. This forms the sphere as an occupation of a space reminiscent of the collective unconscious that is always there, and which has its *raison d'être* in our body.

---

61   "The Gates of Light" or "Sha'are Orah" by Abraham Joseph Gikatilla.

We deduce from the whole a diagram that unites the 5 diapasons that respect the mnemosyne or tetraktys in the two primordial ones, and the three following ones remain as a path to that, the so-called hero's journey that I recounted with the stages of the Tarot in 'La Lira de Hermes'.

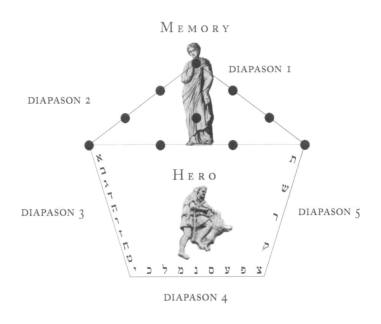

Figure xiii-3: Graphic Kabbalah of the diapason.

Let us account for the quintuple diapason as the five dimensions of reality, the five books, and therefore each diapason alludes to a reality, always delimited by the same quality at both ends, the same colour of light. Thus, the aleph is the same note as the yod and the kof; the tet is the same as the tzadi and the tav. But in between, different unfoldings occur, giving rise to the quality of the lumen. The lower figure represents Hercules (detail from the facade of the town hall of Tarazona, Spain), but it could be Gil Gamesh or any other solar hero. The upper one (Mnemosyne) dresses with the Tetraktys. The pentagonal outline alludes to the hero (initiated man: number five), who as an initiate must find the quintessence or divine presence on Earth (Shekhina) through the kingdom, Malkut. The conception, characteristic of this book, also presents how the first of the sefirot, by analogy with the tetraktys, will be found alone and after having completed the hero's journey. This implies the previous stage -sublunary- being Tartarus and not like the Kingdom-Malkut (Earth). It alludes, therefore, to being only in the presence when one is on the labyrinthine journey of the hero-musician, as it connects the initiate with the memory of each step of the path.

The Sun (solar hero) traverses in Creation the 3 diapasons encompassed in the lower part of the diagram, a direct reference to Robert Fludd's 3 heavens with the occurrences of the note G, gamma, or gnomon, on his monochord and as the origin of the journey. The three heavens, of the elements, spheres, and empyrean, are distinguished in orders of magnitude: x10 in each case. All letters, stages, intervals as numerical ratios, indeed belong to the air, with varying degrees of purity. Ultimately, the prana or vital breath impregnates the hero, and Hera (his matron) represents the philosophical Mercury, symbolized by the peacock, air impregnated with spirit, fixed to the earth. Thus, the hero is the body that fixes this air. Moreover, he completes his journey only with the possibility provided by Mnemosyne, which, undoubtedly, we can now syncretize with the goddess Hera and the dispensation of *charis*, the ambrosial fluid of the initiatory journey. With a high probability, the stratification of the goddess may explain this syncretism since Hera precedes Mnemosyne, although they share Zeus's vehicular lightning. But much about the goddess has been lost, and we can only speculate to a certain extent.

Air, Hera, the letter, the ratio, and the Pythagorean tetraktys fuse into a single sword of keen discernment, to be applied in the education of the speculative whose element is the air.

The vital spirit necessary for hermetic performance is obtained by "breathing like Hera" from the concise ideas (ratio) with which to work in musical study. The diapason, diapente, diatessaron, embedded in the performance of their applied symbolism (for example: Sun, lion, diapente) with which the *musician's mind* operates, enter the body as spirit through breath.

The Hermetic Musician's Kabbalism

A cursory introduction to it would be as follows:

[a] The image of the aleph א functions as a musical unison, unity, and primordial sound. Pure light with which we should not associate any interval as it is the origin and fundamental.

[b] The image of the bet ב refers to the diapason, which encompasses from the sphere of the fixed stars to the mundane. All the light serves in this marked region which we call the visible macrocosm.

[c] The image of the gimmel ג, also as an interval, allows for the sounding of the diapente, a quality that originates the note and calls to dawn and the Sun.

[d] The image of the dalet ד, diatessaron in music, originates the quaternary, and from it nourishes its presence in memory.

[e] The image of the hei ה represents the breath of which we speak, both the one present in pure light and its presence (Hera) on Earth (Kingdom). It is the ditone that enlivens the color of the note and the interval as the third emphasizes the diapente with which it forms a chord. The hei is then like the ditone that gives joy imbued in diapente and diapason, allowing the air to enter as "sensation".

[f] The image of the vav ו refers to the same Adam's fall that generates the seed (light) upon the matrix (earth/water), to the phallus of man. In the word *adam* אדם this symbol is missing, as it is of his fall; a letter we do find in *adom* אדום, red, alluding to clay and the spectrum of the material. Along with the abandonment of the incarnated state of grace referred to as Adam, to his "fall" into incarnation, which is not the same as his fall into temptation (the wordplay conceals the issue of the divine spirit's habitation in the body, not the sin of it), accompanies the semitone, which if framed as the previous simile, functions as a minor chord, and this as the sound of the symbol of the spirit's entry into the body.

Here I pause to imbue the trot with the rain that is to bless our path: from the hei to the vav, the transition from bright to dark chord musically resonates, symbolically marking the entry of prana and its assimilation into the body, where it will lose some of that brightness by embodying the imperfection of a particle of the multiplicity of G.od (fall). For this reason, humans are to continue breathing in pursuit of identifying that duality with the unity they both generate. This unity is better understood through the tetragrammaton yod-hei-vav-hei, as the yod symbolizes the divine, and since its gematria is 10, the interval remains a ditone when reducing the diapason: $10/2 = 5$, $5/2 = 2.5$, $5/4 =$ ditone, just like the *hei*. This is the sought-after identity (only present in divinity) of air with light.

The *yod* is a diapason above the *hei*, and therefore they resonate. The dissonance or lack of perfection would occur with the vav, representative of the human. Thus, both the semitone and its complement, that is, both 6/5 and 5/3, link man with divinity. And if we focus on the number of man, the five, and of spirit, the three, 5/3 or the relationship between yod and vav will constitute the harmony between the divine and the human, the rational relationship by which as the heaven sounds, so does the earth: 5/3 == Φ. In a way, and with this light shed on the page, we find the same Pythagorean and Kabbalistic relationship (mind you, it's the same) in the three diapasons of the hero and five in total. The deified man travels the yang of his yin, the search within himself for form (3 in the 5).

Until the Hebrew aleph-bet is completed, symbolic maps follow that deepen according to the adept's level in them, but undoubtedly offer how to articulate their *raison d'être*, the interval. The last of the reasons that air imprints on flesh through the light of its letters results, if reduced to the octave, in 1.375, a tritone.

Mnemonic Diagrams

Returning to 5/3, the number for the third Muse (see 'La Lira de Hermes': figure of the "Muses and the golden ratio," p. 337), we obtain a ratio sufficiently close to the Φ canon with which to imbue the symbol and bring it satisfactorily to the highest dignity on Earth. It is easy to imagine a space divided into three parts by five and place in it any objects that need to be revitalized in our memory. The hermetic musician can ensure to remember the diapente, its form, associated symbol (as in the example: lion), and reiterate this even with the Hebrew letters to establish a construction of memory in the image and likeness of universal memory.

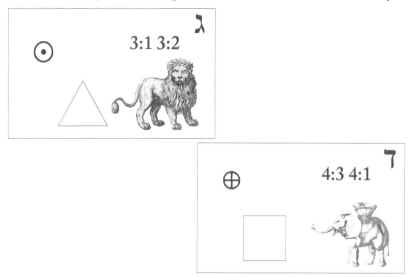

Figure: enclosure of gimmel and enclosure of dalet.

We have discussed extensively the difference between the sonorous and the non-sonorous, and how the non-sonorous refers to the ratio is already well explained. In the proposed image, sound must be placed (imagined). Perhaps initially it may be complex, but by internalizing it without the need for proper listening, the same movement will direct the entry of prana. This is a hermetic quality, akin to how Hermes guides the passage of souls, except in this case, it proceeds to enliven the body and does not refer to the psychopomp. We know that this light embedded in the air exists from the hierarchy. By employing this advanced exercise, the same hierarchy settles the entry of the harmonic beam into the body.

Since this book disseminates Hermetic Music, following the tradition of the Nolano, the aforementioned does not contravene any norms, but I shall not proceed further at this juncture with purely Kabbalistic matters. This dissertation, this essay, this nocturnal golem or perhaps revelatory proposal, concludes with the harmonic spectrum of a note, inviting the reader to contemplate the cradle of order and the images to be placed.

The base note, an A at 108 Hz, is produced by a classical guitar, and the peaks form the representation of the wave in the frequency domain. The 22 peaks from the fundamental (incl.) suffice to define the timbre of the sound, although there are other harmonics subsequently. The entire harmonic language is encapsulated by the Hebrew letters and their archetypal pronunciation, but as mentioned, I will not continue. Anyone wishing to delve into this topic in depth can refer to 'La Lira de Hermes,' the initiatory journey of the musician-hero (through the 22 archetype-intervals).

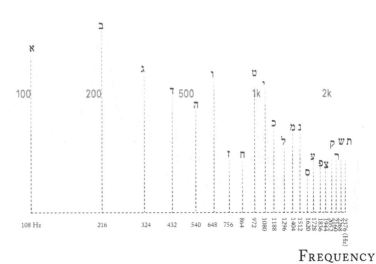

Figure: harmonic series and hebrew letters.

C:.XIV:. STRING THEORY AND 432 TUNING

Or the Principle of Necessary Reunification

Let's delve into something fundamental in speculative music, in Pythagorean philosophy, and for our current moment in terms of cutting-edge science: string theory. What I introduce in these pages serves as a preview of works that, with the blessing of the Muses, will attract Nous to the intersection of modern science —and hermeticism.

Musical String Theory

The Holy Grail has always been to unify all fields that define physical reality. The quantum, the tiny, and the macro, the large, gravitational forces; and in between and throughout, electromagnetism. It was Einstein's dream, and it has not been understood without string theory. Therefore, it serves to develop a theory of everything.

The postulate (initially) of this is really simple: there would exist subatomic particles that would be the result of vibrational states of a string. Looking at the smallest of the small and beyond, we would find that each particle, each electron, each quark, each graviton (the primordial particle of gravity), would not be a fortuitous mass that is there without a genesis of itself, but a consequence of the vibrational state of a string. That string is a mathematical model called the Calabi-Yau manifold.

The string would be vibrating, and depending on its vibrational state, we would observe one particle or another. This vibration transitions into matter when observation becomes pertinent, translating into the realm of sensory perception. Consequently, the string acts as an intermediary between the perceptible and the intelligible, employing Neoplatonic terms.

It's crucial to emphasize its dimensional aspect. In string theory, it's discussed that the mathematical framework necessitates either ten or eleven dimensions for viability. Let's focus on the former scenario. These ten dimensions consist of the three spatial dimensions plus one temporal dimension, with an additional six dimensions related to Calabi-Yau spaces. While we can readily grasp the initial three dimensions, accessing the next dimension requires gnosis, which pertains to the doctrine of cycles or temporal singularities. These six additional dimensions, often sparking controversy regarding the potential pseudoscientific nature of string theory, stem from the mathematical model aimed at ensuring viability. My conjecture is that this approach is adopted due to its allure in achieving a unified model across three realms of scientific theories concerning matter: quantum mechanics, electromagnetism, and universal gravitation.

These 6 dimensions are not observable. They are manifested at wavelengths close to the Planck length, which would make them unobservable by definition. Essentially, conceptually we have a model in which:

[1] At an infinitesimal level, microscopic to the point of almost abstraction, particles would be mere manifestations of vibration states of a string.

[2] This string is not observable.

However, the effects of this theory are what scientists attempt to observe and verify. It's like looking at the projection of light onto matter, the shadow, and, by using intellect, deducing the object on which the light falls. It's a swift move to venture out of Plato's Cave. There is a serious experiment underway[62] seeking energy that is being lost, thereby assuming its existence upon the completion of the experiment. But in this writing, we shouldn't delve too much into the issue, as it will be expanded upon later.

How to reconcile this theory with music?

The next part we are concerned with is how to reconcile this "theory of everything" with music. We cannot simply assume that these changes in vibration equate to notes or something similar. It would be a speculative model at a low level to approach the issue. It's not about that, and it would be quite simplistic. The key, without a doubt, lies in the tetractys. Essentially, we would first have to acknowledge that there are ten states in the whole, which also define reality itself. They define, as well, the link between the material and the spiritual, and would represent the Cosmos as a whole. There is an observable part and a deducible one within it, as demonstrated when it was treated in geometric terms.

The fourth level of the tetractys represents the tangible; the subsequent level, the first spiritual (form, diapente); then, the dual in the second level, and finally the monad. In the case of the tetractys, each level is an elevation of the state of vibration. We transition from the level of matter to the level of spirit, and ascend to the absence of all distinction (unity) by hierarchizing systems of perception. With each level of vibra-

---

62 Super-Kamiokande experiment, based on neutrino detection.

tion that we ascend, we comprehend a greater complexity of reality, from the Neoplatonic perspective and that of any other cosmological philosophy. With string theory, we have 3+1 un-derstandable levels[63]; and then an ontology of 6 levels, which understood through speculation would lead us to the most complete understanding of reality, making the system finite and yet complete at the same time. This understanding of all would lead us to grasp reality and where it is unified; and also how this is possible: how the entire non-sensible world that affects the sensible world is unified. And the sensible world itself.

Secondly, in the tetraktys, the rise is of states of conscious-ness, in an analogous manner until the monad is reached. And at the monad one have total understanding, the Logos. This level is the *eye of G.od*. Could it be that string theory leads to the Logos just as the tetractys leads to the Logos?

On the other hand, there are several states of vibration that cannot be perceived via string theory. The fifth state of the theory of tetraktys is no longer material, it is spiritual. At the sensible world, four points that form a volume, define what's physical. It is from the fifth point that there is abstraction. Just like what happens with the fifth dimension in string theory.

And thirdly, these similarities already speak volumes, but if we take it a step further and consider a hierarchy of the Tree of Life, where we have the ten spheres, we will be even more surprised. In these ten spheres corresponding to the tetraktys, we would also find a similarity with strings, as from that tra-dition we bring the cognitive idiosyncrasy of each sphere, to which attributes of strength are intimately related to particles.

---

63 Equivalentes to the four formative points of volume, the material, the last level of the tetractys.

In essence, it seems that this mathematical-physical-philosophical question that arises, namely the theory of strings (hence the fine line it treads among scientific academics, bordering on pseudoscience), resonates with the Neoplatonic perspective. This connection has been vaguely hinted at throughout various historical moments and contexts. Let us not overlook this similarity, as it is highly probable that this reality constantly influences the human psyche, where there exist ten levels, and those ten, representing completeness, perfection, the sum of the first four natural numbers. This perfection leads to a complete understanding of the cosmos.

432 Hz Tuning

The numerical aspect of musical tuning presents a divergence at the outset but ultimately converges. The number 432 evokes the vast cycles of time within the Mahayuga, cycles that, by repeating every Year of Brahma, serve as a window into the concept of eternal recurrence, inviting contemplation of the correct understanding of temporal dimensions. All is cyclical, and if a note embodies within its number the shared idea of immeasurable eons of Time, it is already sufficient grounds to explore the 3+1 dimensions. Vibration serves as a manifestation of this idea, guiding our steps along the path and molding our feet to the yellow brick road (quantum light).

Mathematically, 3^3 multiplied by 2^4 yields this figure. Musically, the self-operated form is the note A, the sound of the Moon. Among all spheres, the Moon serves as a transmuter of solar energy, nurturing Life with it. It does so within the context of time, as all life is subject to time; however, not from a fatalistic perspective, but a cyclical one. Hence the theories of reincarnation among Platonists and Hindus, among others (metempsychosis, wheel of samsara). For it is a consequence of understanding cycles. Hence the multiple messiahs, heroes, and others that Hostory provides as redemption for what lies beyond the light.

It really doesn't matter whether we say 27, 54, 108, 432, 864, ... it's an A in any case, and thus an archetype, a resonant sonic idea aligned with the dimensions of time and space that allow the animation of the Cosmos.

The archetipal diagram of diapents: *la* (A) as an universal note

Another element can be outlined here, which no one usually mentions as a corollary when talking (always from vague intuitions) about the tuning of 432 Hz. This note, the A, is not only a reference in a tuning system but in the universe. To see this, we must understand that if 3 represents form, quality, and astral force, to arrive at A, we must multiply $3 \times 3 \times 3 = 27$. When octave-shifted four times, 27 leads to $432 = 3 \times 3 \times 3 \times 2 \times 2 \times 2 \times 2$. Disregarding the quadruple octave shift—because as long as we multiply by two doesn't change the quality of the note— we focus on breaking down this number:

[a] 3 = the form, the quality, the astral force.
[b] 3 x 3 = 9 = the form of the quality, the strength of the astral force.
[c] $3 \times 3 \times 3 = 27$ = the form of the form of the quality, the force of the force of the astral force.

From each number (3, 9, 27), we extract a musical note as its vibration, naturally following the order of fifths (G,

D, A). The triplet outlines a progressive order towards the formal, and since it culminates in the utmost form of form, 3^3 = form^{form}, it defines the Spirit in the same way that 3 delineates the Body and 9 the Soul. Nine is the number of the Muses, and it has already been said to precisely concern the journey of the soul. If 3 represents the physical universe, we should find it in its movements. Indeed, the three holds the relationship between Saturn and Jupiter, which are the largest visible planets and form the chronocrators. Specifically, their extreme movements, aphelion and perihelion[64], respectively, are separated by a disdiapente. They mark the boundaries of time, thus forming boundary conditions of the system by linking their extremes with three times the vibration.

Jupiter perihelion: Saturn aphelion =
0°05'29" / 0°1'48"= 3.04

Other places of lesser importance where the number 3 is found (this time with octaves in between) are Mars and Jupiter at their aphelions, or Mars aphelion with Saturn perihelion. We also find relationships, this time of 9, between the aphelion of Venus and that of Saturn, or the aphelion of Mercury with the perihelion of Saturn.

As we have studied the reference with the chronocrators, another one can be found in the relationship between the slowest and the fastest movement of the planetary spheres. Thus, Saturn at aphelion compared to the Moon at apogee will be measured, resulting in a surprising outcome:

---

64   See 'The Models of the Spheres' in the third part of the book. Or refer to 'Harmonices Mundi' by J. Kepler, any edition.

$$apogee\ Moon:\ aphelion\ Saturn =$$
$$= 13°10'35''/\ 0°1'48'' = 439.213 = ca.\ 432$$

It is not at all compromising if the quotient results in 432, even with slight variations (and there are such). These are the two most important boundaries astrologycally speaking- and they turn out to be governed by the Spirit. In this simple manner, it is judged why, from the planetary structure, its quality is that of the diapente; and why the Moon has this as its note, capable of binding all astral light with it (from Saturn's range to the Moon itself). In computation, there are and will be musical intervals faithful to the order imposed by the number according to the circle of diapentes and, specifically with the body of the cosmos (3), the soul of the cosmos (9), and the spirit of the cosmos (27).

A Pythagorean exploration like this is not mere speculation or vague *Christian Kabbalah*, but rather an affirmation. through the celestial movements, of the Truth. If the universe is grounded, sustained, in the number 3, the third power of 3 will be its spirit, that which is fixed and immutable. This affects its active, masculine polarity (a masculine number for the Pythagoreans and an upright triangle in natural philosophy). Therefore, the

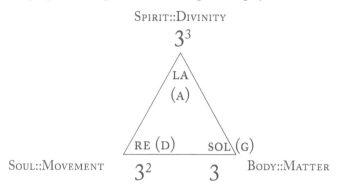

Figure: Context of the universal note.

note LA-A is fixed throughout the cosmos, and comes to structure it. The body represents visible movement, whose echo is
physical bodies and their functions (organs, blood, ...); and the
soul represents the form of movement, its cause, which receives
the will of the spirit and translates it into the bodies it concretizes, linking the notes LA-A and SOL-G in what results in the
interval of a ninth tone 9:8. From the hermetic musical foundations outlined at the beginning of the book, we know that the
Pythagorean tone is the basic unit of the scale (not the limma),
thus the scale will appear as the unfolding of the connection
between universal spirit and body.

Between both vertices 3·3·3/3 = 3·3 = 9 lies the note of the
third, which is a RE-D, and serves as a tone from the Monad (1),
embodied in DO-C. The entirety would be circumscribed within
the Monad (see fig.), which encompasses all sonic possibilities
just as one is in the factorial decomposition of every number.
As an inner circle, the note cannot be the same, as the understanding of unity is not granted to human beings; archetypally,
the cosmos will be encompassed, visibly, by the note FA#-F#,
corresponding to the 360 degrees of the circumference (due to
the vehicular relationship between astrology and music of de-
grees=cycles/second), viewed from within, for from the outside,
the Spirit sees the one and indivisible.

Embedded within the triangle is the realm of matter (elements), which can only reflect the actual notes that exist in the
universe. Symbolized by the square form, it receives octaves
from those notes, thus forming images or replicas of them at
different levels of creation (octaves). It does not respond to just
one note, as naturally, everything that sounds down here receives influences from the notes above. By passing the note LA-A
through the diapason mirror, its octave emerges, and from the
inverted triangle, the order of fifths is also reversed, resulting in

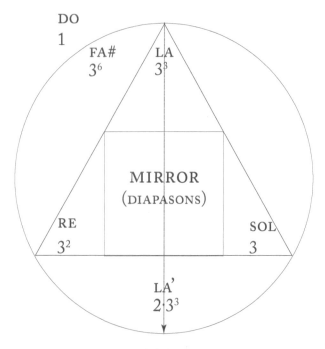

Figure: context (ii) of the universal note.

the notes MI-E and SI-B, in succession. The square is grounded at the base of the triangle, which is why only the note from the upper vertex descends by octaving until it creates the lower vertex. From the spirit's passage through the mirror of matter, the reflection of divinity is born on Earth and in Heaven. The Shekhina, or divine presence, resonates with the same note LA-A as the spirit, but separated by a diapason (immanent divinity, chthonic divinity).

The subsequent notes after LA-A will also be images, receptacles (formation of the inverted triangle) of the stellar light of the spirit. Thus, MI-E is the note of the Sun, and through it, we inhabit Truth and Goodness, in contrast to SI-B, which is the note of Saturn, through which we inhabit temporality, rigor, and death. This also tells us that the LA-A of the lower vertex is the Moon, clearly serving as the boundary function between worlds.

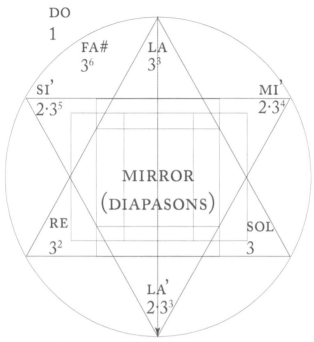

Figure: context (iii) of the universal note.

Looking at the circle of fifths in its entirety, it is worth noting that the mirror only reflects LA-A, which refers to resonance and the concept of universal resonance. The gateway between the supralunar and sublunar realms lies in the vibration of this note. Therefore, when symmetry of the set occurs, the mirror is *duplicated* (number of matter), resulting in a kind of distortion due to the multiplicity of things, and this is where the issue of string theory resides. Each mirror (multiple mirrors) would propose a sieve through which the creative force would manifest in the physical world. The ray of the diapason (creator ray in myths, the Uranus) will pass through external mirrors a and c, and internal mirrors 2, 9, and 6 to exist in the sensible.

The numbered mirrors correspond to time dimensions of the **present** (2, 9, 6); **past** (3, 4, 5), and **future** (1, 8, 7). In all cases, and being triune sets, they form the three axes of space. Mirrors a and c bind the world through time, allowing its existence through it, so that time permeates space, and they are not of equal hierarchy as previously understood. The mirrors of the 'past' also correspond to quantum mechanics, the minuscule, where there is nothing but number theory and statistics, and things are not yet conceived as formed and concrete (or formed and concrete), although in reality, they already are; the mirrors of the 'future' correspond to electro-magnetic energy, the ultimate manifestation of the material in its feared return to the heavens. In it, temporality begins to blur (speed of light) just as in the extreme opposite (particle dynamics).

In the present, the gravitational force prevails, represen-ting nothing but the constant materiality of the world and its renewal in a finite yet boundless moment. The various strings are no longer perceived as such but rather as mirrors that effectively induce a universal motion of the spirit, observable as the particle in each instance. Only one mirror, the central one (9), remains void, causing no particle. Mirrors b and d,

		a		
	3	2	1	
b	4	9	8	d
	5	6	7	
		c		

Figure: musical string theory, multiple mirrors.

though not agents of time, influence space, thereby incorporating time on this occasion. In colloquial terms, we refer to them as life and death, although they are the principles of rhythm that reconcile opposites in the very wave (vibration), of which we recognise its gradations (Robert Fludd's parts of light and matter) as the causes of different spheres (quantum levels of orbits = quantum levels of thought).

Altogether, and without further ado here, we have a set of 9-1+4=12 particles, which amount to 10 if we don't count the ones not accounted for in string theory (b and d). The collective of all mirrors, let's not forget, is 13, also the number of the Moon (due to the astronomical count of maximum full moons in a year), and incidentally the number of Pythagorean limmas that fit within the diapason, as we previously derived as the "lunar scale".

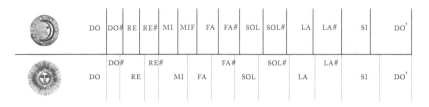

	DO	DO#	RE	RE#	MI	MIF	FA	FA#	SOL	SOL#	LA	LA#	SI	DO'
			DO#		RE#			FA#		SOL#		LA#		
	DO		RE		MI	FA		SOL		LA		SI	DO'	

Figure: lunar scale/solar scale (reset).

The projection of the archetype (divinity) of the note in the shadow returns the multiplicity, this time, in the sensible world. The 13 notes name stages of matter, and since one of them is nothing but the primordial emptiness itself, which does not constitute any entity, there are really 12. The way to regroup everything in a harmonious way is our Pythagorean scale.

C:.XV:. Κάλλος καλλατοσ.
MUSES OR THE RAPTURE OF
MUSICAL DIVINITY

Or of the process and parts of Inspiration

The Muses are *daughters* of the psycho-genetic substrate and the prana, and in turn, the former is the channel of resonance between the inner gods or deep layers of being and the tangible or earthly, visible layers of biological being. The deeper one delves, the closer to divinity. Mythology explains this as daughters of Mnemosyne and Zeus; the former being the daughter of Heaven (Uranus) and Earth (Gaia).

These 9 sequenced parts, which correspond to the celestial spheres, stratify the Hermetic ascent and descent of the musician, or signal it, with the descent of *gratia* (Grace). Since light acquires physical framework through geometry, and it is through this that things in the world reflect beauty, the bridge between the divine and the mundane is subordinated to the nonary number. The ultimate reason advocates simplicity although it may not have it: every regular geometric figure adds up, for each number of its angles, to nine.

The Hermetic musician also contemplates that the translucent presence of the muses is signified by each of the seven spheres, to which he adds correspondence with that of Earth and the fixed stars (Heaven). The framework, therefore, of the muses, is superior to the qualities of the manifest (seven), including musical notes. By imbuing the physical, it constitutes a metaphysical framework, a container for a moving content, which is the soul of the spheres. Hence, they are matched by Ramos de Pareja, among others, and develop a soulful musical system. Therefore, the study of the spheres, to which we have dedicated much in this volume, is advisable, facilitating what I am going to break down. From the terrestrial sphere, immobile, governed by the deaf muse Thalia, and up to the sphere of the stars, in that sense, the notion of the musician ascends; conversely, from those peaks and even more than we do not observe, and down to the musician, inspiration descends. They are two senses of an identical path.

The nature of the inspired state is characterized by the absence of perceptible time and space. The musician broadens their "bandwidth" by precisely understanding the nine mirrors of the musical string theory. Inhabiting these nine spaces of consciousness bestows upon the inspired individual the ability of prophecy, inspired writing (revealed books), and understanding of the universe (music of the spheres). As we saw, {3, 4, 5} constitutes the past; {2, 9, 6} the present; and {1, 8, 7} the future, implying the absence of distinction of the temporal variable and its embedded spatiality. Primarily, this underpins the mystic ratio and the relationship with music in its purest forms, more of the archetype than of the auditory (actual sound).

As for the notion of being inspired, it is something intuited, but not fully understood, by the novice. These lines will address questions such as the seat of consciousness during inspiration, and the real and tangible notion of being in that state. And I say sensed, but not fully understood, because intuition does tune into higher planes (genetic), but remains assimilated as such by those not educated in hermetic music, and does not bring it into the realm, into the tangible with another more solid word. Instead, it remains in the realm of intuition, hence it must be initially directed as to the divine-other. Other musicians, due to their distance from understanding the phenomenon (laziness and arrogance), conceive that the musical (or artistic in general) work is theirs, just as the adolescent plays with their sexuality thinking that energy is eternal: out of ignorance. Ignorance is the inability to conceive the smallness of the human being in the face of the vastness of the unknown, which leads to internal panic in the individual; the opposite, the hard path of learning conceives, from the natural model, the movement of being in the midst of fear of divinity. In the first way, the musician will fall into moral, physical, or spiritual disgrace; in the second, one will receive, if heaven wills it, grace, through ecstatic rapture.

The 'Gratias'

The Apollonian light that they collect sifts its original purity (nakedness of the Charites), becoming colored, ultimately becoming plausible in the biological organism through the different Muses, which guard a relationship with the number of Graces. These, producers of *caris, gratia*, constitute the merciful reward of heaven, the nectar of light, which will be transported by the geometric vehicle (muses). At the foot of Parnassus, where the nine live, the adept drinks from the Castalia fountain, a tributary of the river of memory, to begin his ascent back to union with the divinity of light, by the light of divinity. The graces are Euphrosine (joy), Aglaia (splendor), and Thalia (blooming), respectively: heat, light and humidity. Its feminine representation, together with what I just mentioned, refers us to the Hebrew 'mother letters', also three, of the Sefer Yetsirá. With that:

Figure: light, moisture, and warmth in the Charites.

In the figure, the radiant Aglaia corresponds to the source of light; the lively inspirer Euphrosine to the source of warmth; and the also sublunary Thalia, whose reception of her sisters allows the act to emerge from potentiality, to humidity. Light and warmth are inherent to the solar lumen, so with the third element, it sustains the necessary condition.

> *"(The Sun) stimulates the humors of the human body, especially at the beginning of spring, &c. The female vegetal stimulates its generation and puts the power back into action."*[65]

From the original light emanating from Apollo, as it passes through the triad of vital principles, in the manner in which the light enters the world (myth of the creator ray), this is produced. Thus, the Hebrew words that I have endeavored

---

65 Morin de Villefranche. Astrologia Gallica, liber. XVI. Latin original.

to include (Or = light; Chai = life), complete the meaning. It is evident that humors, man, and humidity go hand in hand as the characteristic of the object to the object. It is through these humors that movements are defined in one way or another. Affected by inspiration, the predominant humors of the human being are transformed through music. Therefore, the Muses as signifiers of music and the bridge between heaven (biological matter in potentiality and supragenerational cycles) and earth (biology in act and planetary cycles), transfigure the intermediate spheres (planets and their regencies) in order to dignify, facilitated by Aglaia (light) and through Thalia (moisture) and Euphrosine (warmth), each nature of the body. As a result, vitality increases in the individual and imbalances or disorder are compensated for by an increase in justice or order.

Rapture

The word "rapture" comes from the Latin *rapere*, which means to violently snatch away. If the question revolves around inspiration, here seems to lie an unyielding oxymoron: the sweet nectar that the muse brings from the Graces cannot serve as a violent action in any way. Inspiration snatches away the notion of time from the one who experiences it and seizes their will exercised in agreement with any chronida[66], chronocrator, time measurer. Perhaps, while not being "violent," inspiration is sudden, and catches the recipient off guard, albeit

---

66 Jupiter (a 'chronida', since he is the son of Cronus) and Saturn (Cronus himself), or, by extension, the 'chronocrators' or time lords-measurers.

not entirely lacking the desire for it. We can speak of rapture in another field, that of love, because after the amorous rapture comes the union of opposites, of what is separated, in a sort of sacrifice of light that occurs, also, without time or space comprehensible to the subject.

In reality, love and inspiration are facets of different but connected natures: love, as the Renaissance understood it and which was the impulse of light, is now what we call in the formal realm that encompasses music, inspiration. Love as such has a nature much better reflected in music than in any other artistic endeavor, and it is not wrongly said that the Muses are the inspirers of all art and queens from the purest realm of all: music. Mystical raptures or seizures in musicians are directed from Hindu (ragams), Arabic (makams), or Greek (tonoi) modes. But our major and minor modes do not reproduce the doors of inspiration that call to the Muses. They need a system that allows them to mirror the movements of the souls of the universe. And these are not just two - like the modes - they will be more out of necessity.

Both the word "muse" and its attribute "music" allude to moisture (in Egypt: maw; from Latin: moys; from ancient Hebrew: mosh), to the womb, and to the pregnant water of the Spirit. We have studied them as vessels from the source of light, the boundary of retained memory between the celestial and the terrestrial (Uranus and Gaia), and the moment through which the divine expresses itself in the work of the mundane, always in need of self-use to align with it.

Humans, through our reason, access the meanings of things according to the internal order we possess. If we are in disharmony, we see accordingly; and if in harmony, likewise. It's a simplification, but if we remove the static from the image and energize the symbol, we have two possible directions: the ordering or the disorder of internal realities, through the ratio of music (number, interval). Human beings, through our rationality, interpret the meanings of things based on the internal order we possess. When we're in harmony, our perception aligns accordingly, and when we're out of sync, our perception reflects that discordance. Simplified, if we remove the static nature of an image and animate the symbol, two potential directions emerge: the coherence or disarray of our internal realities, shaped by the musical ratios (numbers, intervals). This suggests that our internal state significantly influences how we perceive and interpret the world around us.

Now, order comes hand in hand with hierarchy and justice. Without the just layer of each thing, derives almost always the defect. It looks like a clock. All its gears must be placed correctly and sat at their speed so that the whole tunes into the pulse of time, the beat of the universe that we translate into our terrestrial laws to measure our movement (soul). We see these wheels, also with their own speeds, their unique sizes, in each of the surrounding planets of the king of heaven (the planetary periods). And their order is maintained with musical relationships, as we study in the Speculatory, and that mesh a harmonious whole influential in the creation, formation and development of life here on Earth. We relate **life to love, humidity** and **inspiration**.

That external order, cosmos, and space, which however much may seem fateful and be so, creating tensions and relaxations, conflicts and bonds, as classical astrology studies, is, if we distance ourselves enough or penetrate deeply enough into the vision of the thing, an articulated organism of light, operating in the immense macrocosm and subject to laws of which we are not aware here because they impose the absence of life (empty regions between galaxies). Our solar system, therefore, is an intelligent being, it is alive (ratio, numerical ratios between planets), and its harmony, with tensions and relaxations (aspects), is what shapes the hierarchy that allows it to be alive. From it will come the ordaining of the muses. Concerning hierarchy, Liaño[67] says:

> "Dionisio (Areopagita) uses the term 'hierarchy' to designate 'a sacred disposition, an image of the beauty of God, representing the mysteries of illumination itself, thanks to the sacred order of its rank and knowledge'. Hierarchy is, at the same time, order, understanding, and action. By order, one must understand memory (the order that allows memorization), thus hierarchy serves memory, understanding, and will (or action)."

It's worth questioning, *whose* action? That of the musician seeking inspiration. Liaño's masterful hand combines here the movement that the body will perform, along with the symbol of the body and its movement (music), and in turn along with its path of ordination-memory (music of the spheres). Later, he will say that hierarchies, due to their affiliation with divine rotation, are circular in form. Quoting Areopagite again, he says something interesting about love:

> "Divine love has no beginning or end. Like an eternal circle moving from the Good, through the Good, in the Good and towards the Good. Perfect circle, always in the same center, the same direction, the same walk, the same return to its origin".

Consequently, it specifies the force that rotates in circles around the symbol, around the constitutive sphere, whichever body inhabits it. As the spheres succeed in hierarchy, the understanding of the continuum of love advances: unity, some-

---

67   I. Gómez de Liaño. 'El Círculo de la Sabiduría', Ed. Siruela. Págs 638-639.

thing that in lower spheres is "forgotten" (Lethe river, sublunar world), and it is through the ascent through the cycles of Memory that it is remembered. The hierarchy of this path is structured with the Muses (daughters of memory) as quantum states of tuning into perpetual rotation, preserved energy, the zero divergence of light.

How does one become a prey to divine love?

How does one become a prey to divine love? Love propels its strength towards understanding the act of loving creation; said love undergoes the gradual purification until embodying perfect and eternal motion. The musician must ponder, how does one know that they are inspired? How does one know that they are prey to divine love? Same answer, with verb absent. Inspiration is perceptible **through its consequences**, which are the work. We can contemplate retrospectively whether something was endowed with the gift of the Muse or not, but in the precise moment, we can only be aware of it.

This present moment creates a *conditio sine qua non*, yet not sufficient on its own. The inhabited presence establishes the musician's seat, his throne, and needless to say, that without breathing in the here and now, there is no rapturous presence, presence of ecstasy, nor is it expected. But little guarantee lies in this because, like a true quantum state, inspiration does not allow it to be recognized *while*, meaning during the 'discharge', the 'light-release', but only afterwards and only for its work in the world, a reliable witness of the undoubted beauty of the purest strata that underpin the Muses (Charites). In this silence of perception the ancients placed Surda Talía, deaf for not allowing herself to listen to this sound from above.

Ascending through spheres, the notion of inspiration becomes present. Almost as a witness to the ignorance bound to the sublunar world we inhabit. Wisdom grows as the perception of that inspiration, which the neophyte cannot grasp, increases, and which the initiate verifies through analogies. And these analogies are the correspondences in quality with the quantum points of the celestial spheres. As we saw, each Muse has a sphere, for she must find her place on the **ladder of wisdom**, which is the recovery of Memory, and also configure with the corresponding spheres a hierarchy valid for the perception of growing divine love, which the initiated musician conceives as inspiration.

What descends from above is perceived as inspiration and is thus woven by the musician; but it is nothing other than divine love from the long-period spheres (highest memory), and some more in number tending towards the majority, which cohere (love) the entire system like a choral hymn.

"When we say love, you hace to understand desire for beauty. Because this is the definition of love in all philosophers. Beauty is a certain grace, which mainly and most of the time is born in harmony a of the greatest number of things. And this is threefold[68]. Because the grace that is in the spirits is due to the consonance of many virtues. That which is in the bodies is born from the concordance of the lines and colors. And in the same way the highest grace that exists in sounds comes from the consonance of many voices."[69]

---

68 Triple is the shape, and triply triple is the form that moves the astral form. This is what the Muses are when they are nine.

69 De Amore, chap. IV. Marsilio Ficino.

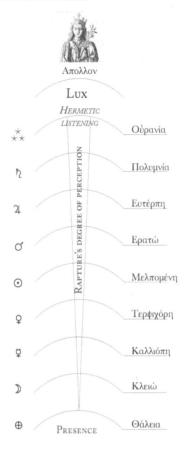

Figure: perception of the rapture.

Triple is the form, and thrice triple is the form that moves the astral form. Hence the ninefold of the Muses. It should be noted: 1) inspiration only occurs if the musician is consciously present, but if there is a present moment there does not have to be inspiration, and 2) as the hierarchical conjecture rises, inspiration is perceived as cohesion -love- with light -divinity-. Although we've studied their names — the reality they present— in conjunction with the musician's experience, would be similar to this, Muse by Muse:

<u>Thalia</u> only perceives outside of the present moment, that is, she embodies the idea that she is deaf to the voice

of Clio (muse immediately above), a voice that contains the first particle if it can be called that way, which as inspiration is perceived by the musician.

<u>Clio</u> perceives inspiration in emotion as it is in relation to the Moon, hence it fleetingly perceives (short cycles) the spring of light. As a corollary, she discerns inspiration in the simple and ephemeral feeling that musical art may be showcasing during the rapture. **Calliope**, as the successor, perceives inspiration in the manner of Clio, and adds the vivacious thought (Hermes), so that the sketch of the idea in successive moments enlivened by the electric manner of Mercury, produces the portion of wellspring that the hermetic musician perceives in this sphere of trance. In a similar way and always enclosing the preceding, <u>Terpsichore</u> represents the perception, in the present tense, of the spring of light from inspiration's rapture, in the idiosyncrasy of Aphrodite's form, and by the sensuality of her movement. <u>Melpomene</u> pertains to the solar plexus and settles in the equity of the sphere of equality, between non-perception and the perceived resonance of the spring.

Successively, each Muse represents the progressive perception of something that already exists, but is not "visible" by the incarnated eye of the Spirit. It thus represents the escalated perception of inspiration anchored to the necessary present moment. It should not be confused with inspiration as such, without any notion of itself. That is, it represents the degree to which we do perceive inspiration in us not because of its result but because of the movement (current) that resolves the coupling between that energy and matter (experience from or in inspiration or divine love):

[a] inspiration: *natural spring*.

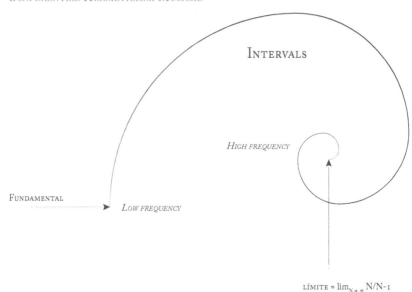

INTERVALS

HIGH FREQUENCY

FUNDAMENTAL

LOW FREQUENCY

$$\text{LÍMITE} = \lim_{N \to \infty} N/N\text{-}1$$

Translation: Harmonic frequencies transition.

[b] notion of *inspiration*: perception (incl. physical sensation) of the natural spring.

It is precisely [b] that enlightens memory, not [a] *per se*. By the time the last muse, Urania, is reached, we have previously gone through <u>Erato</u>, which opens the perceptual window into the loving and poetic, producing a feeling of warmth; <u>Euterpe</u>, whose noticed presence swells the musician's lung capacity and imbues him with full ecstatic enjoyment; and <u>Polyhymnia</u>, which retains it, because, with the constant of work, it unites the perceived spring with Cronus, conveying that it exists in time as such and is perceived in the present moment (inspiration that "has to find you working" - P. Picasso). <u>Urania</u> causes complete absorption into the spring, an indistinguishable union between the seat and the inspiration. Beyond it, nothing can move, but from there, it imprints all movement:

"Mentis Apollinae vis has movet undique Musas".

Apollo embodies light and the origin from which light's grace is formed. By this point, the hierarchy has been grasped through the hieratic musical trance. I stress the comprehension of natural philosophy through the constraining medium of study and its offspring, the cultivation of human virtues. It's crucial to recall the Pythagorean Ypsilon and how the use of substances can constitute a swift path (leading to madness) for those who haven't laid the groundwork thoroughly beforehand.

Apollo's arrow strikes those who attempt to ascend his path without virtue, for it is his, governed by him through motion. Everything relies on action and reaction in terms of the speed of such ascent. The path of ascent and descent is a spiral, like any form of concentration of being at the point or monas. As depicted in 'La Lira de Hermes', it's a trace from the breadth of the outer circle towards the harmonious union at the central point. In fact, the spiral form begins with the fundamental and ends by converging at the point that corresponds, in turn, to the finite and unlimited harmonic point. It's the same journey as light descending into the world, mirrored in the musician's consciousness ascending through the spheres of the Muses.

The limit of understanding or consciousness is epitomized by Apollo, residing beyond the sphere of the Fixed Stars—the observable and influential force at our birth and throughout life. Apollo embodies light itself, the Hebrew Or; he represents the will of light, igniting inspiration in the hermetic musician and the speculative student. This will is perceived through the subject moved by it, serving as the conduit for inspiration. Hence, one doesn't consciously access Apollo but becomes aware of his existence through prior ecstatic experiences (Urania). Yet, this experience isn't solely the entity's responsibility; in our era, it replaces the function of self-help books without rigor, seeking answers. A natural arrangement encompassing culture, initiation, and guidance within and outside the subject is essential. Following Neoplatonism, Apollo remains invisible, as the sphere of the fixed stars exists beneath him.

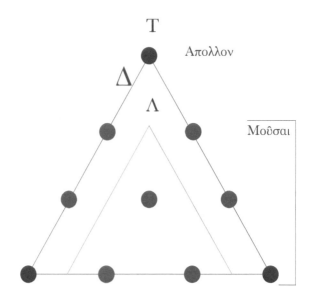

Figure: lambda, delta and pythagorean tetraktys.

Meaning of the Number of the Muses

The staircase of the 9 Muses, *forma formalis*, traverses from the utmost obscurity of the ecstatic stage to unity with the source of divine splendor. The number 9 is broken down as the astral force of light (the form) by itself operated (form of the form), and it is understood as a transition from visible form (3) to invisible form (3·3), since when we associate life (light-humidity-heat) with the former, the latter is configured as the operation that the own formal structure of the universe exerts on each of these three elements: its symbol would be delta, lambda, or tetractys.

The delta and lambda symbols indeed allude to the same concept at this symbolic level, albeit with distinct characteristics: the delta is closed, while the lambda is open. The former symbolizes the divinity of light or geometry, while the latter represents the Jacob's ladder or musical rapture. However, both are connected through the tetractys, which embodies the concept of Memory, the mother of the Muses and the link to geometry (the formation of things through archetypes). It also encompasses the musical disdiapason, the dual Pythagorean scale represented by the lambda's two arms

The joint stroke of inspiration and presence ascends as the true learning of the musician, which is, therefore, also hermetic (the double helix). Without a path to unity like this, to the rapture, to the disengagement of the self, the death of the ego, and the naturalization of being, **the spark that gave the human being the belief that he invented music would never have happened.** The human being expresses music and continues to do so because his vital need is to get closer to the Creator, note by note, muse by muse, scale by scale, until the very visit of the angelic, the geometric fire, emerges for the happy encounter towards the inner powers of the hero-musician.

In the waves of the gentle ecstatic path of the muses, ultimately sails the sole ship capable of warding off the disintegration of the mental body that constitutes our brain with its neuroelectric processes. We need that humidity to live. It is necessary as love is. Where mystique assaults those who drink from it with profusion, and leaves boneless those who rise without permission, scorches those without heart who approach the Sun, the spring of Apollo's acolytes forms the most delightful and beautiful passage that any human being with sincere inclination for truth can experience.

Are the Muses something real? Physical effects

It's almost a rhetorical question if we follow a symbolic language, but from Joseph Campbell's perspective, it's interesting to see each aspect of myth for its face within us, the living beings that we are, and vitalizing the world in which we exist through life. The first thing to say, although it may sound challenging, is that "they are an internal and external reality, in communion with the luminous nature of the biological." They deal with different qualities of being, governed by the different celestial bodies, and their effect equates to the dignity of each of them, to produce their goodness (spirit) and resonate it in base matter (planet, body). The idea is the same as that which gives rise to life: light, warmth, and moisture. The Muse carries them in inspiration, thus enlivening matter, warming coldness, moistening dryness, and hence:

[-] e.g. 1: relieves melancholy by fueling desire
[-] e.g. 2 tempers anger by channeling affections
[-] e.g. 3 activates the initiative in the phlegmatic person
[-] &c.

The musician, if he knows what happens, **educates** himself in the experience of inspiration. This is what hermetic music works on. The musician, if he does not know, if he does not study the laws of nature that happen here, does not educate himself, ergo does not perfect his appetites, senses, ...; nor does he delve into his vital purpose. That is because he dismembers his Dionysian nature with each rapture, evading the arduous knowledge of elevation demanded by Apollo. Permanently subject to ego and flesh

Humidity can be understood as the harmonizing part of the whole that impregnates beings with life, although as such we can think of the humidity that quenches thirst. And in reality it is something like that, except that the analogy will be from the need and satisfying that need. Inspiration shows us how lost we live without it and how subject to the vital rigor that we prove to be in thoughts, actions and words continuously and without harmony with the natural kingdom, animal, vegetable or mineral, to which inspiration water without difficulty because in essence it is life itself.

We have discussed imbalances in the human being, and based on what has already been studied, we can establish a map of the imagination to help us understand the physical effect of inspiration. The four classical humors, well known as melancholic, choleric, phlegmatic, and sanguine, affect the body due to their qualities and the areas they govern. As mentioned, Aglaia would encapsulate the **charis**, which descends through light. This idea is nothing more than an idealization of the effect of sunlight on the planets, which determines the dignity of that light based on their position in the ecliptic. The reflection of radiation from the Sun is uneven on the stars, also depending on the angles of incidence (position relative to the Sun).

Considering the virtues or flaws of the gods, and most likely under the same process of spiritualization of the cause (since that light, whether good or bad, is the cause of the effect on Earth), the 36 decans and the 3 Charites formulate the same conception of the universe: an intelligible spirit infuses truth and goodness into the astral bodies. Hence, the astral force on the spirit (light) of the planets is 9, and the spirit that causes it is 3. The Sun, dispenser of Good and Truth, can already be considered the original triad, hence the imaginative relationship with Apollo. The decans, of Egyptian origin, are twelve times three, signifying the spirit of each of the divisions of the ecliptic, of each of the units of time-space (dozen).

By the sunlight comes its virtue, which is the same light (Aglaia) and the warmth (Euphrosyne). And by contact with water (atmosphere and waters), it activates the moisture (Thalia), which turns potential into act in the vegetal spirit. Understanding the natural functioning, the humors will be understood as the presence or absence of two of the Charites: Euphrosyne, by presence, warms, and by absence allows coldness; Thalia, by presence, moistens, and by absence allows dryness. The seat of the musician is imagined as a house, a building of the imagination that facilitates the divinity (light) its effect on our affections. No other thing is the betyl of Jacob's ladder and the lambda, which, settled in warmth and moisture as legs of the same, sustains the ascent to the apex/vertex of light.

Melancholy, a humor rooted in black bile—cold and dry—requires the most attention among the humors due to its absence of both heat and humidity. The microcosmic temple of the musician requires the entry of both facets of divinity, a duality within the triune that demands equilibrium. Therefore, without proper preparation, music causes imbalance in those who are not adequately educated. This imbalance leads

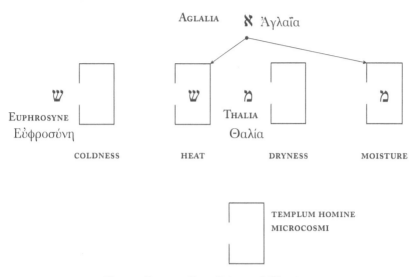

Figure: Rooms of qualities and Charites.

to despair through fantasy. Properly embraced, inspiration rekindles in the melancholic individual the impulse for conversation and the fertility of his solitude.

Anger, a martial emotion, arises from yellow bile, commonly referred to simply as bile, originating in the gallbladder. Its characteristics, dry and warm, necessitate the presence of Thalia's humidity to temper it and prevent actions born from alienation and wandering.

Phlegm engenders the phlegmatic humor, with its essence akin to water, complementing earth and fire as seen in the previous humors—a blend of elemental qualities. Euphrosyne's warmth counteracts the coldness, while her activation sparks the required humidity. Through this interplay, surrender and timidity dissipate, allowing space for righteous actions and advantageous endeavors.

Again and lastly among the humors, the sanguine, whose element for warmth and humidity is the air, because it is inhabited by the blood, specifies and opts for the greatest of the three favors, since it is Aglaia, (light), which acts on the blood to produce inspiration in it (inhale:: air), which is nothing other than establishing in the biological of the blood, and in the soul of the sanguine humor, the light of the spirit that carries the number. So, is it the blood the physical place, biological seat of inspiration? By similarity (it circulates, like the lumen and the aspects between planets) with the macrocosm, it formulates a channel of internal light whose center is the heart (Sun). From the blood, the Spirit (light), and from this will be born the qualities similar to the modulations that the planets make out of light. The function of light is to communicate the order of divine love, and in this is the quality of heat and activation of humidity; In this similar way, blood transports heat and oxygen, as well as nutrients, hormones, vitamins and electrolytes, to the body's tissues.

The origin of the 'Ennead', ninefold, that is, Uranus or the starry sky, frames the descent of the caris to the center which is the Earth, the omega in other words. Its quality is born from light by inquiring into its manifestation as a force, from which the triangle and the diapente emerge, which is the symbol that produces it. The firmament and the earth contain the qualities in the same way that the thresholds of visible light form the same quality of light (color) where purple joins maroon. Blood has that color, and as such it will contain the quality like the spectrum, the color, or the diapason, the interval. With the diapente, movement and quality are activated, coming from the triangle of life. In the Uranus-Gea enclosure (light: blood), beginning and end, alpha and omega, remain at the planetary heptad. In this way, 7 and 2 add up to the number of the Muses. From the Charites arises the diapente that produces the notes, so that it is not reckless to say that the very nature of music responds to the action of the Charites, through inspiration on the world, subject to the spatial and temporal through the dozen (Ecliptic).

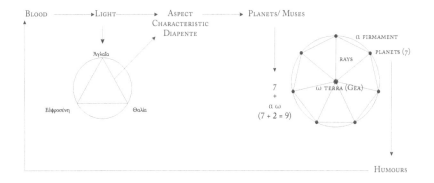

Figure: blood, humors, and ontology of light and the muses/sphere.

Muses's Undulatory

The ecliptic shall encompass the seven qualities of light and their hierarchy, according to planetary periods, until converging on the motionless Earth (reference) of the imagined ray of light by Apollo as the thread that links the spheres, guided by Memory. With the heptagon as a model of the quality, each edge from alpha to omega will encounter a sphere, originating theories of opposites (waves) and, of course, the ontological diagram of light called the Tree of Life, between which and the image cone we can indeed observe identical nature.

The so-called ray that forms within the imago as the natural substrate of the periods, harmonized among themselves (harmony of the spheres), is naturally an undulation by virtue of the duality that provides its substrate, continuity, and foundation. Within it oscillate:

367

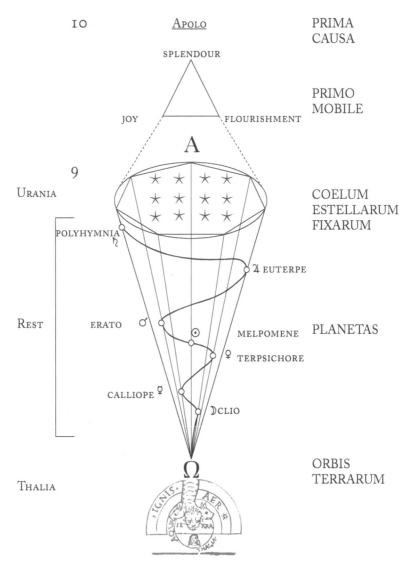

10   APOLO   PRIMA CAUSA

SPLENDOUR

PRIMO MOBILE

JOY   FLOURISHMENT

A

9

URANIA   COELUM ESTELLARUM FIXARUM

POLYHYMNIA ♄

♃ EUTERPE

REST   ERATO ♂   MELPOMENE   PLANETAS

⊙   ♀ TERPSICHORE

CALLIOPE ☿

☽ CLIO

Ω   ORBIS TERRARUM

THALIA

Figure: cone of light established by celestial qualities (planets).

The retaining principle ♄ vs. the expanding principle ♃
The mobile expelling principle ♂ vs. the mobile attracting principle ♀
The mental principle ☿ vs. the emotional principle ☽

The planets appear as active or receptive forces depending on the number, and some will be positive poles, others negative, and the limes of the Sun will lie in equity. Jupiter distinguishes the broader positive polarity, after which that of Venus, cushioned by a factor. The Moon assumes a polarity almost mixed, like Mercury, due to its proximity to balance. Symmetrical to this, Mercury, and in order from lowest to highest negative amplitude, Mars and Saturn. The factors how the amplitude decreases have to do with the body's radiation[70]. The limit, neither negative nor positive, is the source of the radiation, in this case the Sun, from which the Moon receives and shifts the spectrum slightly, and Mercury joins it by proximity of movement, playing the role of the herald.

The positive pole, or Horos, signifies mercy and the expansion of life, while the negative pole, or Stauros, represents the rigidity and contraction of light (matter). Mnemosyne governs the axis of the system, serving as the mother of the mnemonic process, which occurs through the abduction and education of the hermetic-musical student. Acting as the axis mundi, the "zero" point of the wave, Mnemosyne embodies the constant or true light of the Sun, serving as the axis in the realm of the stars and arising as a consequence of the subsequent and invisible Apollonian light. In our ephemeral world of illusions, Mnemosyne is studied from the shadows, from which objects are deduced, and the divine light that projects them is glimpsed. The shadows of the Moon, Mercury, &c., are cast by the light that falls on the body, allowing each muse to study them, as they function as complements to the force of astral movement.

---

70 As a reference, the amplitude will be factored by 1, 0.8019, and 0.445, not including the projections of the lightning's descent, which I won't address here.

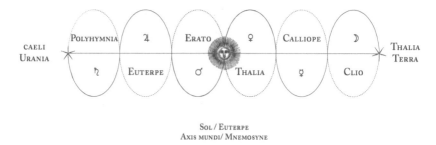

SOL / EUTERPE
AXIS MUNDI / MNEMOSYNE

Figure: muses and stars in the wave of the muses.

Each zero crossing is a wave contraction and energy variation in amplitude. From the contraction of the celestial light of the fixed stars to the sphere of Saturn (Seth, Stauros), a wave whose frequency is nothing but ontological, belonging to the realm of Apollo's *imago*—due to the non-homogeneous variation of planetary periods—descends to the contraction (agglutination) of light towards the sublunar world, that is, the orb of Earth. Thus, thanks to its notable number of three complete waves, the frequency of the wave will be that of 3 cycles covering the distance between Heaven and Earth, which in musical notes is a SOL-G; also the number of the Charites. The Triad of Life: light, heat, humidity transported by the spheres, is demonstrated in terms of how it does and how it serves the muses to do so. Both chronocrators govern the wave as they are the rulers of time itself; thus they are Seth and Horus, Stauros and Horos, Saturn and Jupiter, the two ministers that *wave the soul of the spheres*. Osiris dwells in the axis that sustains them, where the flow of the charis descends. Now, on this final page ends the first volume of the treatise on **Hermetic Music**.

ANNEX

The present annex constitutes the author's commentary on the figure entitled *"idiosyncrasy of light and sound in musical instruments, and their demiurgic archetypes,"* with the aim of expanding its significance and content. Within it (on the following page), the two fundamental principles, masculine and feminine, active and receptive, are depicted in corresponding upright and inverted triangles, alongside the labels "light/sound" and "modulation/arrangement of light/color." The connection with musical instruments is direct, as the action of plucking the string (guitar-type instruments), rubbing it (violin-type), blowing into the tube (wind instruments in group 1), or into the reed (wind instruments in group 2) originates from the solar principle. Whether through friction, blowing, or contraction due to plucking, an absolute sound dependent on length is generated. In strings, there are several systems in parallel, one for each string, with absolute tunings in each; in wind instruments, a single one tuned by its length.

In all these absolute sounds, the wave generated is stationary, trapped by two ends and vibrating according to the space it occupies. This is slightly different in wind instruments, but further discussion of their physics is beyond the scope of this elucidation.

Within the ensemble of the instrument, each sonorous system, whether propelled by friction, breath, or percussion, corresponds to a beam of light. This expresses its inherent nature fundamentally akin to the note that resounds without any modulation. In practice, this absence of modulation is the non-action of the hands (in wind instruments) on the keys or

PASSIVE PRINCIPLE

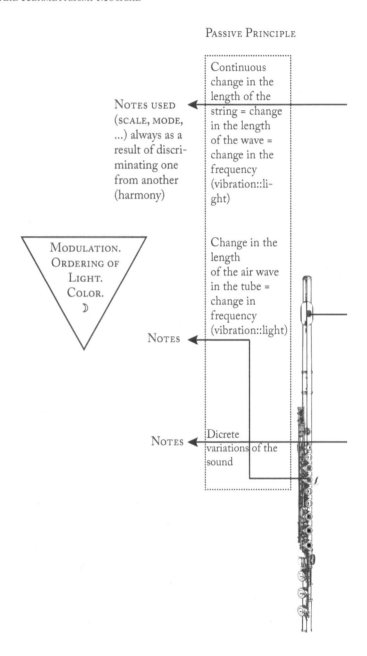

Continuous change in the length of the string = change in the length of the wave = change in the frequency (vibration::light)

NOTES USED (SCALE, MODE, ...) always as a result of discriminating one from another (harmony)

MODULATION. ORDERING OF LIGHT. COLOR. ☽

Change in the length of the air wave in the tube = change in frequency (vibration::light)

NOTES

NOTES

Dicrete variations of the sound

Figure: (expanded) Idiosyncrasy of light and sound in musical instruments, and their demiurgic archetypes.

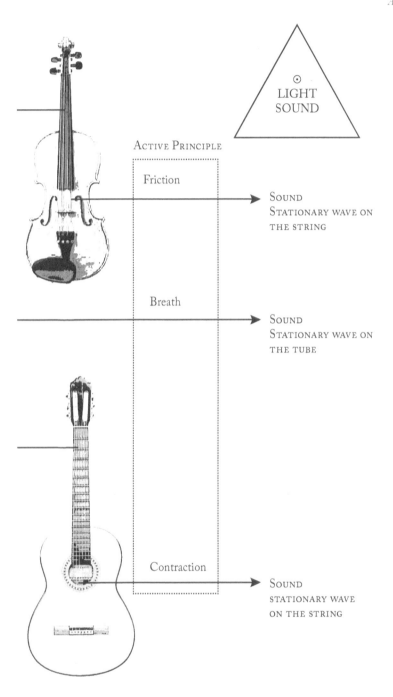

LIGHT
SOUND

ACTIVE PRINCIPLE

Friction

SOUND
STATIONARY WAVE ON
THE STRING

Breath

SOUND
STATIONARY WAVE ON
THE TUBE

Contraction

SOUND
STATIONARY WAVE
ON THE STRING

of the left hand (for the standard right-handed individual) on stringed instruments. Thus, delving into string instruments, the right hand equates to the Sun, while the left embodies the Moon, being the receptor of the rays from the former, which it then modulates.

By modulating the beam, the original light is arranged, resulting in the adaptation to a color, dictated by the variation of vibration of the string. Synesthetic ideas operate within the mnemonic ensemble, enabling the musician to transpose objects from natural philosophy (Sun, Moon, etc.) onto the instrument that orchestrates hermetic music in the physical realm. Sophisticating the system, successive modulations of the foundational beam give rise to musical modes, which serve as a stage for portraying states of the instrumentalist's nervous system—whether attained or aspired—as well as those sentiments induced or sought to be induced in the listener. Moreover, understanding which modes are requisite for specific moments and functions (elaborated upon in "Music Hermetica vol. II"), the practitioner engages in nothing less than modulating the internal light once communication is established with the listener or oneself. This intricate process demands elevated practice and dedicated time.

The significance of discernment and the virtue of Justice, although further elaborated upon in the subsequent volume, impart the idea to the reader that the primary discernment is that of the interval, followed by that of the note. Discrete positions sequentially unfold, selectively succeeding one another akin to the musical hand. This hand operates within memory, while the physical hands maneuver over the instrument, instigating the movements of the latter, and becoming the impetus for the orchestrated sounds in modes and scales.

Furthermore, the Moon invariably emits less light than the Sun, and indeed, when employing the left hand (Moon), the modulation towards the higher register resembles that loss of magnificence in light, no longer offering an absolute, but a relative one: the light of the Moon will always be relative to that of the Sun, as the relative position to the Sun generates more or less luminosity in the Moon's radiance. Hence, the association of Sun-Moon, as explained, finds justification.

Additionally, considering the discussion of a musical scale of the Moon, the notes themselves would hold a ritualistic significance when played on an instrument capable of such tuning, where the lunar hand effectively modulates the solar beam into these sounds—something achievable only with bowed string instruments but feasible nonetheless. What would ensue from a set of 13 notes?

The slight differences between the diapente and diatessaron would produce initial moments of divergence, both sonically and cognitively, with respect to their perfect counterparts. Logically, we should refrain from playing this if, through Justice, we seek the inherent Truth of the Sun. Yet, it is precisely due to the coherence with the illusory in the sublunary world that we find this lunar tonality useful for both the ear and the mind. The lunar diatessaron closest to the solar is the one bearing the ratio 175/128, called high F; and the lunar diapente would be in the ratio $97/64 = 1.515625$, close to $3/2 = 1.5$.

As I express, the divergence from the perfect ordering of light by Pythagorean intervals supports the nature of that which the Moon illuminates—belonging to the realm of illusion, the veil of maya; yet, also belonging to the vegetative realm. It is this sympathetic connection that deems this the scale Orpheus would have played to move the trees and rocks, ascending once again to the celestial sphere. Whether through literal or symbolic translation (vegetative spirit), the music composed with the 13-note or lunar scale is crafted with the 7-sphere-note plus one—amounting to 8 notes. The effect it produces is peculiar. With this, a certain study has been conducted in the manner of a small treatise, not included here, as the core of this is the Hermetic Wave. The annex concludes at this juncture.

END OF VOLUME I

.

. .

. . .

. . . .

Edited by the Author

BIBLIOGRAPHY

I include in these pages consulted literature, derived influence from the same, and sources of specific quotes, as well as recommended literature that has not been consulted in the text but that represents cultural foundations of interest. Podcasts, videos, etc. from Cittara Musica Hermetica, which were used as developed studies and supported this corpus at its inception, are not present.

1. Robert Fludd. Ed. Luis Robledo Estaire: Writings on Music. Madrid, 1979.
2. Albert Poisson. Theories and Symbols of the Alchemists. Obelisco Editions. 2021.
3. Giordano Bruno. Expulsion of the Triumphant Beast. Library of Politics, Economics, and Sociology. Barcelona, 1985.
4. Giordano Bruno. De umbris idearum (The Shadows of Ideas).
5. Giordano Bruno. On the Infinite Universe and Worlds. Ed. Gredos.
6. Frances A. Yates: Giordano Bruno and the Hermetic Tradition. Ariel, 1983.
7. Quadrivium. Vvaa. Librero. Madrid, 2010.
8. Jerónimo Cortés: O non plus ultra of the lunario and perpetual general and particular prognostic amended and translated into Portuguese by Antonio Silva de Brito. Lisbon, Miguel Menescal. Lisbon, 1703.
9. Diego de Torres y Villaroel: Anatomy of everything visible and invisible, compendium of both worlds; fantastic journey (...). Madrid, 1738.

10. Johannes Kepler. Opera Omnia. Frankfurt, 1858-72.

11. Johannes Kepler. Harmonices Mundi. 1619.

12. Altair: Scientific Astrology. Buenos Aires, 1960.

13. Michael Gauquelin: Astrology Facing Science. Plaza y Janés. Barcelona, 1969.

14. Demetrio Santos. Astrology and Gnosticism. Ed. Barach. Madrid, 1986.

15. Demetrio Santos. Investigations on Astrology, vol. I and II. Cycles of the Cosmos, National Publishing. 1978.

16. Demetrio Santos. Harmonics, Cl. Ptolemy. Ed. Miguel Gómez, University Collection, 1999.

17. Demetrio Santos. Astrological Interpretation. Barath. 1989.

18. Demetrio Santos Santos. Theoretical Astrology, fundamental equations. Ed. Barach, 1985.

19. Ignacio Gómez de Liaño. Athanasius Kircher: Itinerary of ecstasy or the images of universal knowledge. Siruela, 1985.

20. Ignacio Gómez de Liaño. Giordano Bruno: World, Magic, and Memory. New Library. Madrid, 1997-2007.

21. Ignacio Gómez de Liaño. The Circle of Wisdom. Ed. Siruela. Madrid, 1998.

22. Ignacio Gómez de Liaño. Greek Philosophers, Jewish Seers. Siruela. 2004.

23. Karl Kerényi. The Greek Heroes. Atalanta Editions. Originally from 1958.

24. Gaspar Calvo Hernández. The Lyre of Hermes, the initiatory journey of the hero-musician. Cronocratores Collection. 2020.

25. Juan Antonio Belmonte Avilés. Pyramids, Temples, and Stars, astronomy and archaeology in ancient Egypt. Barcelona Critic. 2012.

26. Porphyry. Lives of Pythagoras. Ed. Gredos. 1987.

27. Porphyry. The Cave of the Nymphs in the Odyssey. Ed. Gredos. 2008.

28. Sha'are Orah, Abraham Joseph Gikatilla, Yale Publications. 2011.

29. Robert Graves. The Greek Myths. RBA Coleccionables, S.A. 2005.

30. Marius Schneider. The Musical Origin of Animal-Symbols. Ed. Siruela.

31. Hazrat Inayat Khan. The Music of Life. Omega publications, 2005.

32. Hazrat Inayat Khan. The Mysticism of Sound and Music. Shambhala Dragon Editions. 1996.

33. Joseph Campbell. The Hero with a Thousand Faces, psychoanalysis of myth. Fondo de Cultura Económica and Joseph Campbell Foundation. 2014.

34. Joseph Campbell. Selected Essays. The Thread of Ariadne. 2018.

35. Gershom Scholem. Languages and Kabbalah. Ed. Siruela. 2006.

36. Robert Fludd. Utriusque cosmi maioris scilicet et minoris Metaphysica, physica atque technica Historia. 1617.

37. Athanasius Kircher. Musurgia Universalis. 1650.

38. Joscelyn Godwin. The Harmony of the Spheres. Inner Traditions Bear & Company. 2000

39. Sciencia. VV.AA. Ed Librero. 2019.

40. De Radiis. Al Kindi. French edition.

41. Torah.

42. Rabbi Shimon BarYojai. Sefer HaZohar.

43. Michael Maier. The Flight of Atalanta.

44. Fulcanelli. The Philosophical Dwellings.

45. Hesiod. Theogony.

46. Macrobius. Comments on the Dream of Scipio. Ed. Siruela. 2005.
47. Vivian Robston. Fixed Stars.
48. L. & Viji Subramaniam. Classical Music of India. A practical guide.
49. Heinrich Zimmer. Myths and Symbols of India. Joseph Campbell (editor). Present edition from 2008.
50. Cornelius Agrippa. Occult Philosophy, Natural Magic.

Workshops and contact: hermeticmusicinstitute@gmail.com
gaspar@musicaexlumen.com

Made in United States
Troutdale, OR
12/31/2024